HINTERLAND

Caribbean Poetry
from the West Indies & Britain

'The product largely of offshore islands – Jamaica, Trinidad, Britain, etc (Guyana being the exception) – West Indian poetry in English has often been located on the fringes of the central experience. Its popularity is widely associated with local colour, linguistic and tonal innovation, thought to be lacking in the English "mainstream".

   This collection shows that the most vital and challenging poetry of the British Caribbean heritage is both local in its urgency and informed by a hinterland of experience deeper than the geography of the islands' politics' – E.A. MARKHAM

E.A. MARKHAM was born in 1939 in Montserrat, and moved to Britain in 1956. He is Professor of Creative Writing at Sheffield Hallam University, and has taught and held residencies in Papua New Guinea, London and Coleraine.

He edited *The Penguin Book of Caribbean Short Stories* (1996), and has published several books of poetry, including *Human Rites: Selected Poems* (1984), *Living in Disguise* (1986), *Towards the End of a Century* (1989) and *Misapprehensions* (1995) – all from Anvil – and *Letter from Ulster and the Hugo Poems* (1993) from Arc.

Hinterland

CARIBBEAN POETRY
FROM THE
WEST INDIES & BRITAIN

EDITED BY
E.A. MARKHAM

BLOODAXE BOOKS

ISBN: 1 85224 087 3 paperback edition

First published 1989 by
Bloodaxe Books Ltd,
Highgreen,
Tarset,
Northumberland NE48 1RP.

Second impression (with corrections) 1995.
Third impression (with errata list on page 336) 2001.

Bloodaxe Books Ltd acknowledges
the financial assistance of Northern Arts.

Typesetting by Bryan Williamson, Frome, Somerset.

Cover printing by J. Thomson Colour Printers Ltd, Glasgow.

Printed in Great Britain by
Cromwell Press Ltd, Trowbridge, Wiltshire.

To Lystra and Bertrand Osborne
and to
Eudora and Howard Fergus

Contents

MERVYN MORRIS (b. 1937)

JAMES BERRY (b. 1924)

E.A. MARKHAM (b. 1939)

OLIVE SENIOR (*b.* 1943)

LORNA GOODISON (*b.* 1947)

FRED D'AGUIAR (*b.* 1960)

Random Thoughts

1

The threat of compiling an anthology concentrates the mind. It makes you speculate about why you want to do it, and why, indeed, you think it's worth doing. And you hope that such surprises as are thrown up in this exercise in self-consciousness, are not unpleasant or unworthy ones.

When I approached this I tried to bear a few things in mind, one of which was the date at which the job was being put together. A 1989 anthology of selected West Indian and Caribbean heritage, anglophone poets must assume that its potential readership is in important ways aware of some manifestation of West Indian poetry in English, and is inclined to be receptive to it. So we no longer have to put the old case that the work is invisibilised. That it is still marginalised[1] is clear, even though, in recent years, poets from the Caribbean have been "taken on" by the metropolitan publishing houses (and have, in some cases, gained access to recording studios) – six or seven of the fourteen authors represented here having been published, in individual collections, by medium or large houses.

What contributed greatly to the visibility of the product was, of course, the work of earlier anthologists. At the start of the 70s we had Figueroa's *Caribbean Voices* (Evans, 1966, 1970: two volumes) and Salkey's *Breaklight* (Hamish Hamilton, 1971). Then there was Nick Toczek's pan-Caribbean effort, *Melanthika* (LWM, 1977) – mainly poetry with some fiction, criticism and artwork.[2] *Ambit 91* (1983, ed. E.A. Markham and others) was a similar, if anglophone mix, with the first printing of the community-inspired women's play, *Motherland*. James Berry concentrated on black British poetry in his two collections: *Bluefoot Traveller* (Limestone, 1976; rev. Harrap, 1981) and *News for Babylon* (Chatto, 1984) – this last being a general round-up of what was available rather than an attempt to employ aesthetic criteria. Stewart Brown's *Caribbean Poetry Now* (Hodder and Stoughton, 1984) and Paula Burnett's *Penguin Book of Caribbean Verse* [in English] (1986), are two particularly fine collections. Finally, *The New British Poetry* (Paladin, 1988) contains a 'Black British Poetry' section, edited by Fred D'Aguiar, one of a quartet of editors.

These anthologies have been largely successful because of the vigour of what lay behind them – the mass of poetry being performed in the Caribbean; and performed, broadcast and published by Caribbean people in North America (mainly Canada) and Britain over the last twenty years or so. Crucially, before that, in Britain, we must pay tribute to Henry Swanzy's BBC Caribbean Service Programme, *Caribbean Voices* (1945-58) which became the overall title of the Figueroa collection. From the 70s more and more pockets of creative energy were finding outlets. Reggae and dub poets like Linton Kwesi Johnson, Michael Smith and Oku Onuora were attracting huge audiences worldwide. Louise Bennett's ('Miss Lou') once lonely brand of 'dialect poetry' had been institutionalised, not least at the annual National Jamaica Festival competitions; and widely imitated abroad. The Guyanese group of Ken Corsbie, Henry Muttoo, John Agard and Marc Matthews performed widely in the region; and in England, at the same time, the Bluefoot Travellers (which supplied the name for James Berry's first anthology) performed up and down the country.[3]

To this mass of material we must add the small, often irregular publications of resident tutors and local groups as well as the "ground-breaking" cultural organs that have become permanent reference points in Caribbean magazine publishing: *Kykoverall* (Guyana, 1945-61; 1986-) edited mainly by A.J. Seymour; *Bim* (Barbados, 1942, edited by Therold Barnes and then mainly by Frank Collymore till 1973, then by John Wickham, A.N. Forde, Brathwaite and E.L. Crozier); *Focus* (Jamaica, four issues, 1943, 1948, 1956 and 1960, first edited by Edna Manley, and revived in 1983); *Caribbean Quarterly* (Journal of the Extra-Mural Department of the University of the West Indies, Jamaica [first issue, 1949], edited mainly by Rex Nettleford); and the two relative newcomers – *Savacou* and *Artrage*. *Savacou* (Jamaica, 1969), edited by Brathwaite and others, is 'A Journal of the Caribbean Artists Movement', and *Artrage*, the London-based black arts magazine (incorporating its predecessor, *Echo*, 1976), is the cultural arm of MAAS, and has had as its early editors Fay Rodrigues and E.A. Markham.[4]

All of this work is constantly being reinforced by publications which promote poets from this or that island/territory/group in Babylon: *The New Voices* (Trinidad, edited by Anson Gonzalez); several volumes by Howard A. Fergus from the University Centre, Montserrat; *Seven Jamaican Poets* (Bolivar Press, 1971); and *From Our Yard* (Jamaican Poetry Since Independence, edited by Pamela Mordecai and brought out by the Institute of Jamaica Publications, 1987). The list is long.

My impulse initially was to base this new collection on one of the major anthologies above, to make minor adjustments to what could be seen as a new edition. But I found this increasingly difficult. Too many current excitements were being missed; too many old assumptions seem to have settled on the work, and some sort of shift was needed. Let me give an example. In 1987 I participated in a conference on Commonwealth Poetry at the Commonwealth Institute in London, and was surprised to discover that delegates (including some from the Caribbean) seemed quite clear in their minds what sort of thing Caribbean poetry was. It was discussed as if it were a fixed, known thing, almost a monolith, too set now to undergo significant modification. The oddity of this attempt to freeze an aspect of the culture was pointed up by the realisation that most of the celebrated practitioners of Caribbean poetry were alive and well and writing (and the two deaths we continued to mourn were not, in fact, "natural" ones).[5] At that moment, 1987, A.J. Seymour, at 74, was again editing *Kykoverall*; Louise Bennett, at 68, was contemplating life in a new country; both Walcott and Brathwaite, at 58, were pouring out books at a rate which slightly unnerved John Figueroa.[6] Figueroa himself (67) was in our audience, and Martin Carter, at 60, was expected. I say nothing of the youth, like D'Aguiar, who hadn't quite got over the flush of the first book.

So there was need to stress that though certain things hadn't yet happened in Caribbean letters, we had to hold out the possibility of their happening (I'm not referring just to the relative absence in the Caribbean poetic tradition of what might be called the tricks of "Modernism", but of the possibility of new shapes to contain our sound and meaning). It was time to re-check our records and re-interpret them (and not make the mistake of an earlier generation of critics who saw us trying to erect a culture on an historical void). In any case, as Walcott says, talking of drama: 'If there was nothing, there was everything to be made. With this prodigious ambition one began.'[7] I remember Earl Lovelace observing, in an interview, that we in the Caribbean had no tradition of warfare or of surrealism and that that must necessarily reflect itself in the literature produced (presumably South American-type magic realism was out, as was the sort of literature spawned by relentless totalitarian political conditions). But then, how do you account for Tony McNeill?

    un God   on
    the day of the   egg
    may you come
    the light c! omes on
    the valley of cries
    up from the sea
    the egg rises
    into the air

light   the light spilling
downward all day
I have given you voice
said the egg   I have given
you ash said the egg

I have given you music
the bell rang it out
the pebble   slipped up
the nightingale sang it
the piano kissed darkly

I come on the face
in the last church
it is air air
swinging beside us
the music inside me

all day
I had wanted poems like these
the valley recrossed me
I fell on my hands as
the cries rose

And McNeill isn't alone out there. Bongo Jerry comes to mind; and, exercising tight control, Dennis Scott. True, they were responding to the mood of Jamaica at a stressful time;[8] but the suspicion that the surreal permeates all our lives; indeed, it's a defining feature of our condition is reinforced by, perhaps, our most traditional poet.

Eric Roach reminds us in 'Love Overgrows a Rock', that we live the bad dream:

Too narrow room pressed down
My years to stunted scrub,
Blunted my sister's beauty
And my friend's grave force,
Our tribe's renewing faith and pride:
Love overgrows a rock as blood outbreeds it.

We take banana boats
Tourist, stowaway,
Our luck in hand, calypsoes in the heart:
We turn Columbus's blunder back
From sun to snow, to bitter cities;
We explore the hostile and exploding zones.

Unlike Roach, most of us hedge our bets and prepare a way out; we continue to dream of some kind of escape. In the Caribbean the dream of home must contain the most unruly clutch of images: there is the vague longing for being elsewhere, as well as having the security of knowing that as certain types of ambition can't be fully tested where you are, that brings consolation, protection from defeat and exposure. The chafing against physical and social constriction is similarly eased by the recognition that social and political pressures might well be fiercer elsewhere. There is the reality of having to accommodate what Andrew Salkey aptly calls the 'sea-split family'. No, it's not always a relief: it aids the abdication of responsibility, the denial of adulthood. These are all parts of the same dream. Think of the situation of the Mandelas in South Africa/Azania: Winnie and Nelson, thirty-one years a couple, having had four staggered months together (few seem enraged at this aspect of their violated human rights). The aberrations which Caribbean people suffer, either in their own societies or abroad are sometimes less melodramatic than what many other people of the Third and Fourth Worlds might claim; and yet... – I, for instance, was always aware of my father's reality, though distant, of the sound of his voice on the radio; of the fact that he was a prominent clergyman and that the family were not formally estranged. And yet, I met him for a total of five hours – when I was 42. No armies of occupation drove the family apart. This is a West Indian story. I would want some poems to reflect the surreal nature of this – all part of breaking down not the old but the new structures that are forever attempting to rehouse us.

*

One of the pleasant things in writing about Caribbean matters is that it gives you an excuse to write about sport. (We are, after all, dealing with the poetry of what Gordon Rohlehr calls somewhere the 'cricket-playing Caribbean'.) It's charming to think of a successful poem as a beautifully constructed and excitingly executed innings by a master batsman of the day; but there are risks. Sporting metaphors and analogies don't always work for us. Two of our finest writers have been compared with horses (we are not English: this isn't necessarily a step up the evolutionary scale) pitted against each other by their respective punters till the Walcott-Brathwaite race has become somewhat demeaning to the 'thoroughbreds' and embarrassing to others in the starting line. But we are not horses; let's not pursue this.

Let's not pursue this because it encourages a certain slackness of approach, till we find ourselves mixing racing and political metaphors and hailing successors: after the Big Two, how about the Gang of Four? No disrespect to the considerable talents (or to the persons) of Mervyn Morris, Dennis Scott, Tony McNeill and Wayne Brown to say that presenting them as inheritors of the Kingdom (Chiang Ch'ing, Zhang Chunquao, Yao Wenyuan and Wang Hougwan after the rule of Daddy-Mao) tends to divert us into the games critics play. With all these men inheriting the Kingdom, might not Caribbean women poets – working as far afield as Canada and Australia – feel the need to break away, declare UDI and make themselves visible?[9]

Awareness of these separatist tendencies are prompted by my living in Britain where questions of Caribbean *versus* the Caribbean diaspora surface from time to time during debates about culture. Obviously, we can't get into a position where writers of Caribbean extraction, due to long residence abroad, become merely poets of nostalgia but still claiming to represent a Caribbean reality that is vital. At the same time, people living in the Caribbean can't assume that a writer of Caribbean heritage living near, say, the nuclear power plant at Sellafield in Cumbria is expressing a non-Caribbean concern in warning about the effects of radiation contamination on the surrounding soil, the air, the Irish Sea.[10] (And, to be sure, Cuba has nuclear power stations.)

Few West Indians are so self-contained as to regard the island/territory of birth as fulfilling the sum total of their aspirations. (Remember Eric Roach looked towards the entire anglophone Caribbean, and was disappointed.) Simply to go to school or to work elsewhere constitutes leaving some of your emotional credit in that place – which you will call on from time to time. We must stop being on the defensive about this, and learn to exploit its possibilities. After all, the geography of most Caribbean poets' lives suggests dual or multiple citizenship: Linton Kwesi Johnson came to Britain when he was eleven, in 1963, and having lived here for the best part of twenty-six years, has proclaimed himself here to stay: he has two countries. James Berry arrived in 1948 when he was 25, having already lived in the USA. That's over 40 years' experience in Britain – more than that of a third of the population – white or black – born in the country. A.L. Hendriks, 'Shake' Keane and others have spent years on the continent of Europe attempting to work in languages other than English. Andrew Salkey, having lived in Britain for 25 years, has been in the USA now for the past 13. We are multi-national; cosmopolitan – some of us multi-lingual in ways that encompass and extend beyond the standard-English nation-language debate and have residences on earth which defy the makers of treaties and the laws of immigration.

2 *Another View of Our Times*

We who represent the First, Third and Fourth Worlds (some of us live in the First, we are grounded in the Third and we have sympathies with those of the Fourth seeking a homeland) have lost the luxury of whose who, once claiming to be on the margins of society, celebrated disintegration at the centre. Suddenly (or gradually) our margins have become the "front line" and so we have had to shed early assumptions of what the centre holds. The centre holds us.

That earlier comfort in disintegration of society which was seen as the expression of others' Will (i.e. the personality and aesthetic preferences of others) is tainted by anxiety. This isn't the apocalyptic despair of a W.B. Yeats or a De Gaulle; more the recognition that when old empires break up their successors inherit the mess – a condition well meditated upon by Brathwaite in *X/Self* (1987):

> Rome burns
> and our slavery begins

There is a temptation, then, to think of the world you might inherit, less in terms of the size of the estate than in the level of pollution that hangs over it. And there is (again) something surreal here, in the spectacle of people essentially without power taking responsibility, in fact, for the world.

But for the smaller things, too, that matter – old journeys being retraced: 'We turn Columbus's blunder back/From sun to snow, to bitter cities' no longer, I think, like Brathwaite's Tom (remember him?)

> So to New York London
> I finally come
> hope in my belly
> hate smothered down
> to the bone
> to suit the part
> I am playing

We're a generation at least away from this world of Hollywood, from the cultural violence of Laurence Olivier *playing* Othello; we're closer to the stance of cultural resistance of Linton Kwesi Johnson, which caused his one-off TV programme to be 'delayed' so that the 1983 British General Election could take place in an atmosphere of minimum dissent. No, some of these small journeys being retraced – a West Indian with a cardboard suitcase on route to England, a pioneer disguised as an immigrant – to test (not consciously but nevertheless serving to test) the proposition that acts have consequences and that distant historical events still need contemporary chapters to be written. Orthodoxies are being challenged by persons who are in no way heroes – the West Indian in the mid-50s electing to paint the front door of his dreary London house bright green, sick-making yellow. Or people very much like him, now sending their children back to the Caribbean to be educated, having lost confidence in what seems to be on offer here. They have found new allies – with women who will no longer accept that the impossibility of getting a pram and two young children through the London rush hour is their fault. And more. This is all part of a revaluation of Caribbean people on their stand versus the developed world.

And then there is Africa. Shortly after the independence of Ghana in 1957 many African-Americans and some West Indians went on pilgrimage to that country, and subsequently to other African states gaining independence. Over the intervening years, however, Africans in the diaspora and Africans at home have negotiated new contracts for creative contact, in which measurable skills were identified as a factor. The result is (in theory) that the African in the diaspora returns neither as penitent nor as conqueror, but to share in the process of reconstruction: the pioneering element still present. We learn now that there are charismatic churches in the Ivory Coast sending missionaries abroad, to Europe, to christianise France; and we have Cuban armies (for our purposes, a Caribbean army – not that we feel comfortable with armies) rewriting the history of the Middle Passage,[11] going to the aid of an African community in crisis, in Africa. All these things contribute to the person from the Caribbean experiencing a shift from the edge to the centre of the world – from periphery to hinterland.

In talking of that shift and thinking of poetry *four* things immediately come to mind. One is the way in which the language of Caribbean poetry has been extended and revolutionised by the use of dialect/nation-language. Second (and linked, perhaps, to the first) is the responsibility of poet as performer. Third, is the validation of the voice (and the life) of the West Indian woman; and finally, there is the death of the poet.

Nation-language has been important in declassing poetry. Both its practitioners and audience are no longer *necessarily* part of a social or, indeed, an educational elite; and this must lead to some shift in the patterns of cultural and information exchange, and to new relations of stress between those in (conventional) power who seek to conceal information, and the new disseminators of it. Hence, among other things, the death of the poet.

Now, the poet as performer. She/he presents the poem to a live audience. The poet differs from an actor performing, in at least two important ways: the poet is not backed/protected by the *text*, by an absent author; and the live audience can challenge the validity of the product in more intimate ways than walking out (which is the usual course of action employed by the disappointed theatre-goer). For the poet/performer, the protection of middle-man is removed.

This, perhaps, militates against the poetic mountebank succeeding indefinitely (though, the parallel problem of the good poet but bad performer reading her/himself off the circuit remains). The poet as performer is coming out this side of not being quite the preacher/teacher/activist/comic/apologist/bore, stripping the sermon/lesson/protest/joke/cause of outside authority, thereby admitting to a degree of vulnerability, thereby working against structures (most of them oppressive) which, in order to deny/conceal that vulnerability, wear the face of authority. In this spirit, performance is a continuous process of becoming.

The contemporary West Indian woman's voice would be important if she wrote no poetry. So here, part of the additional importance is not just that she has broken through the ghetto of invisibility but – from Louise Bennett to Judy Miles to Olive Senior to Dionne Brand to Amryl Johnson to Grace Nichols to Jean Binta Breeze and Lorna Goodison – we have a sense here that people who have been responsible for making certain things work in the society – through a continuous rather than a sporadic attachment to them; making certain – often nebulous – structures cohere, have assumed a special responsibility for that society, and derive part of their authority from that fact. They now have the confidence to articulate it, and an international climate ready to receive it.

Of the death of the poet I will say only this. Death in terms of silencing and harassment is a popular sport which governments find fascinating, as perusal of the journal *Index On Censorship* can testify. This isn't necessarily the general climate. It is one of the climates that prevail. But here, we are talking about two specific and literal deaths, the first, self-imposed by Eric Roach, who swam out to sea (Trinidad, 1974). The enormity of the act, the unlikeliness of it, the standing on its head of an old West Indian certainty that you took to the sea in search of a new life, must, at the very least, make us modify our view of the sea.

And then there is Michael Smith (1954-83). Suddenly we're not the poor relation to the Mandelstams of this world. From Michael Smith's death, we come forward with a sense of equality with the horrors found in *Index On Censorship*. We no longer have to march outside other people's embassies (because they take poets seriously and we don't) to gain significance by association. The minds of all are concentrated in a new way. Note Brathwaite's astonishing poem 'Stone', his tribute to Michael Smith. The stone that killed Michael Smith drained some of the innocence, some of the romantic excess from our poetry; indeed, from Brathwaite himself.

3 Points of Departure

As we have indicated, earlier anthologists have done their work, and what many people have been asking for now (schools and colleges among them) is assistance in selecting a manageable number of Caribbean and Caribbean heritage poets who can be expected both to give pleasure and to repay study. I wanted in this to identify and celebrate a broad range of aesthetic experience – those verbal, intellectual and musical constructs that both trap and release aspects of our particular history, geography, racial and social tension – while keeping a sharp eye against anything that might resemble "local colour", self-parody. It's no longer useful, I think, to pitch our discussion of the language of Caribbean poems in terms of standard English *versus* nation-language (Paula Burnett, in her introduction to the *Penguin Book of Caribbean Verse* aligns them broadly with the literary and oral traditions, respectively, and then goes on to show how they're now coming to co-mingle). The question I'm concerned with is how our thinking is able to match up to our living, and how our language is able to do justice to that. We're talking about the *appropriateness* of the language to the demands placed on it – demands of depicting states of private contentment, yes, but also states of mental and social disorientation, of political and sexist aggression (often the same thing); of cosmic doubt – as well as recording the unobtrusive, potentially lost gesture of affirmation. Language, for the poet, must retain the gift of risk. And language, as we say, is where the culture is.[12]

We note, with some satisfaction, the general revival of interest in pioneering figures like Claude McKay (Jamaica/USA, 1889-1948) and Una Marson (Jamaica, 1905-65). McKay's somewhat visionary quality and his early use of nation-language and Marson's near-feminist perspectives and wide social sympathies appeal to the present time. A.J. Seymour (Guyana, *b*. 1914) and Eric Roach could have been our starting points – as, indeed, could Louis Simpson[13]

(Jamaica/USA, *b*. 1923), a more substantial poet than any of the above. But it seemed to me that Louise Bennett (Jamaica, *b*. 1919) and Martin Carter (Guyana, *b*. 1927) are seminal figures who help us both to understand the tradition so far, and also to define new challenges for the practitioner.

Louise Bennett's marriage of the oral tradition – of popular songs, folk songs, Anancy stories, proverbs – to a rigorous (if, at times, stiff) scribal craft, is now much admired. Through her we can be said to have a direct line back to the earlier "newspaper poets", the Barbadian Edward Cordle (1857-1903) and James Martinez (*c*. 1860 - *c*. 1945) from Belize. Through her we certainly have a line forward to poets like James Berry and Valerie Bloom where the Jamaican proverbs, idiom and little social dramas of market women find expression in a new setting, or at least, to a new audience (in Britain).

Bennett is a marvellous story-teller and, as such, has a sense of drama (the Trinidadian, Paul Keens-Douglas [*b*. 1942] is someone from a later generation who comes to mind, who has perfected these skills); so her poems are really occasions to play out social scenes, which she does with wit and humour, and in the unliterary language of the people. The texture of Jamaican street life is felt everywhere in the work: the peddler hawking goods on the pavement; crafty, sharp-tongue, but never giving up on the possibility of a sale, even though the police are on her heels. And you have the feeling that this South Parade Peddler gets something out of it in the end, even if it's just the satisfaction of having abused the reluctant customer. (The fact that these particular peddlers are now put behind Corporation stalls 'thus reducing their nuisance value to passers-by', doesn't diminish the value of the poem.)

The numerous walk-on parts of street characters in Bennett suggest a richer, more populous *Miguel Street*; the Census man must be lied to – in a witty way – for questions he asks are either emotionally or economically embarrassing to admit to; Aunt Tama's niece in 'Yuh Nephew Sue', apparently out of her depth at a meeting of coconut plantation owners getting together to claim for storm damage, has to admit, with shame, that she is claiming for two, not two thousand trees (and even then she's inflated the figure by 100%). But in an odd way she comes out ahead *because she comes out telling the story against herself*. And with humour.

Jamaicans – West Indians – have a history of migration, as immigrants, as pioneers – from the late 19th century to Panama, elsewhere in Central America, Haiti, Cuba, then to the USA/Canada and from

the late 1940s to Britain/Europe. And, from the 19th century, to
Africa. Bennett, unlike most Caribbean writers, sees the comedy in
this. Those who go away and change accent, styles, colour are a
rich, though at times, disturbing vein in her humour. The boy who
spent six months in 'Merica' coming back to display 'not even lickle
twang' is a source of shame to his mother. And when in 'Tan a Yuh
Yard', the poet commends a man for staying put, the reality of what
going abroad can mean ('Pass fi White') is part of the experience
that informs this.

But really, the challenge that Bennett poses is not to "them" but
to us. In 'Uriah Preach', the stand-in preacher takes the opportunity
to get back at his "enemies" from the immunity of the pulpit: when
the laughter subsides, we are left with the feeling that we are adopting
roles and developing habits that will be hard to shake off when we
no longer have scapegoats to validate this.

There is a note of poignancy that comes through some of the
poems – a note that we perhaps more readily associate with the short
story: a sense of pathos. In 'Speechify', the bride and groom are
being toasted. Gradually, we learn that the courtship has been going
on for thirty years, but now it's all come good. No matter 'dem head
grey now, dem teet drop out'. The speaker uses the occasion to ask
young girls not to force the issue of marriage. Now, this isn't just
an anti-Hollywood Ad. This is a challenge to us. In a society whose
many insecurities include the quixotic nature of courtship, a thirty-
year long courtship must be akin to a war of attrition. Today, though
the new generation of women poets strive to treat these matters
differently – Lorna Goodison, for instance, in 'The Mulatta as
Penelope' – they are admitting one way or another, to the unequal
nature of the emotional contract between man and woman. Bennett's
view of Jamaican woman's independence ('Jamaica Oman') is equally
(but perhaps, unintentionally) disturbing. But part of Louise Ben-
nett's achievement is that she makes us laugh first and then conscious
that we have laughed.

Martin Carter (Guyana, *b*. 1927) spans an enormous arc of
experience from exuberant public statement to betrayed introspec-
tion. The journey from optimism to disillusionment within the same
generation is a problem for someone identified with a "new society".
Carter's move from a poetry of Innocence – *Poems of Resistance* (1954)
– to a poetry of Experience, is natural enough; it's the nature and
"texture" of the "experience" that is of concern. Martin Carter was
the youngest of the Guyanese triumvirate associated with that
country's literary renaissance. But unlike Wilson Harris – a poet

when young, before turning to prose – whose verse was heavy with an environmental presence peopled with figures, uncreolised, from classical mythology – Hector, Agamemnon, Achilles – etc; and unlike A.J. Seymour with his interest in heroes of history and literature, Carter's main concern was with the politics of the day, with political revolution, with the reality of colonial oppression.[14] Hence, the great lyrical trumpetings: 'I Come from the Nigger Yard'; 'This Is the Dark Time, My Love'...In 'Looking at Your Hands', he concludes: 'I do not sleep to dream, but dream to change the world.' Yes, you could say that in 1951 and mean it. 'University of Hunger' displays all the early Carter generosity, exuberance and sense of being on the cusp.

But Carter was never an armchair revolutionary. In 'On the Fourth Night of the Hunger Strike' and 'Death of a Comrade', we feel the emotional engagement, the desperate courage devoid of bravado, matched to a language no longer listening to itself. The outcome of political events, the failure of things to match their promise led to the draining of the public voice into something more private. By the time we get to 'Groaning in this Wilderness' (1962) the poet, not speaking but listening (interestingly, still on the street) is reeling to find that speech has become a brutish sound, and that the corruption is contagious. It is a tough and courageous admission. True, the possibility of political engagement is now dismissed ('There Is No Riot', 1975); but in returning to the puzzle of how things get corrupted and die, the rhythm cheats on the thought, Carter's voice refuses to go flat and ('How Come?' 1972) there is bounce; there is life.

This survey is not strictly chronological in terms of following the poets' birth dates. I tried to give some thought of where best to place a poet in terms of when she/he made an impact on other poets and on the general public. And in dealing with people living in more than one society this is difficult. In the slightly larger anthology planned, I had thought of putting A.L. Hendriks (Jamaica, *b.* 1922) after Martin Carter, although he is a few years older than Carter, mainly because his work was slower to percolate. James Berry (Jamaica, *b.* 1924), though some years older than Walcott and Brathwaite, follows them, and the much younger duo of Scott and Morris, because his impact came later, and in Britain, where he is something of a conduit between West Indian and black British modes of expression (and perhaps, of perception).

The point of the (sadly missing) Hendriks' inclusion was not only his pleasing, well-crafted poems, 'lyrical and sometimes metaphysically

crafty', as Pam Mordecai says about them...work that 'resonates
with a powerful sense of the Jamaican place'; but that Hendriks was
part of a generation of poets with intimate contact with non-
anglophone cultures and whose work defies the English-British
Caribbean cultural Trade Route. Poets in this category would
include John Figueroa (Jamaica, *b*. 1920), whose maternal grand-
father came from Cuba (his name is John Joseph Maria), and who
has worked in Puerto Rico, Nigeria as well as in Britain; Shake
Keane (St Vincent, *b*. 1927), whose experience as a jazz musician
and long residence in Germany have informed his work; Andrew
Salkey (Panama/Jamaica/London/Amherst) whose Chilean poems
represent a new level of sensitivity in the political poetry of the
cricket-playing Caribbean and, of course Hendriks, whose mother
was French, and who lived in Germany for some years. They rep-
resent an anti-parochial spirit, so much more generous than that of
most of their English counterparts. Here is Hendriks' 'St Paul-de-
Vence' (from *The Islanders* [1983]):

> They sat in the garden, separate,
> Each with secure, clear thought.
>
> Mireille holding her palette
> Dreaming of subtler tints,
> Alex visioning timber
> And steel and concrete and glass,
> Guillaume putting on paper
> Words upon words upon words.
>
> Nobody spoke to the silence,
> No one mentioned the date.
>
> The sun cascaded,
> Drenching their figures with light,
> And the wind moved like a dancer,
> Sinuous, confident, strong.
>
> The dog slept in the shadow,
> Moaned in his dream,
> Following scents lost forever;
>
> And behind,
> The Provencal house
> Sprawled
> With a cargo of books
> And pictures
> And music
> And fruit.
>
> Nobody spoke to the silence,
> No one mentioned the date.

Derek Walcott was born in 1930 in St Lucia but spent most of his working life in Trinidad where, in 1959, he founded the Trinidad Theatre Workshop which he directed until 1977. In recent years, he has tended to live in the USA.

Walcott is, quite simply, one of the finest poets writing anywhere in the world today. Just about everyone agrees – from Robert Graves back in 1962 to Joseph Brodsky, winner of the Nobel Prize for Literature in 1987 – that Walcott is among the finest writing *in English*. This sometimes gets Walcott into trouble about the sort of English he traditionally uses – whether it's sufficiently folk, sufficiently distanced from the English and American masters of the colonial past and present. But these are often ideological snipes, and a failure fully to appreciate the linguistic subtlety of the poet.

Walcott's lyrical gift is rare; his range of sympathy wide, suggesting an imaginative engagement with a world of unusual complexity: a large world filled with strange longings and a rich vocabulary. But it's our world. Often, with Walcott, it's like being in the presence of an inspired and somewhat unlikely guide to a world of treasure we don't quite believe we've inherited. His amazing autobiography *Another Life* (1972) is itself a treasure-trove. Here Walcott attempts in poetry what had hitherto been achieved in the Caribbean only in prose: 'the growth of consciousness through development from child to young man while portraying a uniquely Caribbean consciousness'.[15] It's rich in texture and variety; large enough to register loss, love, regret, sensuality, joy; the metaphysics of sea, sky, place, love of painting, without the feeling that any one state had to be nudged aside to make room for another, or was planted artificially to make a point or to complete the scheme. And it avoids sentimentality.

Walcott is self-consciously the poet, and his mode is largely self-exploration. Of his African and European ancestry, he muses:

> I who am poisoned with the blood of both
> Where shall I turn, divided to the vein?
> I who have cursed
> The drunken officer of British rule, how choose
> Between this Africa and the English tongue I love?
>
> ('A Far Cry from Africa', *In a Green Night* [1962])

This sometimes somewhat embarrassing self-consciousness runs through all the collections, from the precocious *25 Poems* (1948) through *Another Life* and into the territory of ageing and sexual anxieties (*The Star Apple Kingdom* [1980], *The Fortunate Traveller* [1982]), to *The Arkansas Testament* (1987), where his flirting with U.S. citizenship drenches the title poem in a mood of anxiety and hopefulness of a man looking over a house he might buy – a house whose reputation for ill might not be in the past. The neighbours know more than they say.

One of Walcott's early images was of the Castaway, logging conditions of shipwreck. It is the thought of this solitary pursuit, and Walcott's admission of the tool he sought to perfect it:

> I seek
> As climate seeks its style, to write
> Verse crisp as sand, clear as sunlight
> Cold as the curled wave, ordinary
> As a tumbler of island water
>   ('Islands', *In a Green Night* [1962])

that has upset certain critics who feel the poet's role to be more communal.[16] And many of Walcott's early statements have been taken, not as the privileged glimpse inside a writer's mind trying to relate achievement to objectives, but as literary manifestoes.[17] Maybe a late statement by Walcott, redefining his stance, might be helpful:

> I think for a poet the struggle from the beginning is to really find the confidence and authority of your own voice, not only in terms of historical style but how you get to the point where what you're writing on the page is metrically and in terms of tone, the exact voice in which you speak
>   (Radio Ulster, 1988)

Yes, this has something to do with accepting your physiology, your biography. But it also has something to do with getting beyond the ego – as Heaney points out in connection with Sylvia Plath – 'in order to become the voice of more than the autobiography'; so that the marrying of sound and meaning triggers or confirms something deeper than literal sense, something that might unite poem, poet and reader/listener 'in an experience of enlargement'.[18] This is Walcott's quest.

Edward Kamau Brathwaite (*b*. 1930, in Barbados) burst on the poetry scene almost ready-made with three book-length poems in two years: *Rights of Passage* (1967), *Masks* (1968) and *Islands* (1969). (Poems written earlier were published in a later collection *Other Exiles* [1975]). The explosive force of the Brathwaite eruption is hard to imagine. The impact on the normally non-poetry-reading Caribbean youth was immediate (Brathwaite made records and that helped). If the volume of work seems scarcely credible, what seemed an entirely new way of composing poems made us suspect that a revolution of some kind was taking place. And remember, this was '68 with Kent State and the Provos in Amsterdam; "Free Universities" (i.e. an assertion of student power) were springing up in

England, including Cambridge, Brathwaite's university. In Paris and Prague, success seemed closer, defeat more numbing. October '68, Walter Rodney was leading a protest on the Mona Campus of the University of the West Indies; so we were prepared for the shock of the new. But not for this:

> E-
> gypt
> in Af-
> rica
> Mesopo-
> tamia
> Mero
> ë
>
> the
> Nile
> silica
> glass
> and brittle
> Sa-
> hara, Tim-
> buctu, Gao
> the hills of
> Ahafo, winds
>
> of the Ni-
> ger, Kumasi
> and Kiver
> down the
> coiled Congo
> and down
> that black river
> that tides us to hell

('The Journeys', *Rights of Passage* [1967])

This was certainly different from tidy rows of lines roughly matching one another in length, varying the caesura this way, that way, changing the rhyme scheme. The new shape often looked like something struggling to be formed. Yet it had the authority of recognition. It matched Brathwaite's subject which was migration, exile, wanderings. Then there was the suggestion that these stumblings across the page, along a dried river-bed, into the spring of memory were to be accompanied by sound: the drum. The work song. Gospel music. Blues. Calypso, Jazz. Read to this music, what seemed at first perverse or eccentric, now not only made sense, but (when it worked, which it often did) brought release. Add to these sounds, Ska. Rock Steady. Reggae. People hitherto cowed by "good talk", "good writing" no longer felt tongue-tied, and a whole flood of personal reminiscence and statement-making ensued from people who had been given the go-ahead to "mash up" language; given "nation-language". A main difference between Brathwaite and his imitators is that his music isn't external to the lines but contained within them.

Of course it wasn't all new. Caribbean novelists had used dialect before to give articulation to the underclass; there are echoes of Césaire (of Martinique) and of Nicolás Guillén (of Cuba),[19] but these epics, this heroic scale was new to Caribbean anglophone poetry.

The other startling factor, of course, was the treatment of Africa. Africa, from being a vague memory in the West Indian literary consciousness, was given definition by Brathwaite. During his stay in Ghana from 1955 to 1962, he used his professional skills as historian to give authority to his study of the Caribbean folk tradition.

Brathwaite's is the communal voice par excellence (he comes over almost like the empathy figure in the traditional drama) charting us through often uncomfortable territory. In *Rights of Passage* we move restlessly from the Caribbean to the USA and back. *Masks* reverses the journey from Africa, and *Islands* tries to make sense of what has come to be called the West Indies. Two great cycles, two trilogies have been completed (as well as other work including, importantly, critical work) and the poet is about to embark on a third cycle.

Brathwaite's revolution has gathered its own momentum; imitators abound. But it is interesting that this most communal of poets (and accessible of men) whose various personae serve to guide us through these journeys, still seems to reside at a distance from his reader/listener, which is not always the case of a more "literary" poet. Even in the touching tribute to Brathwaite by Pam Mordecai, the subject is more comfortably accommodated in the third person, at the start of the poem, than when addressed directly towards the end. And the poem, though beautiful, carries a slight suspicion of parody.[20]

Editors, like people running for President, always talk about having to make tough choices; but unlike the elected Presidents, editors generally have to honour these promises. So which two of the Gang of Four? It turned out in the end to be Mervyn Morris and Dennis Scott: Wayne Brown (Trinidad, *b.* 1943) is an elegant poet, and his collection, *On the Coast* (1972), which won many awards, reveals him to be fine poet in the Walcott mould. Tony McNeill (Jamaica, *b.* 1941) is like the old romantic poet-figure brought up to date. He bares himself in the act of radiating poetry. His is a tormented spirit from a Dostoyevskian world updated with new terrors of race-strife, nuclear madness, man's technological toys out of control: his ability, mentally, to cope not helped by a drug culture. So there is a desperate search for sanity, balance. McNeill adopts the guise of the flamingo (rather than the John Crow scavenger): with this 'exotic but comical' bird on one side and the dream of a Rasta "healing" community on the other, McNeill, punishingly, keeps the performance going.

McNeill's sense of the surreal is carried through in **Dennis Scott** (Jamaica, *b*. 1939); and in neither poet is this an attempt to escape the realities of Jamaican society. It is their perception of the madness in the society that feeds the vision. They, like Mervyn Morris, are privileged people in the society (both socially and in their heightened consciousness as artists; hence the great number of poems – particularly in Scott – on the role of the poet). The menace of violence is everywhere, in subject, in imagery. Indeed, Scott's bird imagery is like an update of early Ted Hughes, except that the violence is not now of the natural world, but something more cosmic. Or, as in 'For the Last Time, Fire', at least apocalyptic. All these middle-class poets have learnt to use "nation-language", tellingly, as an effective tool – Scott in 'Uncle Time', Morris in 'I Am the Man' etc, and in so doing at least show themselves to be ideological men of their times.

Mervyn Morris (Jamaica, *b*. 1937) is the minimalist[21] whose poems are bound tight with irony, and, because of his brevity, has probably fewer dead trees on his conscience than the rest of us. Morris seems different from other Caribbean poets because of the type of filtering you suspect to have taken place before the poem announces itself on the page. (In others, Walcott, for instance, the filtering is an important part of the process of making the poem; it's the sensual unfolding of the lines that is so satisfyingly part of the subject.) So in Morris, we are disposed to have a certain respect for the *result*. This is a slightly unusual contract for a poet to make with his reader.

Edward Baugh (Jamaica, *b*. 1936) is another who should be in this anthology, but has at present two things going against him: first he hasn't had a major volume out; and secondly, as an academic and critic, he has spent much time promoting other people's poetry at the expense of his own. His 'Sometimes in the Middle of the Story' should be read as a taster.

The 70s scene was just as active in Britain among people from the Caribbean. In the wake of CAM, Caribbean and black poets became prominent on the poetry-performing circuit. Linton Kwesi

Johnson, with his band, was able to attract up to 1500 people at a
"gig". One of the aims of CAM was to make Caribbean writing in
Britain more visible and poetry seemed to benefit more from this
than other genres.[22] One of the people at the heart of organising
poetry events – to live audiences, on radio and, latterly, on television
– was James Berry (Jamaica, *b*. 1924). Berry, though an older figure,
was able to establish rapport with the new generation of black writers
in Britain. (This was particularly important after the departure of
Andrew Salkey to the U.S. in the mid-70s – for Salkey had per-
formed a similar role, over a larger field.) Berry was the driving
force behind The Bluefoot Travellers troupe, which gave often
unpublished writers the opportunity of an audience; then sub-
sequently, with his two anthologies, *Bluefoot Traveller* and *News For
Babylon* brought them to the notice of readers.

Berry's own literary traditions are embedded in the Jamaican folk,
his proverbs and letters home – adopting the persona of an unlettered
Jamaican woman in *Lucy's Letter* (1975) – recall those newspaper
figures behind Louise Bennett, while the proverbs, as we have said,
recall Bennett. And younger writers (some of them, like Fred D'Agu-
iar, non-Jamaican) have attested to Berry's role as a conduit to their
understanding of that tradition. With his high profile, in schools
and in the media, Berry has helped to gain acceptance for nation-
language as a vehicle for conveying complex and mature thought
and feeling.

It's unwise to treat Linton Kwesi Johnson as a purely British
phenomenon, so we'll return to him.

It has been said that the two most exciting events in Jamaican
poetry of the seventies have been the emergence of "dub" (more of
this later) and the impact of women poets on what has been – despite
the influence of Bennett and Marson – a predominantly male trad-
ition. This recovery of the woman's voice is reflected in a couple of
anthologies, *Savacou*'s special 'New Poets' issue where seven of the
thirteen poets represented are women; and Heinemann's *Jamaica
Woman* (1980) – a collection of fifteen poets. Beverley Brown, whom
Savacou published in an individual edition, *Dream Diary* (1982),
emerges as someone of outstanding promise; but it's her somewhat
older contemporaries Olive Senior and Lorna Goodison who have
arrested our attention.

Olive Senior (Jamaica, *b*. 1943) shouldn't, perhaps, by our own
criteria, appear quite so soon in the story as her first (and, to date,
only) book, *Talking of Trees* (Calabash Press, Mona, Jamaica)
appeared only in 1985, but it's so far from being a "first book" that

we must assume her influence has long been felt. Senior must be
– apart from Walcott – our most elegant and graceful poet. The
thing that immediately strikes one is her control of tone – like a
singer having perfect pitch. There is a cleanliness to the writing, a
sureness of diction that is always pleasing. What is remarkable about
this is that Senior's world is not divorced from the stress of life, the
threat of day-to-day existence. This threat is usually represented by
man, maleness. Her father's house the night before the bird-shooting
season commences 'turns macho' while 'contentless women' do their
duty and little girls come out on the side of the birds. In 'Portrait',
it is the father's dark shadow that fills the doorway. Armed, this time
('One Night, the Father') he takes on the family in a bizarre one-
sided attempt at a shoot-out. Inevitably, there is the question of
incest ('The Mother'). Here, Uncle Paul is certainly, and the father,
possibly, a culprit. The mother colludes: how can she cope when
her pressing worry tonight is the young son running wild in the city
– possibly armed? The reality of the city is the more frightening
because of the delicacy with which the horrors are depicted. We
have to remind ourselves that there are guns guns guns everywhere,
madness. The threat of living in the apartment is evident, the caught
moment of sadness, is felt. And in 'tie up tight/in crocus bag' there
is a very real corpse.

But with the tone, the temper is maintained. There can be empathy
with men – the man in 'Hill Country', for instance, who knows that
sentiment for his unproductive bit of land won't be transferred to
his sons, won't help them to resist the pull of the city. In her feeling
for the country, as opposed to the town – in her talking of trees –
Senior is prepared to recognise new allies.

There is humour, too; a lightness of touch. In Kingston, a well-
placed Mistress Marshall of reactionary views ('The Lady') wants
to escape to Miami (to Miami!) to improve her skin pigment and
distance herself from fellow black people; and she wants, in effect,
to live in a supermarket. Yet (as with those poems of Louise Bennett)
she is not *just* a figure of fun. The reality which turns these people
crazy is not addressed. Mistress Marshall wakes to a hangover; her
husband is cheating on her – this is the husband without whom she
can't presumably get to Miami! – cheating on her 'with a girl/who's
not slim'. So 'she must go to the gym/to keep fit and trim'. Senior's
update of Apollinaire's *'Il Pleut'* manages to be as elegant as the
original and to be a poem against war, against the rape of nature –
this promise, this threat of *RAIN*.

Lorna Goodison (Jamaica, *b.* 1947) is more overt and self-conscious than Olive Senior as someone developing a feminist voice, a "woman's" voice. She is closer to the confessional poets of the USA a couple of decades ago, or of the feminist poets on both sides of the Atlantic now. Though this is only one of her modes; she can be metaphysical in her conceits, as in 'Keith Jarrett – Rainmaker' when the heat of her Africanness, and the treasures she stores, need to be cooled/nourished by the 'waterfalls of rain' that his hands could divine on the keyboard. This quality is also present in her "political" poem, 'Bedspread' – a woman's poem in that it enlarges the concept of "political" beyond the usual malespeak. Here, after the women of Azania had woven a blanket, in ANC colours

            with slender
    capable hands
    accustomed to binding wounds
    hands that closed the eyes of
    dead children

the police raided Winnie Mandela's home, and arrested the blanket. Goodison celebrates her mother ('For My Mother...') in a poem of sensuality; of pain of hope betrayed; of the maturity of acceptance. She celebrates women generally ('For Rosa Parks', 'Nanny') and rewrites the old Penelope myths, not, one feels, to fulfill a feminist programme but in her determination to reconnect with an organic, female, suppressed, principle.

There is a raw edge of anger, too, as she examines how women are forced to deny their sexuality, to censor themselves. Some become mermaids 'sex locked under/mother-of-pearl scales'. And there is the familiar game of woman waiting for man, gone to sea/gone abroad.

    I will not sit and spin and spin
    the door open to let the madness in
    till the sailor finally weary
    of the sea
    returns with tin souvenirs and a claim
    to me
            ('The Mulatta As Penelope', *I Am Becoming My Mother*)

Here, she invests, emotionally, in child rather than husband. Is the child a boy? Is this another victory for patriarchy?

Linton Kwesi Johnson (Jamaica, *b.* 1952) came to Britain when he was eleven and made the biggest public impact of any of the Caribbean/black poets in Britain by the time he was twenty. He captured the popular imagination partly because he performed with a band; partly because much of his work (like Brathwaite's) was recorded, usually to a reggae beat; and partly because his social message struck a chord with young people, black and white. Secure in his Jamaican roots, LKJ firmly identified himself with the black British, and has continued to draw creative energy from both sources: he now has a large and loyal following in many countries.

There is something hypnotic in the rhythm of LKJ's beat:

Shock-black bubble-doun-beat bouncing
rock-wise tumble-doun sound music;
foot-drop find drum, blood story,
bass history is a moving
        is a hurting black story.
('Reggae Sounds')

but this isn't romantic excess. This is a form of release. It is also an attempt to control the frustrations which living in a society that is often openly racist and violent engender. (It's as if Olive Senior's background tenement-dwellers suddenly found their voice and a language which we can empathise with.) He issues albums but the words are his starting point ('The music just grew out of the poetry'), though the fusion is so complete – even when there is no band – that the question is academic. In poem after poem ('Five Nights Bleeding') we get a confrontation with violence – knives, blood – and yet we get the feeling that it is this resistance by the minority that prevents greater violence. Of course things have consequences and an ambivalence to violence by the victims of violence is a condition that LKJ dramatises. The warnings/threats come thick and fast ('Time Come'); but if your situation is desperate and your probable allies ('Di Black Petty-Booshwah') let you down and you dream to sing

dere'ill be peace
in da valley
some day

you must fight now against the peace of genocide.

So the campaigning element in LKJ is paramount ('Experience' to Carter's 'Innocence'). He draws attention to Home Office scandals – as with the anti-SUS poem 'Sonny's Lettah' and generally castigates the powers that be for the urban squalor they create. It is the poor and black who most need the country's public spaces. If these are allowed to contract (Health, Education, Housing) or to be polluted (the media; the climate of tolerance, the unacquisitive tradition) the victims must protest.

After reggae came "dub". This was another expression of the post-60s feeling of protest that swept the Caribbean as well as the metropolitan centres. The result in poetry was in some ways a "downmarket" extension of Brathwaite. The "dub" poets work with musicians and are heavily influenced in style by the disc jockeys. In Jamaica these DJs are themselves often celebrities, part of their act being to improvise – talk, rap, chant, abuse, gossip, sometimes provide witty political and social commentary. They could do this because 'records were manufactured with a "dub" side, that is, an instrumental version of the song with the vocal track removed ("dubbed out")'.[23] The most notable dub poets are Michael Smith (Jamaica, 1954-83), Oku Onuora (Jamaica, *b*. 1952) and Mutabaruka (Jamaica, *b*. 1952). These poets see themselves (like LKJ in England) with a mission to articulate the condition of the oppressed, using the language and music of the oppressed.

Michael Smith was a magnetic performer, having perfected his extraordinary technique at the Jamaican School of Drama, of which he was a graduate. He had a colossal international reputation for someone who made his first record in 1980 and was dead before the end of 1983 – murdered in the street during the Jamaican elections. Between those two dates he appeared at Carifesta in Barbados in 1981; gave a memorable performance at the First International Bookfair of Radical Black and Third World Books, in London in 1982 (and did a BBC commentary – as, indeed, he'd done after the Carifesta appearance) as well as a hugely successful UNESCO performance in Paris later that year.

Michael Smith's performances of 'Mi Cyaan Believe It', 'Say, Natty-Natty' and 'I and I Alone' are like nothing else in the language. If there is consolation to be drawn from any of this, it is that we have his voice on tape and his memorable presence on film.

Michael Smith's development was arrested. At the stage where he was cut down, he claimed to be suspicious of lyricism; in his own words, of 'lamentations for the dead'. Much of his work is, of course, lyrical. But it remained stubbornly male – a strong characteristic of Reggae/dub/Rasta culture. The stone that cut down Michael Smith robbed us of the adult phase that might have come.

Grace Nichols (Guyana, *b*. 1950) is what Alice Walker would call "womanist " because she seems to easy in her womanness. She reminds us, *I is a long memoried woman*, and the streams of memory which flow through her have more moisture than the arid landscape that Brathwaite tried to reclaim in *Masks*. Nichols' poems have a wholeness, an intouchness barely discernible in her male colleagues. Though many of her themes are common with Goodison her angle of approach and her modes of celebration are different. Nichols is

economical – even in her book-length sequence, quoted above –
and witty.

IT'S BETTER TO DIE IN THE FLESH OF HOPE
THAN TO LIVE IN THE SLIMNESS OF DESPAIR
('The Fat Black Woman's Motto on Her Bedroom Door')

This is from *The Fat Black Woman's Poems* (Virago, 1984) – a title which
raised a few delicate eyebrows – as, indeed, her equally impressive
Lazy Thoughts of a Lazy Woman (Virago, 1989) will do. But Nichols
is an honest poet, and in these poems effects a corrective to the
male fantasy of 'African Queen' – long-necked and Hollywood.
Nichols' fat black women are regal in their assuredness, in their
sensuality, in their vulnerability, in their humanity. There is a per-
vading sense of fun in her work, even when the challenge is sharp
– as it is against men who don't surrender to the spell of the fat,
black woman's charms.

Grace Nichols' skill at slipping in and out of modes of English is
as good as any and she manages to make "nation-language" seem
not a duty, not a deliberate act of "rooting", but a gift, joyfully received.

The journeys continue. **Fred D'Aguiar** (London/Guyana/Lon-
don, *b*. 1960) was sent from London to Guyana to be educated –
'posted home for a proper upbringing', and the wisdom of this is
evident in his first book, *Mama Dot* (Chatto, 1985). This short book
(48 pages) has a mock-heroic quality which is pleasing in the context
of so much contemporary poetic earnestness. There is 'Town
Daddy' who visits the country cousins with presents – like the father
home from sea; there is 'Pappa-T' – the grandfather who actually
did learn his Tennyson at sea, slipping out of his poetic voice to
reprimand the inattentive, young audience:

If yu all don't pay me mind,
I goin ge yu a good lickin an sen yu to bed...

and best of all, there is 'Mama Dot'. Yes, she is the archetypal
grandmother, an elemental force: 'She gesticulates and it's sheet
lightning on our world.' She is feared as she should be; her bush
remedies work perfect obeah, frightening the child back to health,
and when she warns against flying a kite on Good Friday, you know
the rascal who disobeys her is going to be punished by an unseen
hand (remember those grandmothers who ruled the household, who
outlawed ironing on a Sunday: remember the burnt, flat-iron designs
on Sunday pants and white shirts as a result?).

But 'Mama Dot' is not an ogre. The warmth, the sensuality, the
fullness of life, pervade the whole. (This is also true of Nichols, as

we've noted, and of that other Guyanese "poetsonion" and magnetic performer, John Agard.)

Part of the pleasure of these poems is the subtlety of their shaping. Some have strong endings, like stories; but the more arresting of these aren't punch-lines. They are proverbs, sayings or half-threats – *Neva see come fo see*; *Bwoy, we goin ge yu a chance, run!* etc – which the entire poem "sits" on so that this "knowledge" can explode. This quality is also present in some of James Berry's 'Lucy' poems.

4 Hinterland

It seems right, when naming your book, to show some loyalty to the subject rather than to the publisher (The *Penguin* book of…The *Faber* book of…The *Bloodaxe* book of…) What if tobacco companies, say, or unattractive governments started publishing poetry? Yet, without publishers there are no books, in the normal sense; so maybe poets should quietly write their publishers love letters, and in exchange, keep control of the book titles.

Caribbean Poetry in English is what we want to celebrate here; and this led us to look in the main areas where this work is produced: the "cricket-playing" Caribbean, naturally, the UK and Canada. The fact that none of the fine Caribbean-heritage poets working in Canada survived into the final manuscript, doesn't change the *concept* of the enterprise, doesn't make it a West Indies and black British exclusive.[24]

A more disappointing feature is that the book (though, with Olive Senior and Fred D'Aguiar, not solidly Afro-Caribbean) has no Indo-Caribbean representation. This is not ideological. Until the very end there was the possibility that one Dabydeen,[25] at least, might be fitted in; but the more people "fitted in", the thinner the representation of each, and that would defeat the purpose of the anthology.

Having stressed all along the central rather than the peripheral nature of the Caribbean people's position in the contemporary world – either because they live in metropolitan centres and make the machines which "date" us; or absorb the stress of those societies; whether, living on the archipelago, they have sometimes woken up to gunboats and other surprises, and now to a sea polluted by toxic waste from abroad; or whether as "newer" societies having to take responsibility for the lapses of "older" ones – we wanted to show that the most arresting poetry grew out of this hinterland of experience. Part of the shift we spoke of earlier, is being able to release certain concepts that both traditional and fashionable disciplines have colonised. *Hinterland*, having been chosen, all sorts of things surfaced to confirm its rightness. This is Brathwaite, from an early essay:

> In the Caribbean, whether it be African or Amerindian, the recognition of an ancestral relationship with the folk or aboriginal culture involves the artist and participant in a journey into the past and hinterland which is at the same time a movement of possession into present and future.[26]

Finally, a note of explanation about two things. One: the length of the introduction was intended not just to give a feel for the context of the work, but to draw attention to source-material not always easily accessible. Two: for some of the more established poets, I've taken interviews and statements made relatively early in their careers, to prevent the revisionism of hindsight.

E.A. MARKHAM
Montserrat & University of Ulster
1989

Notes

1. In Britain, for instance, Caribbean heritage poets are still not accorded dual-citizenship when it comes to entry into prestige collections of British poetry. None appeared in the *Penguin Book of Contemporary British Poetry*, edited by Blake Morrison and Andrew Motion (1982) and in the recent *New British Poetry* (Paladin, 1988) they were accorded their own *Black British Poetry* section. Similarly, in the massive portmanteau of world poetry, *The Rattle Bag*, edited by Seamus Heaney and Ted Hughes (Faber, 1982), Louis Simpson and Derek Walcott are represented by one poem each – the *only* two from the Caribbean amongst nearly 500 poems.

2. The Anne Walmsley/Nick Caistor *Facing the Sea* (Heinemann, 1986) is an ambitious update of the pan-Caribbean idea, though sticking to literary creative work. O.R. Dathorne's *Caribbean Verse* (complete with elaborate notes) had appeared in 1967 from HEB.

3. This loose association of Caribbean and black poets in Britain was one of the many cultural offshoots of the Caribbean Artists Movement started by John La Rose, Edward Kamau Brathwaite and Andrew Salkey in London in 1966. (Other manifestations of CAM are the Savacou Publishing enterprise in Jamaica and the annual Radical, Black and Third World Book Fair held in London and other British cities.)

4. MAAS (Minorities' Arts Advisory Service) provides information, advice and training for people involved in or interested in Black Arts in Britain. As part

of this service it compiles a register of black artists in Britain, and produces the quarterly arts magazine *Artrage*. This is, therefore, a Black Arts, not a Caribbean magazine.

5. The death of Eric Roach (1915-74, born in Tobago) was self-imposed. Michael Smith (1954-83) was stoned to death in Kingston, Jamaica, his birthplace.

6. See Figueroa's review of *X/Self* by Edward Kamau Brathwaite and *The Arkansas Testament* by Derek Walcott, in *London Magazine* (August/September 1988, pp.116-9).

7. 'What the Twilight Says': An Overture; introduction to *Dream On Monkey Mountain & Other Plays* (Farrar, Straus & Giroux, 1970), p.4.

8. Gordon Rohlehr reminds us that in Trinidad five poets were among the 1970 detainees; Jack Kelshall, a Guyanese, became a poet after he was wrongfully imprisoned in the 1970s, and that Martin Carter had of course experienced this under the British two decades earlier. 'Under such stasis, such unchange, some writers have chosen the amnesia of alcohol. Others, like Mittleholzer, Leroy Calliste, Eric Roach, the painter and folklorist Harold Simmons, committed suicide by rope, poison, the knife or fire' – 'Trophy and Catastrophe', address given at the Guyana Prize for Literature, 1987. Eric Roach of course drowned himself.

9. There is, as it happens, a flourishing industry in feminist/women's publishing with – in Britain – Virago, the Women's Press, Sheba and (perhaps) HEB in the ascendant. Heinemann, in 1980, published *Jamaica Woman*, poems edited by Mervyn Morris and Pamela Mordecai; and in Jamaica, in 1977, *Savacou* 13 was devoted to 'Caribbean Women', but had very few poems. The women's publishing scene is, if anything, more vibrant in North America.

10. Its original name, Windscale, had become unattractive to the authorities, partly because it was associated in the popular mind – because of numerous leaks over the years – with danger, with death.

11. Brathwaite, of course, also reverses the Middle Passage voyage – in *Masks* – and returns to Africa.

12. It might be worth pointing out the obvious, that purely formal experiments with language – concrete poetry, etc – might occasionally yield unexpected results; a case not of language matching the life but the other way round. It might be useful to point out, also, the danger of having a too-fixed ideology of language as social tool. When Michael Smith (in 'Say, Natty-Natty') warns us 'be ware of de cultural smuggler', he is talking to most of us.

13. Louis Simpson went to the USA from Jamaica at the age of 17 in 1940, and served with the US Army in 1943-45. None of this – including the fact that he is a US citizen (so was Claud McKay) – disqualifies him from appearing in this book. Nor even the fact, as some claim, that his numerous literary awards – the Prix de Rome, the Pulitzer Prize in 1964 – are thought to pay tribute to American rather than Caribbean literary achievement. (No one really doubts that the novelists Austen Clarke [Barbados/Canada] and Paule Marshall [Barbados/USA] are Caribbean novelists.) Though, with Simpson, one gets the sense of someone whose imagination has been fed first by the Russia of his mother's birth, and later by the USA; whereas the Caribbean interlude seems to have engaged him less.

14. Another poet who was concerned with public issues, with the political struggles in Jamaica from the late 1930s, was George Campbell (*b.* 1916, in Panama – like Andrew Salkey – of Jamaican parents). He was associated with *Focus* magazine in the 1940s, and – like Martin Carter – helped to legitimatise the protest tradition in Caribbean poetry.

15. Paula Burnett, *Penguin Book of Caribbean Verse*; introduction.

16. Brathwaite, though generous in his acknowledgement of Walcott's 'brilliance' is often critical of his trend towards individual rather than communal wholeness.

17. Chinua Achebe, the Nigerian novelist, is fond of pointing out that when you are a pioneer in literature from the Third World, one of your traditional functions has been to make statements on the world's stages. You can't be expected to be held to all of them.

18. *The Government of the Tongue* (Faber, 1988).

19. Many people have pointed out the T.S. Eliot influences on *Other Exiles*; and in the later poetry – *Mother Poem*, for instance – there are wonderful echoes of Walt Whitman. This is not a criticism. Brathwaite is large enough to absorb these influences from white Europe/America as well as those from Africa.

20. 'Eddy'
(with indebtedness to Edward Kamau and 'The Glory Trumpeter')

Eddy	blow my mind
eddy	blow my mind
eddy plays	with the thrum
eddy plays on	of a drum
a life	with the blues
with his ripples	black good news
of words	of a whole
catch the song	soul for me
catch the song	eddy
how I listen	eddy play
and long	eddy play
for its rope	on my life
in the neck	with your ripples
of my mind	of words
how I listen	watch my throat
and long	watch my throat
for the point	Let the whirl
of its hook	catch my song
in my throat	and I choke
on some note	on the note
on some tremulous	of your stream
note still	
on air	
still on air	

[Pam Mordecai, *Caribbean Quarterly*, 26 nos.1-2 (March-June 1980).]

21. Caribbean critics tend to disagree on the achievement of Morris. Writing in the *Journal of Commonwealth Literature* (12 no.2 [December 1974]), K. Ram-

chand and A. Alleyane suggested that Morris was 'too committed to the fiction of order either to reject compromise or to open himself up to radical questionings'. But Pam Mordecai has pointed to the 'central ambivalence, ambiguity and irony' that pervade his work, and the 'light metaphysical cogency' which is opposite of complacency or fence-sitting (*Caribbean Quarterly*, 25 no.4 [December 1979]).

22. Though the major anthologies of British poetry failed to reflect any of this. One might absolve Michael Horovitz, in 1969, for being unaware of the Caribbean literary naissance in Britain, when he edited the highly popular *Children of Albion* (Penguin); and it did save the blushes of those who would not wish to be deemed 'Children of Albion' – Michael X, as poet, being the sole black/Caribbean representative asked to blush. The other anthologies of the time – the Jamaican Edward Lucie-Smith's *British Poetry Since 1945* (Penguin, 1970), Jeremy Robson's *The Young British Poets* (Chatto, 1971; Corgi, 1972) etc – ignore the Caribbean/black poets (who are still unrepresented in Lucie-Smith's revised and enlarged edition of his anthology, published in 1985).

23. Paula Burnett, *Penguin Book of Caribbean Verse*; introduction.

24. Another curious "statistic" is that there are no poets from Trinidad and Tobago in the final 14. If this were an old-fashioned West Indian cricket team, I would, of course, have shifted a Jamaican (or, better still, a Montserratian) to make room for a Trinidadian; but I think we're over such considerations now. A quick glance at the available Trinidad talent would give us a formidable XI. How about: Eric Morton Roach (1915-74), 'Lord Kitchener' (*b*. 1922), Leroy Clarke (*b*. 1938), Judy Miles (*b*. 1942), Paul Keens-Douglas (*b*. 1942), Amryl Johnson, Wayne Brown (*b*. 1944), Faustin Charles (*b*. 1944), Christopher Laird (*b*. 1946), John Lyons, Dionne Brand (*b*. 1953), And there are more.

25. David Dabydeen (*b*. 1953) won the Commonwealth Poetry Prize for his collection *Slave Song* (Dangaroo Press, 1984), and Cyril Dabydeen (*b*. 1945) and now a Canadian citizen, is a member of the Canadian League of Poets and has been Poet Laureate of the city of Ottawa. Cyril Dabydeen's collections include *Poems of Recession* (Georgetown, 1972), *Distances* (Fiddlehead, 1977), *Goatsong* (Mosaic, Ottawa, 1977), and *Heart's Frame*.

26. 'Timehri', in *Savacou* 2 (September 1970), p.44. Another extract from this essay is included in Brathwaite's section of this anthology.

LOUISE BENNETT

Louise Bennett was born in 1919 in Kingston, Jamaica. She began
writing and performing poems in Creole as a teenager, and started
collecting Jamaican folk songs and stories. In 1945 she moved to
London to study drama at RADA, and worked as resident artist
with the BBC (West Indies section) and in the theatre for repertory
companies in Coventry, Huddersfield and Amersham. She
returned to Jamaica in 1955 to become a drama specialist with
the Jamaica Welfare Commission, and from 1959 to 1961 lectured
in drama and Jamaican folklore at the University of the West
Indies.

   As 'Miss Lou', the persona of her poems, she became a house-
hold name in the Caribbean, and published several collections of
"dialect verses". Her records featuring folk songs, stories and
singing games as well as her own poems have been highly popular
in Jamaica, and one recording, *Yes M'Dear*, was released by
Island Records in London in 1983. Her books of poems include
Jamaica Labrish (Sangster's, Kingston, 1966) and *Selected
Poems*, edited by Mervyn Morris (Sangster's, 1982).

   She is the pioneering figure of the century in the oral tradition
of Caribbean poetry, but while her work has always enjoyed great
popularity with the public, she had to wait until vernacular poetry
was accepted as "literature" in the 1960s before she was recog-
nised as a great Caribbean writer. In 1965 she represented
Jamaica at the Royal Commonwealth Arts Festival in Britain,
and has since received many awards for her work as a writer,
performer and folklorist, including the MBE.

Interview with Louise Bennett

by DENNIS SCOTT

DS: *Louise, I heard you say once – 'I believe in laughter.' This is one way, your way of looking at the world, but tell me, how far does your use of dialect depend on this attitude? If you were a Jeremiah, for example, would the dialect serve you just as well?*

LB: I have found a medium through which I can pretend to be laughing. Most of the time when we laugh it is so that we may not weep. Isn't that so?

We can laugh at ourselves . . . The nature of the Jamaican dialect is the nature of comedy, I feel. As it is used by the people to express their feelings, the dialect is very adaptable. You can twist it, you can express yourself so much more strongly and vividly than in standard English. Maybe I feel this because I think in the dialect; but I haven't really answered you. Now what I think is, that you have to feel deeply about what you do. My business of believing in laughter forces me to look for the medium through which I can express that attitude. And the greatest medium I can find is the Jamaican dialect – the dialect I know, I feel; the dialect that I understand; the language, the comedy that I understand. And your other question: If I did not believe in laughter would the dialect serve me just as well. Well – I can't say – I could say something in dialect that could make you cry right now, but I don't know because I don't feel tragedy as strongly as I feel comedy. I can portray the tragic side of things or the serious side of things; but immediately the comedy of it comes to mind and that's what I want to express.

DS: *Quite apart from your own intentions do you think that this is a particular quality of the dialect?*

LB: It is a quality of the dialect. The nature of dialect is almost the nature of comedy though it may be difficult to define either of them. Why do people talk a dialect? Why do people laugh? I mean, look how many years we have been using it. They say it came out of slavery – the mixture of different languages – (I am talking about Jamaica now) but we find dialect all over the world.

DS: *And do you feel that this inability to be serious without being funny as well is a particular quality connected with people of negro origin? It certainly is there in the American blues tradition, in the whole field of jazz. Even when you are closest to tears there is a bit of an ironic twist in your expression – there is a joy as well.*

LB: Well, I don't know all that much about other dialects or other countries but I know something of the Cockney, for instance, and I have found some of this very quality there. The quality I think, is stronger among the negro people in that we have a certain quality of forgiveness. I don't care whether people agree with me or not; I find that the negro people have the greatest capacity for forgiving of any people I can find anywhere. I can't think of any other race that has suffered as much as the negro has all over the world that could behave as the negro does, the ordinary negro – knowing what is happening and has happened to negroes all over the world. To behave as we do, to laugh at things as we do – well really! To make fun of ourselves and other people as we do in the midst of unhappiness!

DS: *It's very interesting to hear you talk as generally as this because, forgive me, but it seems to me that in a strange kind of way you go your own sweet way and talk as you are now doing far more seldom than many of the rest of us writers and so on who are always shooting off our mouths with other creative writers. Is this true, is this impression true?*

LB: My dear Dennis, I have been set apart by other creative writers a long time ago because of the language I speak and work in. From the beginning nobody ever recognised me as a writer. 'Well, she is "doing" dialect'; it wasn't even writing you know. Up to now a lot of people don't even think I write. They say 'Oh, you just stand up and say these things!'

DS: *I take your point about yours having been a hard fight for recognition. But today one is constantly coming across statements in print by West Indian critics and writers who are very much impressed and concerned with what you have been doing in dialect, and with dialect.*

LB: Yes, and I am very gratified, very pleased that this has happened at last. But we have to face the fact that in the beginning this wasn't so. You know, I wasn't ever asked to a Jamaican Poetry League meeting? I was never thought good enough to be represented in that anthology *Focus*. The anthology which appeared in 1962 was the first time that anything representing the community of writers contained anything of mine in it. Most people thought that after all they couldn't discourse with me at all because I was going to talk to them in Jamaican dialect which they couldn't understand.

DS: *Do you think that one cause of your having to wait so long for the recognition we all agree you do deserve is that you work in an extremely theatrical way and so often in the theatre itself – so that one tends to think of you as a performing artist primarily?*

LB: Definitely, though I did start to write before I started to perform! My work does lend itself so much to performance because it is oral in its tradition, legendary. People are not as accustomed to reading the dialect as they are to listening to it, and I found it a wonderful medium for the stage.

You know, one reason I persisted writing in dialect in spite of all the opposition was because nobody else was doing so and there was such rich material in the dialect that I felt I wanted to put on paper some of the wonderful things that people say in dialect. You could never say 'look here' as vividly as 'kuyah'.

DS: *Talk for a little about how you began to write, how you began to write dialect, how you began to write comedy.*

LB: From the time I was quite young, I wanted to write. At first I started to write things about birds, and bees and trees. But then I realised that I was not doing what I really wanted to do. There was life going on around me and people living their lives, and what I was writing had nothing to do with what was really happening around me. So then I started to take a greater interest in people – to listen to what they were saying and how they were saying it, and the first dialect verse I wrote was about a tramcar. I remember a country woman in it said ''pread out yuself, one dress-woman a come'.

I remember it was a wonderful description. I was just a schoolgirl but all dressed up to go to pictures and looking well developed. At about this time I began to wonder why more of our poets and writers were not taking more of an interest in the kind of language usage and the kind of experiences of living which were all around us, and writing in this medium of dialect instead of writing in the same old English way about Autumn and things like that. I have always been fascinated by the hills and I used to write a lot about them. The hills were everywhere; even going up Orange Street on the tramcar there were the hills ahead of us. Well, I wrote a poem once about running to the hills and breezes and so on and at the end of it I found myself wondering about the people who lived there. I think it ended 'the people work and play much cooler than we do'. This, mind you, at the end of a deadly serious poem. You see, even as early as that, I was finding a sense of comedy along with the most serious subjects. To cut this short then: being interested in people and what the people were doing and the "now" of their lives, these were my preoccupations and the themes I tried to develop.

DS: *And do the poets whom you read have any influence on your own work?*

LB: I should think so. I'll tell you! At the beginning of my career what I knew most about were the English poets at the time. But I think I was most interested in their rhythms and techniques, and I think I have been greatly influenced by their techniques. Not consciously. Perhaps at the beginning, but nowadays I am quite certain that the things that strike me in contemporary writers – certain qualities, certain things that are said that impressed me, work on me quite unconsciously. And when I say impress me I mean, I feel 'this is true, this is real'. And I try to say the same things in my way. I am sure that most of our writers are very sincere about what they are saying and the way they say it. They are not just writing because it is fashionable, they feel what they write. But the language in which they say these things is not the language in which I would say them, or that I feel. Our people – the people that I keep on studying and portraying – they have a wonderful sanity and clarity in their language – though it's not "acceptable"! But this is really a digression. The answer to your question is yes.

DS: *Among the current crop of writers whose work do you particularly enjoy?*

LB: Dennis, do you know that everybody has influenced me in some way? Just as in my reading of poetry. I couldn't ever say that I have a favourite poet or novelist or essayist among West Indian writers. There are certain things that certain writers say that I like and remember, but I have not got a favourite writer. I have favourite quotations, favourite speeches, favourite lines.

DS: *Your position in this country, it seems to me, Louise, is that of a middle-class professional entertainer. Or perhaps "professional entertainer of the middle-classes" or –*

LB: Oh, never that.

DS: *Who then do you speak for in your poetry, and who do you speak to?*

LB: I think I speak to all Jamaica. In a performance for instance – I don't want to talk about my *writing* – a large cross section of the community from the Governor-General to the man in the street can react to the lines and the situations I present. So I can't feel that I belong to any class or that I write for any class. The Jamaican

peasant who speaks the dialect – not only the peasant, for we all
speak the dialect to some extent – he is an extremely self-aware
and perceptive individual and expresses his awareness of the soc-
iety, as I have said already, in colourful and accurate terms. Even
when he seems deliberately to be expressing himself in nonsense
rhymes, for example, he is actually sayng things very vividly.
Take the folk songs for instance, do you remember 'London Tor-
bun' you know: 'You no heari' wha' me heari?' 'No, no, sah.'
Now this recalls a sad incident. Some turbine on an estate had
exploded and people died in the accident. It's a sad tale, but
because a Jamaican does not dwell on the sorrow of an occasion
exclusively, the song is not a sad one so it has a feeling of lightness
and cheerfulness and on first hearing sounds like almost like a
child's nonsense song. 'Me heari seh London Torbun/boiler
bottom burs'/Kill over nineteen man!/Me heari seh, los' can'
fin'...' and so on: 'Miss Matti man los' cyan fin/De likkle bwoy
los' cyan fin'.' And even the animals enter the picture in later
verses, you know, 'The goat head los' cyan fine.' And of course
it's all part of another tradition – the practice of singing a "dinky"
to cheer up the family of a dead person so that they don't cry.
What is interesting is that when you look between the lines you
find all the sorrow there and all the facts too, but if you don't
search for it, if you don't care, well then you won't find it.

DS: *So then if as you say (and I agree with you), your work
appeals to so large a cross section of our people, how do you
explain the fact that it took so long for people to regard your art
as "respectable"?*

LB: Because for too long, it was considered not respectable to
use the dialect. Because there was a social stigma attached to the
kind of person who used dialect habitually. Many people still do
not accept the fact that for us there are many things which are
best said in the language of the "common man".

DS: *One last question then – Because of this quality of laughter
in your work it is easy sometimes for us, for the audience to miss
the social seriousness, the serious social intent behind the work.
Is this true and is this deliberate on your part?*

LB: This is true. Many people do miss it. Sometimes their missing
of the *point* is deliberate. They prefer to pretend that it's all in
fun. And I don't mind. I go along with them. As long as I myself
am sincere about what I am doing I feel that the truth of a thing
must reveal itself to the right people.

DS: *And are you content with this situation? Would you like*

people to see what's behind the humour as well? More people, I
mean.
LB: Yes I would, but I know that it takes time.
DS: *And about anger finally. Is your work "angry"?*
LB: [*Pause.*] Not obviously. Not *obviously* angry.

[1968]

Independance

Independance wid a vengeance!
Independance raisin Cain!
Jamaica start grow beard, ah hope
We chin can stan de strain!

When dawg marga him head big, an
When puss hungry him nose clean;
But every puss an dog no know
What Independance mean.

Mattie seh it mean we facety,
Stan up pon we dignity,
An we don't allow nobody
Fi teck liberty wid we.

Independance is we nature
Born an bred in all we do,
An she glad fi see dat Government
Tun independant to.

She hope dem caution worl-map
Fi stop draw Jamaica small,
For de lickle speck cyaan show
We independantness at all!

Moresomever we must tell map dat
We don't like we position –
Please kindly teck we out a sea
An draw we in de ocean.

What a crosses! Independance
Woulda never have a chance
Wid so much boogooyagga
Dah expose dem ignorance.

Dog wag him tail fi suit him size
An match him stamina –
Jamaica people need a
Independance formula!

No easy-come-by freeness tings,
Nuff labour, some privation,
Not much of dis an less of dat
An plenty studiration.

Independance wid a vengeance!
Wonder how we gwine to cope?
Jamaica start smoke pipe, ah hope
We got nuff jackass rope!

South Parade Peddler

Hairnet! Scissors! Fine-teet comb!
– Whe de nice lady deh?
Buy a scissors from me, no, lady?
Hair pin? Tootpase? Go weh!
Me seh go-weh aready, ef
Yuh doan like it, see me.
Yuh dah swell like bombin plane fun –
Yuh soon bus up like Graf Spee.

Yuh favour – Shoeslace! Powder puff!
Clothes hanger! Belt! Pen knife!
Buy someting, no, nice young man?
Buy a hairnet fi yuh wife.
Buy someting wid de change, no, sah,
An meck de Lawd bless yuh!
Me no sell farden hair curler, sah!
Yuh fas an facety to!

Teck yuh han outa me box!
Pudung me razor blade!
Yuh no got no use fi it, for yuh
Dah suffer from hair raid!
Nice boonoonoonoos lady, come,
Me precious, come dis way.
Hair pin? Yes, mah, tank yuh, yuh is
De bes one fi de day.

Toot-brush? Ah beg yuh pardon, sah –
Me never see yuh mout:
Dem torpedo yuh teet, sah, or
Yuh female lick dem out?
No bodder pick me up, yaw, sah!
Yuh face look like a seh
Yuh draw it outa lucky box.
No bodder me – go weh!

One police man dah come, but me
Dah try get one more sale.
Shoeslace! Tootpase! Buy quick, no, sah!
Yuh waan me go to jail?
Ef dah police ever ketch we, Lize,
We peddler career done.
Pick up yuh foot eena yuh han.
Hair pin! Hair curler! Run!

Jamaica Oman

Jamaica oman cunny, sah!
Is how dem jinnal so?
Look how long dem liberated
An de man dem never know!

Look how long Jamaica oman
– Modder, sister, wife, sweetheart –
Outa road an eena yard deh pon
A dominate her part!

From Maroon Nanny teck her body
Bounce bullet back pon man,
To when nowadays gal-pickney tun
Spellin-Bee champion.

From de grass root to de hill-top,
In profession, skill an trade,
Jamaica oman teck her time
Dah mount an meck de grade.

Some backa man a push, some side-a
Man a hole him han,
Some a lick sense eena man head,
Some a guide him pon him plan!

Neck an neck an foot an foot wid man
She buckle hole her own;
While man a call her 'so-so rib'
Oman a tun backbone!

An long before Oman Lib bruck out
Over foreign lan
Jamaica femala wasa work
Her liberated plan!

Jamaica oman know she strong,
She know she tallawah,
But she no want her pickney-dem
Fi start call her 'Puppa'.

So de cunny Jamma oman
Gwan like pants-suit is a style,
An Jamaica man no know she wear
De trousiz all de while!

So Jamaica oman coaxin
Fambly budget from explode
A so Jamaica man a sing
'Oman a heaby load!'

But de cunny Jamma oman
Ban her belly, bite her tongue,
Ketch water, put pot pon fire
An jus dig her toe a grung.

For 'Oman luck deh a dungle',
Some rooted more dan some,
But as long as fowl a scratch dungle heap
Oman luck mus come!

Lickle by lickle man start praise her,
Day by day de praise a grow;
So him praise her, so it sweet her,
For she wonder if him know.

Census

But Government fas, eeh mah? Lawd!
Me laugh so tell me cry,
Me dis done tell de census man
A whole ton-load a lie.

Him walks een an sidung like is
Eena my yard him grow,
An yuh want hear de fimiliar tings
De man did want fi know.

Him doan fine out one ting bout me,
For fi-me yeye so dry
Me stare right eena census face
An tell him bans a lie!

Me tell him seh dat all me parents
Dem is still alive –
But me modder she dead twelve ears
And me fader him dead five!

Me tell him seh de fowl an goat-dem
Doan belongs to me,
Me dah care dem fi me sister
Daughter son what gawn a sea.

Him ask me if me married, me
Get bex and tell him 'Gwan!'
For no man never ax me dat
Deh question from me bawn.

Him ax me when me bawn, me tell
Him dat ah is not sure
But me nable-string plant wid de ole
Cotton tree outa door.

One time him question me so fas
Me couldn lie so quick,
Me hole awn pon me heart an belch
An form like seh me sick.

Him ax me ef me feel bad, ah seh
'Jus like ah gwine to dead':
Me stumble, so him hole me han
An lead me to me bed.

Him seh him gawn, hear me: 'Goodbye'
– Me meck me voice soun sof.
Him tip-toe go weh; an me jump up
An bus out in a laugh!

Uriah Preach

Fi-me fambly is no peaw-peaw,
Me daughter Sue dah teach;
An when rain fall or parson sick
Me son Uriah preach.

Sunday gawn rain come so till parson
Couldn lef from out him yard;
People did eena church, an so
Uriah get weh broad –

Him climb up pon de pulpit, him
Lean over an look dung,
Him look pon all we enemy
An lash dem wid him tongue.

De fus one him teck awn was Lize
Who tell de lie pon me:
Him stare eena har face an seh,
'Thou art de mouti-mouti!'

Him seh, 'Thou art de meddlesome,
Thou art de rowersome!'
An den him look pon me an seh,
'Thou art de slaughtered lamb.'

Him teck awn Teacher Brown, for when
Him was a lickle tot
Teacher beat him one day because
Him call Teacher 'Top-Knot'.

So Riah get him revenge now,
For him stare straight pon Brown
An seh, 'Let him dat sittet on
De house top not come down.'

Riah tun pon Butcher Jones who noted
Fi sell all scrapses meat
An seh, 'Thou shalt not give thy neighbours
Floolooloops to eat!'

Him tell dem off, dem know is dem,
Dem heart full to de brim;
But as Uriah eena pulpit
Dem cyaan back-answer him.

So when chuch-member mel me
Ah doan answer till it reach
A rainy day when parson stay home
An Uriah preach.

Speechify

Young ladies an young gentlemans
An odders in de room,
Mas Charlie, Auntie Mary,
Missis Bride an Missa Groom:

Let I takes in hand wine glasses,
Let I full it to de tip,
While Miss Clemmy share de cakeses
Let I rise an let I sip.

De whole distric got frightration
On dis ceremonial day,
After so much courtenation
Fi see Tom married to May!

Tirty years him wasa courten her,
But time longer dan rope;
May seh 'wait no kill nobody'
An she always live in hope.

An teday as we look pon her face
We know her heart a sing:
'Me hopes reward, me patience gain,
At last me get de ring.'

Me an Tom was always buddy
An ah know May from she small;
Dem head grey now, dem teet drop out,
But dem face no change at all.

Same way Tom forehead buck, same way
May bottom lip heng dung;
Tom stop suck him big finger, but
May still dah suck her tongue.

Ah glad fi see dem combination
Tun qualification,
An ah wish dem long duration
In dem new participation.

One warnin wud: Young gals, no force
No man fi married yuh –
Me naw call no name, but is one
Special gal me talkin to!

Ef yuh force him yuh gwine lose out,
Him dah meck up fi run weh;
Ease up de pressure, loose de rein!
Das all me haffi seh.

Yuh Nephew Sue

Aunt Tama, dear, me sad fi hear
How storm wreck Jackass Tung;
But wus of all, yuh one deggeh
Coaknut tree tumble dung!

Las week dem had a meetin fi all
De coaknut growers what
Lose coaknut tree eena de storm,
So me was eena dat.

Bans a big-shot money-man was deh.
Some a dem get out cross
An start fi talk bout omuch hundred
Tousen tree dem loss.

Me did meck up me mine, Aunt Tama,
Fi get up an talk free,
Fi touch dem pon dem consciance
Meck dem gi yuh back yuh tree.

But when me hear de man-dem mout
Dah gwan like distric bell
Me heng me head, fole up me wing
An draw eena me shell.

De chairman pint pon me an seh
'How much yuh lose, Miss Sue?'
Me did feel shame fi seh 'one', so
Me sofly whisper, 'Two'.

Him frowns an seh, 'Two hundred or
Two tousen tree, Miss Sue?'
Hear me, 'Percent is hundred, but
Per tree is so-so two.'

De chairman cough an blow him nose.
'Thank you, madam,' him seh.
De tarra man-dem look pon me
Like me no business deh.

Dem chat bout resolution an
Dem chat bout committee,
Dem vote and dem decline, but dem
No seh 'kemps' bout yuh tree!

But me hear seh dem gwine buil back
All de house-dem new an pretty,
An yuh can stop seh 'Jackass Tung'
An call it 'Race Horse City'.

Inclose please fine corn fi me fowl
An bread fi cousin Lou,
Tropence fi buy yuh saal, while I
Remains yuh nephew, Sue.

Tan a Yuh Yard

Teng Gad, massa, yuh neber go!
Tan weh yuh deh, Mas Jone!
Quiet yuhself, no meck no fuss –
Lef Merica alone!

Gwan do yuh lickle bolo job,
Glad fi yuh lickle pay;
Me wi tun me han an we can live
Pon de four-bit a day.

Win yuh mine offa foreign lan –
Koo how some a de man-dem
Run back home like foreigner
Dis set bad dog pon dem!

Ef backra even poas ticket
Come gi yuh, bwoy, refuse i!
Better yuh tan home fight yuh life
Dan go a sea go lose i.

De same sinting weh sweet man mout
Wi meck him lose him head –
Me read eena newspaper seh
Two farm-man meet dem dead!

Ef a lie, a no me tell i,
Ef a label, me no know!
So me buy i, so me sell it,
So me reap, a so me sow.

But whedder true or lie, me bwoy,
Coward man kip soun bone;
Tan a yuh yard an satisfy –
Lef Merica alone.

Proverbs

'When ashes cowl dawg sleep in deh';
For sence Ma dead, yuh see,
All kine a ole black nayga start
Teck liberty wid me.

Me no wrap up wid dem, for me
Pick an choose me company:
Ma always tell me seh: 'Yuh sleep
Wid dawg yuh ketch him flea.'

Me know plenty a dem no like me,
An doah de time so hard
Me kip fur from dem, for 'Cockroach
No biniz a fowl yard.'

Ah teck time gwan me ways an doan
Fas eena dem affair;
Me tell dem mawnin, for 'Howdy
An tenky bruck no square.'

Sometime me go a parson yard
Sidung lickle an chat –
'Ef yuh no go a man fire-side, yuh no know
Ow much fire-stick a bwile him pot.'

Sake-a dat, as lickle news get bout
Dem call me po gal name;
Me bear it, for doah 'All fish nyam man,
Dah shark one get de blame.'

But when me go look fi parson
Me ongle talk bout me soul,
For Ma use fi tell me: 'Sweet mout fly
Follow coffin go a hole.'

Das why ah miss me mumma, yaw:
Ef she wasa live tedeh
All dem liberty couldn teck wid me,
Dem couldn a seh me seh.

She was me shiel an buckler,
She was me rod an staff.
But 'Back no know weh ole shut do fi i
So tell ole shut tear off.'

Colonisation in Reverse

What a joyful news, Miss Mattie;
Ah feel like me heart gwine burs –
Jamaica people colonizin
Englan in reverse.

By de hundred, by de tousan,
From country an from town,
By de ship-load, by de plane-load,
Jamaica is Englan boun.

Dem a pour out a Jamaica;
Everybody future plan
Is fi get a big-time job
An settle in de motherlan.

What a islan! What a people!
Man an woman, ole an young
Jussa pack dem bag an baggage
An tun history upside dung!

Some people doan like travel,
But fi show dem loyalty
Dem all a open up cheap-fare-
To-Englan agency;

An week by week dem shippin off
Dem countryman like fire
Fi immigrate an populate
De seat a de Empire.

Oonoo se how life is funny,
Oonoo see de tunabout?
Jamaica live fi box bread
Out a English people mout.

For when dem catch a Englan
An start play dem different role
Some will settle down to work
An some will settle fi de dole.

Jane seh de dole is not too bad
Because dey payin she
Two pounds a week fi seek a job
Dat suit her dignity.

Me seh Jane will never fine work
At de rate how she dah look
For all day she stay pon Aunt Fan couch
An read love-story book.

What a devilment a Englan!
Dem face war an brave de worse;
But ah wonderin how dem gwine stan
Colonizin in reverse.

MARTIN CARTER

Martin Carter was born in 1927 in Georgetown, British Guiana, now Guyana. After studying at Queen's College, Georgetown, he worked in the Civil Service for four years until forced to resign because of his involvement in the early nationalist movement. When Britain imposed direct rule in 1953, he was imprisoned for some months, and wrote his *Poems of Resistance*, published in London in 1954. After independence, he became Minister of Public Information and Broadcasting in Prime Minister Burnham's government, and represented Guyana at the United Nations. He is a widely respected historian as well as a poet and politician.

His later books of poems include *Poems of Shape and Motion* (1955), *Conversations* (1955) and *Jail Me Quickly* (1963), all published in Georgetown, and *Poems of Succession* (New Beacon Books, London, 1977), which includes selections from earlier collections, and *Poems of Affinity: 1978-1980* (Release, Georgetown, 1980).

Interview with Martin Carter

by PETER TREVIS
(*extract*)

PT: *Martin, could you describe your own experience of poetry
as a child at home and at school?*
MC: Essentially, through the hymns we sang as children in prim-
ary school, that is between six and, say, ten. In addition to which
we would have had texts originating in Britain of poems by people
like Hemans – 'The boy stood on the burning deck...' sort of
thing. They have a facile rhyme and metrical pattern which
everyone in Guyana, of my generation, would have come in contact
with. We must also remember that when slavery was abolished
in 1834 the greatest impact on the population in the sense of
language was from the Bible because the missionaries, the London
Missionary Society, which was very active in those areas, taught
ex-slaves from the Bible, the Old Testament and the New Testa-
ment. So you would find in speech of places like Guyana a tremend-
ous influence of the patterns and vocabulary of the Old and the
New Testament and I must say of course that one could hardly
find a better form to learn from.
PT: *At what stage did you begin to feel that your interest in
language was such that you wanted to pursue it in your own writ-
ing?*
MC: I couldn't say. What I was very interested in as a child were
the references to Greek mythology, which we read in very simpli-
fied form but, nonetheless, as it's clear, mythology is a narrative,
that is what mythology is about, that is the story of a hero or gods
as the case may be. So that, whether you're learning from the
Greek text or from a simplified text, what does come through is
the story, the narrative, and mythology is a narrative.
PT: *The literature that you have described is set in a landscape
very different to the landscape you must have experienced as a
child. Was there a literature available to all that actually took on
that landscape, that experience that you'd had as a child? Was
there a black literature available, a Caribbean literature?*
MC: No, not at all, when I was a child. As a matter of fact what
you had would have appeared in the newspapers and the nearest
thing to what you are calling black literature would have been
versions of folklore in the vernacular, if I may use that word: the
vernacular in the sense of oral speech being written down; no

attempt to make it literary. That was the closest we had at that time.

PT: *In later years, has the literature of Latin America and the Americas in general exercised an influence on you at all?*

MC: The literature of the Americas, interestingly enough, that would have influenced a lot of us – I don't say alone – were translations from the Spanish into English. Let us take for instance the case of Pablo Neruda, who would have written in Spanish as you know, heavily influenced by the Surrealists in France and then translated back into English from the Spanish; and the translator would have used Whitman as a model or pattern to translate Neruda into, when in fact Neruda's influence was very heavily Surrealist: that is the early 20th century on the Continent, the European Continent. So that it was filtered to us from many sources, and I think what happened to the many young writers in the Caribbean was a sort of unconscious selection from the materials in assimilating them to our own speech patterns and ways of expressing ourselves.

PT: *In the 1950s you were heavily involved in the political activities in Guyana. I wonder if you could briefly outline for us the political context in Guyana early 1950s?*

MC: Yes. In 1950, the last war in Europe, the Second World War, had a tremendous influence on the people of the Caribbean because many young people left the Caribbean to come to Britain to join the air force and to fight in various services. After the war was over some of them were given scholarships and various things and in due course they came back to the Caribbean, to Guyana let us say, bringing with them their experience of life in Britain and on the Continent, and people at home would have come into contact with them: they would have brought books and ideas which would have helped a lot to liberate, if you like, Guyanese and West Indians from the provincialism of small colonial societies. As a consequence, we had in 1950 the emergence of a popular movement called the People's Progressive Party, led by Dr Cheddi Jagan and his wife Janet Jagan who is an American citizen and who introduced, to some extent, Marxist literature, mostly from Britain, from the Communist Party in Britain; and people would never have come into contact with that sort of material before. It was very simplified, over-simplified, and they took it literally: theses about capitalist society and so on were taken literally. But it had a tremendous impact on people who had never before seen themselves as active people in a social milieu.

So you had the emergence of the PPP, the People's Progressive
Party. I became a member of the PPP, and I became an executive
committee member. I was very active, and in 1953 I was invited
to a conference in Romania, to which I went. On going home I
was told on the ship off Martinique that I was banned from
going to Trinidad, which was the place we go from to Guyana. I
arrived in Trinidad and was arrested, a prohibited immigrant.
In due course I got back home only to arrive there the time when
warships from Britain had gone to suspend the constitution of
Guyana.

I was arrested and put in a detention camp at a place called
Timehri – not long, for three months. We came out and continued
agitating and talking to people and sharing out stuff that we
printed ourselves. Some poems were seized by the British Govern-
ment – by the British Army, sorry – on the grounds that they
were subversive, but I'd written poems before all this happened
and they were collected and published in Britain in 1954 under
the title *Poems of Resistance*. So that is the sort of background
to it.

PT: *Were any of these poems actually read at political meetings
or not?*

MC: Oh, yes, they were.

PT: *What was the effect of that?*

MC: Repetition. People repeating lines.

PT: *You say at the end of one of your poems, a poem called
'Looking at Your Hands': 'I don't sleep to dream but dream to
change the world'. Could you say a little bit about that, what that
actually means, those lines?*

MC: It means exactly what it says: one dreams to change the
world knowing that the world is not changeable in the ordinary
sense, and therefore what you get there is hope that other people
will want to change the world – not expecting anyone to change
the world physically, but if your mind is changed, the world is
changed. If I see the world differently, that's a different world.

PT: *So presumably one of the roles of your poems is to make
people see the world differently? Would that be fair?*

MC: Let's put it this way: as a result, it's not a motive – because
I'm talking about personal independence, independence as a
human being – but one hopes that that would be a result, too.

PT: *So they're not didactic in the sense of changing the world
physically, that's not the crude aim of them but hopefully because
you're telling the truth...*

MC: That is it precisely. That is very well put.

PT: *In the early poems I get a very strong sense of internationalism and of optimism: you refer to the struggles in Kenya, the struggles in Malaya, the struggles in Eastern Europe, and the struggle in Guyana. Has that optimism survived?*

MC: Well, it's not a question of optimism or of pessimism, it's a question of emphasis and relevance. Speaking from a distance now and answering your question in critical terms, the invocation of the experience in Kenya or Malaya or what have you, artistically invoked, is inexplicably bound up with what one is living, so that possibly if I were as young as I was then, writing now, I would speak of South Africa. So there's nothing fixed about the reference because if poetry is anything it is spontaneous, and that is why placed against the computer, let us say, poetry remains poetry because the computer can't be programmed to be spontaneous. It can be programmed but it can't be programmed to be spontaneous. As a friend of mine once said, 'I've never seen a computer laugh.' It cannot laugh because laughter is spontaneous.

PT: *You say that it's a question of emphasis and relevance rather than of optimism. Is there a sense that you still see history moving in a particular direction?*

MC: Yes.

PT: *And that direction is not reversible, there are setbacks on the way but it will carry on...*

MC: Not reversible.

PT: *You said earlier on that in Guyana the influence of European Marxism had been very strong and there is a strand in Marxist criticism that goes back through people like Lukács, that requires and makes great emphasis on classical definitions and the terms of classical literary criticism.*

MC: A great English historian, a Greek authority, George Thompson, makes the point very clearly; and just to refer further back: Emmanuel Kant also made the point very clearly of dead languages – meaning Greek of course – that had reached their limit. Now we have an interesting point here between the dead languages and the unwritten languages. By unwritten I mean the speech of the people in the street. By dead, I mean that which has been written down but not been spoken, so you get a beautiful antithesis of the spoken but not written and the written but not spoken. So no matter how we try to intellectualise it away, there is a connection between the language written but not spoken and the language spoken but not written. I suspect that what we are dealing with here is not language in the ordinary sense of the word, what we are dealing with is the power of speech which is only realised in words. In other words a dumb man can speak.

PT: *Could you tell us a little bit about how you actually go about the business of writing a poem, how much re-drafting do you do?*

MC: It depends on the poem. Sometimes you write it and it's very easy.

PT: *Could you give me an example of a poem that came easily?*

MC: Oh yes. I remember exactly when I wrote that. It's a poem entitled 'The Great Dark'.

[Recites 'The Great Dark']

PT: *That was a poem that came easily?*

MC: Yes, very easily. Simpler ones are much more difficult. I suspect it's a combination of factors at work but the simple ones are very difficult because the tendency is to overwrite them. But if they are difficult when they come, you can't overwrite them because they are difficult already, if you want to use the word difficult in the sense of complexity.

PT: *In an earlier conversation you talked about sculpting and carving away the meaning. Would that fit in there with the simpler poem? You are constantly having to take away and take out from it?*

MC: Yes, that is correct.

PT: *Do you enjoy re-reading your own poetry?*

MC: It's difficult because one has to pay so much attention to every word and when you wrote them you were close to them but after years you become foreigners.

PT: *Yes, I was going to say some of these poems are over thirty years old now. Does it feel like a different man, a different person almost?*

MC: No. At the beginning, but the words start removing themselves and the patterns start emerging and the pattern then takes over. In the more recent ones the words dominate, but in the less recent ones the pattern takes over. So that I can't remember a poem from my head but if you tell me the first line and I get the rhythm I will be able to fit it in.

PT: *And what about the experiences that are related to the poems? Do they come back with the poem?*

MC: They don't come back. No, they're totally different. When I say totally different they are not the same things. Now and then you can remember a situation, but that is not frequent.

PT: *Moving on to the poetry that you wrote in the late sixties,*

to me it appears more private, less public and in many ways more difficult. Is that just my observation or is that a fair observation about those poems?
MC: I find that very difficult to answer because one does not choose to be difficult or complex. The material you deal with requires a certain way of doing it and that is not a choice, it's a situation you find yourself in. For instance in a sequence of poems, let us say you wrote five poems in one year; four of them may be very difficult and yet the one that is necessary to the sequence may be as limpid as anything so that it's not a question of setting out to write a simple poem or a difficult poem, it's a question really of having written a poem to ask yourself whether it's the right poem. I like the word "right" you see. Philip Sidney in the 16th century made the point about a *right* poet, not good, *right*; and I think that is the correct way of looking at it. So, in a cluster of poems, five may be as you say difficult where one may be limpid. But all the poems are *right* poems, right for what they have done.

[1986]

Conversations

by MARTIN CARTER

They say I am a poet write for them:
Sometimes I laugh, sometimes I solemnly nod.
I do not want to look them in the eye
Lest they should squeal and scamper far away.

A poet cannot write for those who ask
Hardly himself even, except he lies:
Poems are written either for the dying
Or for the unborn, no matter what we say.

That does not mean his audience lies remote
Inside a womb or some cold bed of agony
It only means that we who want true poems
Must all be born again, and die to do so.

*

I dare not keep too silent, face averted
That tells too much, it gives the heart away
Quick words distract attention from the eyes
And smiling lips are most acceptable.

In any case it is not good to show
The nature of the silence of the heart
To talk is just as easy as to walk
And laughter can be one of a thousand kinds.

I must be casual even over death
This fools the fool whose triumph is a coffin
Shallow as grave pit is the mock concern
Which murders men as surely as a knife.

To cherish silence in the memory
Is to be full of utter loneliness.
It must be right when born with such a curse
To laugh and talk and drink like any boor.

*

The wild men in prisons, they who rot like rust!
The loud men who cry freedom and are so full of lies!
The drunk men who go dancing like shadows down the street
These all surround me, shouting to God for help!

I really do not see how God can help them.
For each one wants the same thing – who can share
To prisoners, politicians and drunk men
What only souls that blaze and burn can win?

                        *

Trying with words to purify disgust
I made a line I simply can't remember:
For hours now I've poked through memory
A desperate child in a jam-packed garbage can.

It should have been a line with nouns and verbs
Like truth and love and hope and happiness
But looking round it seems I was mistaken
To substitute a temple for a shop.

To see a shop and dream of holy temples
Is to expect a toad to sing a song
And yet, who knows, someone may turn translator
When all these biped reptiles crawl again.

                        *

Now there was one whom I knew long ago
And then another to whom I paid respect:
The first I would salute, the second praise
But all is gone, all gone, the murderer cried.

Along what road they went he cannot say
So many roads there are, so many bends.
There is no short cut to integrity
All, all is gone, all gone, the murderer cried.

They did not mean to kill only to burn
But then one act can transform everything
A brother into charcoal, love to crime
Yes, all is gone, all gone, the murderer cried.

                        *

Groaning, in this wilderness of silence
Where voices hardly human shout at me
I imitate the most obscure of insects
And burrow in the soil and hide from light.

Speaking with one on a pavement in the city
I watched the greedy mouth, the cunning eye
I reeled and nearly fell in frantic terror
Seeing a human turn into a dog.

Recovering, I studied this illusion
And made a stupid effort to be strong:
I nodded and agreed and listened close.
But when I tried to utter words – I barked!

                              *

In a great silence I hear approaching rain:
There is a sound of conflict in the sky
The frightened lizard darts behind a stone
First was the wind, now is the wild assault.

I wish this world would sink and drown again
So that we build another Noah's ark
And send another little dove to find
What we have lost in floods of misery.

[1961]

Do Not Stare at Me

Do not stare at me from your window, lady,
do not stare and wonder where I came from.
Born in this city was I, lady,
hearing the beetles at six o'clock
and the noisy cocks in the morning
when your hands rumple the bed sheet
and night is locked up in the wardrobe.

My hand is full of lines
like your breast with veins, lady –
So do not stare and wonder where I come from.
My hand is full of lines
like your breast with veins, lady,
and one must rear, while one must suckle life...

Do not stare at me from your window, lady.
Stare at the wagon of prisoners!
Stare at the hearse passing by your gate!
Stare at the slums in the south of the city!
Stare hard and reason, lady, where I came from
and where I go.

My hand is full of lines
like your breast with veins, lady,
and one must rear, while one must suckle life.

Looking at Your Hands

No!
I will not still my voice!
I have
too much to claim –
if you see me
looking at books
or coming to your house
or walking in the sun
know that I look for fire!

I have learnt
from books dear friend
of men dreaming and living
and hungering in a room without a light
who could not die since death was far too poor
who did not sleep to dream, but dreamed to change the world!

And so
if you see me
looking at your hands
listening when you speak
marching in your ranks
you must know
I do not sleep to dream, but dream to change the world.

Listening to the Land

That night when I left you on the bridge
I bent down
kneeling on my knee
and pressed my ear to listen to the land.

I bent down
listening to the land
but all I heard was tongueless whispering.

On my right hand was the sea behind the wall
the sea that has no business in the forest
and I bent down
listening to the land
and all I heard was tongueless whispering
as if some buried slave wanted to speak again.

University of Hunger

is the university of hunger the wide waste.
is the pilgrimage of man the long march.
The print of hunger wanders in the land.
The green tree bends above the long forgotten.
The plains of life rise up and fall in spasms.
The huts of men are fused in misery.

They come treading in the hoofmarks of the mule
passing the ancient bridge
the grave of pride
the sudden flight
the terror and the time.

They come from the distant village of the flood
passing from middle air to middle earth
in the common hours of nakedness.
Twin bars of hunger mark their metal brows
twin seasons mock them
parching drought and flood.

is the dark ones
the half sunken in the land.
is they who had no voice in the emptiness
in the unbelievable
in the shadowless.

They come treading on the mud floor of the year
mingling with dark heavy waters
and the sea sound of the eyeless flitting bat.
O long is the march of men and long is the life
and wide is the span.
O cold is the cruel wind blowing.
O cold is the hoe in the ground.

They come like sea birds
flapping in the wake of a boat
is the torture of sunset in purple bandages
is the powder of fire spread like dust in the twilight
is the water melodies of white foam on wrinkled sand.

The long streets of night move up and down
baring the thighs of a woman
and the cavern of generation.
The beating drum returns and dies away.
The bearded men fall down and go to sleep.
The cocks of dawn stand up and crow like bugles.

is they who rose early in the morning
watching the moon die in the dawn.
is they who heard the shell blow and the iron clang.
is they who had no voice in the emptiness
in the unbelievable
in the shadowless.
O long is the march of men and long is the life
and wide is the span.

Till I Collect

Over the shining mud the moon is blood
falling on ocean at the fence of lights.
My mast of love will sail and come to port
leaving a trail beneath the world, a track
cut by my rudder tempered out of anguish.

The fisherman will set his tray of hooks
and ease them one by one into the flood.
His net of twine will strain the liquid billow
and take the silver fishes from the deep.
But my own hand I dare not plunge too far
lest only sand and shells I bring to air
lest only bones I resurrect to light.

Over the shining mud the moon is blood
falling on ocean at the fence of lights –
My course I set, I give my sail the wind
to navigate the islands of the stars
till I collect my scattered skeleton
till I collect...

Letter 3

It is not easy to go to sleep
When the tramp of a soldier marches in your brain.
You do not know whether to sleep or wake:
When a rifle crashes on the metal road...

This is all they want me to hear;
A soldier marching with a long black rifle,
A guard commander lining up his squad,
The stamp of feet upon the floors of sunset.
The yawn of darkness swallowing up the world...

It is not easy to go to sleep
When the tramp of a soldier marches in your brain.
You do not know whether to sleep or wake
When the long night comes and takes you in its arms...

On the Fourth Night of Hunger Strike

I have not eaten for four days.
My legs are paining, my blood runs slowly.
It is cold tonight, the rain is silent and sudden,
And yet there is something warm inside of me.

At my side my comrade lies in his bed watching the dark.
A cold wind presses chilly on the world.
It is the night of a Christmas day, a night in December,
We watch each other noting how time passes.

Today my wife brought me a letter from a comrade.
I hid it in my bosom from the soldiers.
They could not know my heart was reading 'Courage'!
They could not dream my skin was touching 'Struggle'!

But comrade now I can hardly write at all,
My legs are paining, my eyes are getting dark.
It is the fourth night of a hunger strike, a night in December.
I hold your letter tightly in my hand...

Death of a Comrade

Death must not find us thinking that we die.

Too soon, too soon
our banner draped for you.
I would prefer
the banner in the wind.
Not bound so tightly
in a scarlet fold –
not sodden sodden
with your people's tears
but flashing on the pole
we bear aloft
down and beyond this dark dark lane of rags.

Dear Comrade,
if it must be
you speak no more with me
nor smile no more with me
nor march no more with me
then let me take
a patience and a calm –
for even now the greener leaf explodes
sun brightens stone
and all the river burns.

Now from the mourning vanguard moving on
dear Comrade I salute you and I say
Death will not find us thinking that we die.

Shape and Motion Two

I walk slowly in the wind
watching myself in things I did not make:
in jumping shadows and in limping cripples
dust on the earth and houses tight with sickness
deep constant pain, the dream without the sleep.

I walk slowly in the wind
hearing myself in the loneliness of a child
in woman's grief which is not understood
in coughing dogs when midnight lingers long
on stones, on streets and then on echoing stars,
that burn all night and suddenly go out.

I walk slowly in the wind
knowing myself in every moving thing
in years and days and words that mean so much
strong hands that shake, long roads that walk and deeds
        that do themselves.
And all this world and all these lives to live.

I walk slowly in the wind
remembering scorn and naked men in darkness
and huts of iron riveted to earth.

Cold huts of iron stand upon this earth
like rusting prisons.
Each wall is marked and each wide roof is spread
like some dark wing
casting a shadow or a living curse.

I walk slowly in the wind
to lifted sunset red and gold and dim
a long brown river slanting to an ocean
a fishing boat, a man who cannot drown.

I walk slowly in the wind.
And birds are swift, the sky is blue like silk.

From the big sweeping ocean of water
an iron ship rusted and brown anchors itself.
And the long river runs like a snake
silent and smooth.

I walk slowly in the wind.
I hear my footsteps echoing down the tide
echoing like a wave on the sand or a wing on the wind
echoing echoing
a voice in the soul, a laugh in the funny silence.

I walk slowly in the wind.
I walk because I cannot crawl or fly.

Black Friday 1962

were some who ran one way.
were some who ran another way.
were some who did not run at all.
were some who will not run again.
And I was with them all,
when the sun and streets exploded,
and a city of clerks
turned a city of men!
Was a day that had to come,
ever since the whole of a morning sky,
glowed red like glory,
over the tops of houses.

I would never have believed it.
I would have made a telling repudiation.
But I saw it myself
and hair was a mass of fire!
So now obsessed I celebrate in words
all origins of creation, whores and virgins:
I do it with a hand upon a groin,
swearing this way, since other ways are false!

For is only one way, one path, one road.
And nothing downwards bends, but upward goes,
like leaves to sunlight, trees to the sun itself.
All, all who are human fail,
like bullets aimed at life,
or the dead who shoot and think themselves alive!

Behind a wall of stone beside this city,
mud is blue-grey when ocean waves are gone,
in the midday sun!
And I have seen some creatures rise from holes
and claw a triumph like a citizen,
and reign until the tide!

Atop the iron roof tops of this city
I see the vultures practising to wait.
And everytime and anytime,
in sleep or sudden wake, nightmare, dream,

always for me the same vision of cemeteries, slow funerals,
broken tombs, and death designing all.

True, was with them all,
and told them more than once:
in despair there is hope, but there is none in death.
Now I repeat it here, feeling a waste of life,
in a market-place of doom, watching the human face!

Who Can Share?

The wild men in prisons, they who rot like rust!
The loud men who cry freedom and are so full of lies!
The drunk men who go dancing like shadows down the street!
These all surround me, shouting to God for help!

I really do not see how God can help them.
For each one wants the same thing – who can share
with prisoners, politicians and drunk men
What only souls that blaze and burn can win?

The Great Dark

Orbiting, the sun itself has a sun
as the moon an earth, a man a mind.
And life is not a matter of a mother only.
It is also a question of the probability of the spirit,
strength of the web of the ever weaving weaver
I know not how to speak of, caught as I am
in the great dark of the bright connection of words.

And the linked power of love holds the restless wind
even though the sky shudders, and life orbits
around time, around death, it holds the restless wind
as each might hold each other, as each might hold each other.

Under a Near Sky

A near sky, no stars, another night.
Without warning I think of you,
and the blown away spatter
of rain, on a window sill.

Unable to learn what dreams are storing up.
Closing my eyes that sleep might suddenly fall
like rain or visions, I, in urgent mood
know certain things are certain in one life.

The beat of water on the faraway sand
comes, bringing to me all your woman figure
dress blown away, and hair alive as foam
or rioting leaves or blossoms without peace.

You have not lost what I have taken from you
and cherish in my violent memory.
Come. Let us race across the ocean, ebbing
under a near sky.

How Come?

So now
how come
the treason
of the spirit?

The beggar man
pretends his tongue
is heavy;
and yet his crutch
his wooden limb
is light!

And he can fling it up
like any hat
and sail it in the air
just like a bird.

So now
how come
the treason
of the spirit?

So now
how come
the bafflement of speech?

So now
how come
the long delight of air
the sense of power
and the sense of passion
created by the dead and wooden
crutch of the spirit
and tongue?

My Hand in Yours

As in sleep, my hand in yours, yours
in mine. Your voice in my hearing
and memory, like the sound of stars
as they shine, not content with light
only. My fingertips walk on your face
gently. They tiptoe as a dream does
away from sleep into waking. In a tree
somewhere a bird calls out. And I wake up
my hand still in yours, in the midst
of the sound of stars and a far bird.

There Is No Riot

Even that desperate gaiety is gone.
Empty bottles, no longer trophies
are weapons now. Even the cunning
grumble. 'If is talk you want,' she said,
'you wasting time with me. Try the church.'
One time, it was because rain fell
there was no riot. Another time,
it was because the terrorist forgot
to bring the bomb. Now, in these days
though no rain falls, and bombs are well remembered
there is no riot. But everywhere
empty and broken bottles gleam like ruin.

On the Death by Drowning
of the Poet, Eric Roach

It is better to drown in the sea
than die in the unfortunate air
which stifles. I heard the rattle
in the river; it was the paddle stroke
scraping the gunwale of a corial.
Memory at least is kind; the lips of death
curse life. And the window in the front of my house
by the gate my children enter by, that window
lets in the perfume of the white waxen glory
of the frangipani, and pain.

DEREK WALCOTT

Derek Walcott was born in 1930 in Castries, St Lucia, grew up
in St Lucia, and studied at the University of the West Indies,
Jamaica, and later in New York on a Rockefeller Fellowship. He
founded the Trinidad Theatre Workshop in 1959, which he
directed until 1977, producing many plays there including several
of his own, such as *Dream on Monkey Mountain* (1967), whose
later production by the Negro Ensemble of New York won the
Obie Award, *The Joker of Seville* (1974) and *O Babylon!* (1976).
He has won numerous literary awards, including the Nobel Prize
for Literature in 1992. While still based in the Caribbean, he now
spends much of each year in the USA, and teaches at Boston
University.

His poetry books include *In a Green Night: Poems 1948-1960*
(1962), *The Castaway and other poems* (1965), *The Gulf* (1970),
Another Life (1973), *Sea Grapes* (1976), and *The Star-Apple
Kingdom* (1980), all published by Jonathan Cape in London, and
the last four by Farrar, Straus & Giroux in America. His later
books are published by Farrar in America and Faber in Britain:
The Fortunate Traveller (USA 1981, UK 1982), *Midsummer* (USA
1983, UK 1984), *Collected Poems* (USA & UK 1986), *The Arkan-
sas Testament* (USA 1987, UK 1988), and *Omeros* (USA 1989,
UK 1990).

Leaving School

by **DEREK WALCOTT**
(extract)

I spent those vacations from school at the large, wooden roadside hotel of a farmer-spinster who had been my father's friend, writing poems which I showed her; one or two a day, preparing myself for the life I had chosen. She treated me with amused respect, introduced me to the writings of Whitman, and at other times she would indulge in reminiscences of my father whom she had loved.

I had come from a genteel, self-denying Methodist poverty. My mother, who was headmistress of the Methodist Infant School, worked hard to keep us at college, even if my brother and I had both won scholarships, by taking in sewing. My mother's friends, those who had survived my father, had been members of an amateur dramatic group, some cultural club which had performed Shakespeare and given musical concerts, when my father was their 'moving spirit'. These friends included a violinist, an ex-merchant seaman, an inveterate reciter who had seen Barrymore's Hamlet, and a professional painter named Harold Simmons.

Their existence, since most of them were from a religious minority, Anglican, Methodist or lapsed Catholic, had a defensive, doomed frailty in that steamy, narrow-minded climate. Perhaps because of this they believed in 'the better things of life' with a defiant intensity, which drew them closely together. Their efforts, since the pattern would be repeated for my brother and me, must have been secretly victimised. Their presentations were known as 'The Anglican consette' (concert) or 'The Methodist School' or 'Teacher Alix Concert', with all the vague implications of damnation. My brother Roderick and I would go through the same purgation later.

All through adolescence I had experienced some of this mockery and persecution, even public damnation. The hell of others, of limbo and purgatory was something that, being an outsider, I learned to envy. I learnt early to accept that Methodists went to purgatory or hell, a Catholic hell, only after some strenuous dispensation. I was thus, in boyhood, estranged not only from another God, but from the common life of the island.

We had been invited to study painting with Harry Simmons on Saturday mornings when he heard that we were interested in art,

that Dunstan St Omer was a prodigious draughtsman for his age,
that Henry and I wrote verse and painted, and that Theobalds,
apart from being an athlete, was also his father's son.

Wherever you grow up as a writer, even with the limitations of
a colonial boyhood, you depend with filial piety on older intelli-
gences that help to shape your mind. I had been very lucky. In
addition to the intelligent indulgence of the farmer-spinster, my
adolescence fed on the approval and faith of teachers, professional
and instinctual who had loved my father, and those who were
amazed at my industry. These included one of the Brothers of
the Presentation, a college master who gave me extra lessons in
French poetry and who read my verse, a Dominican lawyer and
that astigmatic, garrulous, and benevolent man who had been
botanist, editor, anthropologist and painter.

Harold Simmons had been my father's friend. It was my father
who had interested him in painting. My father had died in his
thirties, when my twin-brother and I were a year old, my sister
three, but on the drawing room walls of our house there were
relics of his avocation: a copy of Millet's *The Gleaners*, a romantic
original of sea-birds and pluming breakers he had called *Riders
of the Storm*, a miniature oil portrait of my mother, a self-portrait
in watercolour, and an avenue of pale coconut palms. These
objects had established my vocation, and made it as inevitable as
that of any craftsman's son, for I felt that my father's work,
however minor, was unfinished. Rummaging through stuffed,
dark cupboards, I sometimes came across finely copied verses,
evidence of a polite gracile talent, and once on a sketchbook of
excellent pencil studies. I treasured the books he had used: two
small, blue-covered volumes on *The English Topographical
Draughtsmen* and on *Albrecht Dürer*, and the thick-ridged, clas-
sical albums of John McCormack and, I think, Galli Curci. It was
this veneration that drew his friends to me.

They may have realised that I had no other ambition. Below
where I stood on the balcony was a plaque on the Fourth Form
wall with a gilded list of Island Scholars who had become doctors
and lawyers, or, infrequently, engineers. There was no writer or
painter among them, and I had failed to win the Island Scholarship
because of my poor mathematics. In Foxy's era it had been
awarded biennially on achievement in the London Matriculation.
I had failed the exam once, and I might have won the Scholarship
if, as happened under the Brothers, it had been awarded for
special subjects, but by the time the Higher School Certificate

was introduced I was seventeen and too old.

Those boys who knew the hopelessness of their one chance, for whom a "classical" education meant a rut for life in the Civil Service grabbed at the opportunity to make money working in the oil refineries of Curaçao. By the time I had reached the Sixth, they had left in batches, their school life broken, their education incomplete. They left as frightened boys and returned hardened men. The life there was rough. It was tireless, materialistic, but you could not afford to break, because there was nothing to return to, you were indentured anyway, and sending part of what you made back home, or else, on that sterile, cactus ridden boom-camp, where everyone spoke papiamento, you whored on Campo Allegre, or gambled, or tried at nights to educate yourself.

Until Curaçao, for every doctor, or lawyer the Board numbered it destroyed the ambitions of his classmates. It even took its toll among the winners, some of whom collapsed from tension and the exhaustion of new studies in Edinburgh, Oxford, London or McGill. It was a grinding, merciless system. Those who surrendered hope and became Civil Servants went through accepted, brief periods of protest with idleness or drink, then settled desperately into what they had feared, early marriage, a large family, debt and heavy drinking. Some who had slid to the gutter preferred to stay there, or go mad. They had 'missed it by one mark', or by being born a month too soon. But the 'The Schol' was what made or broke you. It was the only way out, and once every two years, it let just one boy through.

For me, though, everything [love for the beautiful schoolgirl, 'A'] was beginning, the culmination of a secretive childhood spent in reading, writing, and playing with my brother for hours with stick-puppets in our backyard, elaborating our own cowboy and detective plots, into public poems, plays, and paintings like those at Luna Park. Some months before, when I felt that I was ready to be "published", I had sat on the landing of the stairs and asked my mother, who was sewing at the window, for two hundred dollars to put out a booket of poems. She did not have that kind of money, and that fact made her weep, but she found it, the book was printed, and I had hawked it myself on street corners, a dollar a copy, and made the money back. It went into a "second edition". I was writing plays or sketches for the school and for a group we had formed, and I had already painted two huge backdrops for a Convent Concert that had taken me six months.

What made me feel more "professional" was that Harry would

let me have the use of his studio on Saturdays and during vaca-
tions. This meant permission to play his classical records on the
grey-metal, red-buttoned radiogram as loudly as I wanted, the
use of his neat, battered Royal typewriter, his library and his
liquor cabinet. I was drinking a lot, for I was now moving in a
circle that included hard, talkative, and intelligent drinkers: Sim-
mons himself, and the Dominican lawyer, another lawyer who
had won an Island scholarship and had recently returned, an
English architect and his painter wife.

What names, what objects do I remember from that time? The
brown covered *Penguin Series of Modern Painters*: Stanley
Spencer, Frances Hodgkins, Paul Nash, Ben Nicholson: the pocket-
sized Dent edition of Thomas's *Deaths and Entrances*, the Eliot
recordings of *The Four Quartets*, dropped names like Graham
Sutherland, and Carola and Ben Fleming's and Harry's reminis-
cences of ICA student days, and Harry's self-belittling anecdote
of how he had once heard that Augustus John was aboard a cruise-
ship and he had rushed up to see him with a pile of canvases and
how John, agreeing to look at them, had glared back and said
'you can't paint a damn, but I admire your brass!' BIM magazine,
Henry Swanzy's Caribbean Voices programme, Caribbean Quar-
terly, and the first West Indian novels, *New Day* and *A Morning
at the Office*. Once Mittelholzer had sat in our drawing room and
warned me to give up writing verse-tragedies, because 'they' would
never take them.

That year I was hardly ever at home. My life lay between A's
house at Luna Park and along the path that wriggled up the hill
to Harry's Morgue. At school, I now felt more sympathy with the
Brothers. They were at least young and outspoken. Besides, I found
in their accents and in their recollections of Irish events and places,
in their admiration for Synge and Yeats, for Pearse, and even
for Joyce, an atmosphere, fortified by those martial Irish tunes
that the school choir was taught, by the morning and evening
litany droned out by the assembled school under the galvanised
iron roof of the college yard, an atmosphere that summoned that
of my current hero, the blasphemous, arrogant Stephen Dedalus.

'Help Of the Sick,
We are Sick of Help,
Towers of Ivory,
Pay for Us,
Comforter of the Afflicted
We are afflicted with Comfort...'

I was now consumed by poetry, whatever expression it took. I shared with one of the Brothers, a flushed, tubercular-looking mathematician, who also wrote verse and had composed the new school song (did we have one before?), a new cynicism for the Empire and a passion for James Clarence Mangan's poem:

> O, my dark Rosaleen,
>   Do not sigh, do not weep!
> The priests are on the ocean green,
>   They march along the deep...

for Fergus and Cuchulain, and in the struggle and wrestling with my mind to find out who I was, I was discovering the art of bitterness. I had been tormented enough by the priests, and had even been savaged in a review in the *Port of Spain Gazette* by the Catholic Archbishop. Like Stephen, I had my nights of two shilling whores, of 'tackling in the Alley', and silently howling remorse. Like him, I was a knot of paradoxes: hating the Church and loving her rituals, learning to hate England as I worshipped her language, sanctifying A. the more I betrayed her, a Methodist-lecher, a near-Catholic-ascetic, loving the island, and wishing I could get the hell out of it.

My adolescence was over.

[1965]

Self Portrait
by DEREK WALCOTT

The loneliness of Van Gogh.
The humbleness of Van Gogh.
The terror of Van Gogh.

He looks into a mirror,
and begins to paint himself.

He discovers nobody there
but, Vincent Van Gogh.
This is not enough.

He cuts off an ear.
He looks into a mirror:
there is Vincent Van Gogh
with a bandaged ear.

It resembles his portrait,
he is attempting to remain,
first, he must disappear,

he will arrive by reductions
beyond any more terror
by a lonely process

when the mirror will proffer
neither fame nor pain,
neither no nor yea

or maybe, or once, or
no. Nobody there,
not Vincent Van Gogh,

humble, frightened and lonely,
only
a fiction. An essence.

[1980]

Ruins of a Great House

> *though our longest sun sets at right declensions and*
> *makes but winter arches, it cannot be long before we lie*
> *down in darkness, and have our light in ashes...*
> BROWNE: Urn Burial

Stones only, the *disjecta membra* of this Great House,
Whose moth-like girls are mixed with candledust,
Remain to file the lizard's dragonish claws;
The mouths of those gate cherubs streaked with stain.
Axle and coachwheel silted under the muck
Of cattle droppings.

               Three crows flap for the trees,
And settle, creaking the eucalyptus boughs.
A smell of dead limes quickens in the nose
The leprosy of Empire.

               'Farewell, green fields'
               'Farewell, ye happy groves!'

Marble as Greece, like Faulkner's south in stone,
Deciduous beauty prospered and is gone;
But where the lawn breaks in a rash of trees
A spade below dead leaves will ring the bone
Of some dead animal or human thing
Fallen from evil days, from evil times.

It seems that the original crops were limes
Grown in the silt that clogs the river's skirt;
The imperious rakes are gone, their bright girls gone,
The river flows, obliterating hurt.

I climbed a wall with the grill ironwork
Of exiled craftsmen, protecting that great house
From guilt, perhaps, but not from the worm's rent,
Nor from the padded cavalry of the mouse.
And when a wind shook in the limes I heard
What Kipling heard; the death of a great empire, the abuse
Of ignorance by Bible and by sword.

A green lawn, broken by low walls of stone
Dipped to the rivulet, and pacing, I thought next
Of men like Hawkins, Walter Raleigh, Drake,
Ancestral murderers and poets, more perplexed
In memory now by every ulcerous crime.
The world's green age then was a rotting lime
Whose stench became the charnel galleon's text.
The rot remains with us, the men are gone.
But, as dead ash is lifted in a wind,
That fans the blackening ember of the mind,
My eyes burned from the ashen prose of Donne.

Ablaze with rage, I thought
Some slave is rotting in this manorial lake,
And still the coal of my compassion fought:
That Albion too, was once
A colony like ours, 'Part of the continent, piece of the main'
Nook-shotten, rook o'er blown, deranged
By foaming channels, and the vain expense
Of bitter faction.

                    All in compassion ends
So differently from what the heart arranged:
'as well as if a manor of thy friend's...'

Sea Canes

Half my friends are dead.
I will make you new ones, said earth.
No, give me them back, as they were, instead,
with faults and all, I cried.

Tonight I can snatch their talk
from the faint surf's drone
through the canes, but I cannot walk

on the moonlit leaves of ocean
down that white road alone,
or float with the dreaming motion

of owls leaving earth's load.
O earth, the number of friends you keep
exceeds those left to be loved.

The sea-canes by the cliff flash green and silver
they were the seraph lances of my faith,
but out of what is lost grows something stronger

that has the rational radiance of stone,
enduring moonlight, further than despair,
strong as the wind, that through dividing canes

brings those we love before us, as they were,
with faults and all, not nobler, just there.

A Letter from Brooklyn

An old lady writes me in a spidery style,
Each character trembling, and I see a veined hand
Pellucid as paper, travelling on a skein
Of such frail thoughts its thread is often broken;
Or else the filament from which a phrase is hung
Dims to my sense, but caught, it shines like steel,
As touch a line and the whole web will feel.
She describes my father, yet I forget her face
More easily than my father's yearly dying;
Of her I remember small, buttoned boots and the place
She kept in our wooden church on those Sundays
Whenever her strength allowed;
Grey-haired, thin-voiced, perpetually bowed.

'I am Mable Rawlins,' she writes, 'and know both your parents';
He is dead, Miss Rawlins, but God bless your tense:
'Your father was a dutiful, honest,
Faithful, and useful person.'
For such plain praise what fame is recompense?
'A horn-painter, he painted delicately on horn,
He used to sit around the table and paint pictures.'

The peace of God needs nothing to adorn
It, nor glory nor ambition.
'He is twenty-eight years buried,' she writes, 'he was called home,
And is, I am sure, doing greater work.'

The strength of one frail hand in a dim room
Somewhere in Brooklyn, patient and assured,
Restores my sacred duty to the Word.
'Home, home,' she can write, with such short time to live,
Alone as she spins the blessings of her years;
Not withered of beauty if she can bring such tears,
Nor withdrawn from the world that breaks its lovers so;
Heaven is to her the place where painters go,
All who bring beauty on frail shell or horn,
There was all made, thence their *lux-mundi* drawn,
Drawn, drawn, till the thread is resilient steel,
Lost though it seems in darkening periods,
And there they return to do work that is God's.

So this old lady writes, and again I believe.
I believe it all, and for no man's death I grieve.

Mass Man

Through a great lion's head clouded by mange
a black clerk growls.
Next, a gold-wired peacock withholds a man,
a fan, flaunting its oval, jewelled eyes;
What metaphors!
What coruscating, mincing fantasies!

Hector Mannix, waterworks clerk, San Juan, has entered a lion,
Boysie, two golden mangoes bobbing for breastplates, barges
like Cleopatra down her river, making style.
'Join us,' they shout. 'O God, child, you can't dance?'
But somewhere in that whirlwind's radiance
a child, rigged like a bat, collapses, sobbing.

But I am dancing, look, from an old gibbet
my bull-whipped body swings, a metronome!
Like a fruit bat dropped in the silk-cotton's shade,
my mania, my mania is a terrible calm.

Upon your penitential morning,
some skull must rub its memory with ashes,
some mind must squat down howling in your dust,
some hand must crawl and recollect your rubbish,
someone must write your poems.

Extract from For the altar-piece of the Roseau Valley Church, St Lucia

I

The chapel, as the pivot of this valley,
round which whatever is rooted loosely turns
men, women, ditches, the revolving fields
of bananas, the secondary roads,
draws all to it, to the altar
and the massive altar-piece;
like a dull mirror, life
repeated there,
the common life outside
and the other life it holds
a good man made it.

Two earth-brown labourers
dance the botay in it, the drum sounds under
the earth, the heavy foot.

                          This is a rich valley,
it is fat with things.

Its roads radiate like aisles from the altar towards
those acres of bananas, towards
leaf-crowded mountains
rain-bellied clouds
in haze, in iron heat:

This is a cursed valley,
ask the broken mules, the swollen children,
ask the dried women, their gap-toothed men,
ask the parish priest, who, in the altar-piece
carries a replica of the church,
ask the two who could be Eve and Adam dancing.

II

Five centuries ago
in the time of Giotto
this altar might have had
in one corner, when God was young
ST OMER ME FECIT AETAT whatever his own age now,
GLORIA DEI and to God's Mother also.

It is signed with music.
It turns the whole island.
You have to imagine it empty on a Sunday afternoon
between adorations

Nobody can see it and it is there,
nobody adores the two who could be Eve and Adam dancing.

A Sunday at three o'clock
when the real Adam and Eve have coupled
and lie in re-christening sweat

his sweat on her still breasts,
her sweat on his panelled torso

that hefts bananas
that has killed snakes
that has climbed out of rivers,

now, as on the furred tops of the hills
a breeze moving the hairs on his chest

on a Sunday at three o'clock
when the snake pours itself
into a chalice of leaves.

The sugar factory is empty.

Nobody picks bananas,
no trucks raising dust on their way to Vieuxfort,
no helicopter spraying

the mosquito's banjo, yes,
and the gnat's violin, okay,
okay, not absolute Adamic silence,
the valley of Roseau is not the Garden of Eden,
and those who inhabit it, are not in heaven,

so there are little wires of music
some marron up in the hills, by AuxLyons,
some christening.

A boy banging a tin by the river,
with the river trying to sleep.
But nothing can break that silence,

which comes from the depth of the world,
from whatever one man believes he knows of God
and the suffering of his kind,

it comes from the wall of the altar-piece
ST OMER AD GLORIAM DEI FECIT
in whatever year of his suffering.

III

After so many bottles of white rum in a pile,
after the flight of so many little fishes
from the brush that is the finger of St Francis,

after the deaths
of as many names as you want,
Iona, Julian, Ti-Nomme, Cacao,
like the death of the cane-crop in Roseau Valley, St Lucia.

After five thousand novenas
and the idea of the Virgin
coming and going like a little lamp

after all that,
your faith like a canoe at evening coming in,

like a relative who is tired of America,
like a woman coming back to your house

that sang in the ropes of your wrist
when you lifted this up;
so that, from time to time, on Sundays

between adorations, one might see,
if one were there, and not there,
looking in at the windows

the real faces of angels.

Another Life
Extract

CHAPTER 1

i

Verandahs, where the pages of the sea
are a book left open by an absent master
in the middle of another life –
I begin here again,
begin until this ocean's
a shut book, and, like a bulb
the white moon's filaments wane.

Begin with twilight, when a glare
which held a cry of bugles lowered
the coconut lances of the inlet,
as a sun, tired of empire, declined.
It mesmerised like fire without wind,
and as its amber climbed
the beer-stein ovals of the British fort
above the promontory, the sky
grew drunk with light.
                              There
was your heaven! The clear
glaze of another life,

a landscape locked in amber, the rare
gleam. The dream
of reason had produced its monster:
a prodigy of the wrong age and colour.

All afternoon the student
with the dry fever of some draughtsman's clerk
had magnified the harbour, now twilight
eager to complete itself,
drew a girl's figure to the open door
of a stone boathouse with a single stroke, then fell
to a reflecting silence. This silence waited
for the verification of detail:
the gables of the Saint Antoine Hotel
aspiring from jungle, the flag
at Government House melting its pole,
and for the tidal amber glare to glaze
the last shacks of the Morne till they became
transfigured sheerly by the student's will,
a cinquecento fragment in gilt frame.

The vision died,
the black hills simplified
to hunks of coal,
but if the light was dying through the stone
of that converted boathouse on the pier,
a girl, blowing its embers in her kitchen,
could feel its epoch entering her hair.

Darkness, soft as amnesia, furred the slope.
He rose and climbed towards the studio.
The last hill burned,
the sea crinkled like foil,
a moon ballooned up from the Wireless Station. O
mirror, where a generation yearned
for whiteness, for candour, unreturned.

The moon maintained her station,
her fingers stroked a chiton-fluted sea,
her disc whitewashed the shells
of gutted offices barnacling the wharves
of the burnt town, her lamp

baring the ovals of toothless façades,
along the Roman arches, as he passed
her alternating ivories lay untuned,
her age was dead, her sheet
shrouded the antique furniture, the mantel
with its plaster-of-Paris Venus, which
his yearning had made marble, half-cracked
unsilvering mirror of black servants,
like the painter's kerchiefed, ear-ringed portrait: Albertina.

Within the door, a bulb
haloed the tonsure of a reader crouched
in its pale tissue like an embryo,
the leisured gaze
turned towards him, the short arms
yawned briefly, welcome. Let us see.
Brown, balding, a lacertilian
jut to its underlip,
with spectacles thick as a glass paperweight
over eyes the hue of the sea-smoothed bottle glass,
the man wafted the drawing to his face
as if dusk were myopic, not his gaze.
Then, with slow strokes the master changed the sketch.

Parades, Parades

There's the wide desert, but no one marches
except in the pads of old caravans,
there is the ocean, but the keels incise
the precise, old parallels,
there's the blue sea above the mountains
but they scratch the same lines
in the jet trails –
so the politicians plod
without imagination, circling
the same sombre garden
with its fountain dry in the forecourt,
the gri-gri palms desiccating

dung pods like goats,
the same lines rule the White Papers,
the same steps ascend Whitehall,
and only the name of the fool changes
under the plumed white cork-hat
for the Independence Parades,
revolving around, in calypso,
to the brazen joy of the tubas.

Why are the eyes of the beautiful
and unmarked children
in the uniforms of the country
bewildered and shy,
why do they widen in terror
of the pride drummed into their minds?
Were they truer, the old songs,
when the law lived far away,
when the veiled queen, her girth
as comfortable as cushions,
upheld the orb with its stern admonitions?
We wait for the changing of statues,
for the change of parades.

Here he comes now, here he comes!
Papa! Papa! With his crowd,
the sleek, waddling seals of his Cabinet,
trundling up to the dais,
as the wind puts its tail between
the cleft of the mountain, and a wave
coughs once, abruptly.
Who will name this silence
respect? Those forced, hoarse hosannas
awe? That tin-ringing tune
from the pumping, circling horns
the New World? Find a name
for that look on the faces
of the electorate. Tell me
how it all happened, and why
I said nothing.

Preparing for Exile

Why do I imagine the death of Mandelstam
among the yellowing coconuts,
why does my gift already look over its shoulder
for a shadow to fill the door
and pass this very page into eclipse?
Why does the moon increase into an arc-lamp
and the inkstains on my hand prepare to press thumb-downward
before a shrugging sergeant?
What is this new odour in the air
that was once salt, that smelt like lime at daybreak,
and my cat, I know I imagine it, leap from my path,
and my children's eyes already seem like horizons,
and all my poems, even this one, wish to hide?

Edward Kamau Brathwaite was born in 1930 in Bridgetown, Barbados, and studied history at Pembroke College, Cambridge. At Sussex University he wrote his doctoral study, *The Development of Creole Society in Jamaica, 1770-1820* (OUP, 1971). He taught in Ghana from 1955 to 1962; then at the University of the West Indies; and most recently at New York University.

In 1966 he helped to found the Caribbean Artists Movement in London, which published books through *Savacou* in Jamaica, the influential magazine he edited from 1970. He has published several critical works on Caribbean history, culture and literature, including *History of the Voice: The Development of National Language in Anglophone Caribbean Poetry* (New Beacon, 1984).

Most of his poetry books have been published by Oxford University Press, including *Rights of Passage* (1967), *Masks* (1968) and *Islands* (1969), reissued as *The Arrivants: A New World Trilogy* in 1973. *Other Exiles*, largely earlier poems, appeared in 1975. His second, Bajan trilogy comprises *Mother Poem* (1977), *Sun Poem* (1982) and *X/Self* (1987), published by OUP, plus the offshoot of *MiddlePassages* (Bloodaxe Books, 1992). An outstanding performer of his poetry, he has released several recordings, including (on the Argo label) one of each of the books of *The Arrivants*. He is now known as Kamau Brathwaite.

Rohlehr on Brathwaite

The critic, Professor Gordon Rohlehr, who has written an authoritative study of Brathwaite, *Pathfinder* (1981), talks to E.A. Markham about his approach to Brathwaite's work.

There are a number of possible ways I might have gone about it. I could have selected a number of concerns in the Trilogy, for example, spoken about imagery. I felt that as a first exploratory work on the Trilogy, I should retrace in my criticism the journey which the Trilogy was about. The Trilogy is about a journey, or several journeys, which are all tributaries of a single journey. And it's interesting when you take that line, how many things come together. For example, I used that word tributaries, right away you've got the river, and the image of several branches coming in to form a stream, and you've got the idea of the trail. Then you've got that central image in the Trilogy of Anancy, the spider's web. You can see the spider's web, the trail, the river, the strands, the themes, all come together in such an intricate way that what you have is a network or a web; several tissues or strands joining together.

There is a remarkable coherence in what Eddy was doing in the Trilogy. One exciting way of approaching Eddy would be to jump in anywhere, or you might take a single word or a single image and see what has happened to this throughout the thing, and you find yourself moving in all kinds of directions. I decided that I'd take the chronological approach poem by poem, right through to the end. On the other hand I decided that I must also capture something of the sense of growth and the dimension that you gain as you move through the Trilogy.

You ask me about the criticism of Eddy's work. One of the things I have found is that for all the acclaim that his work has got, there isn't really much authoritative statement on the work. You've had this mixture of admiration and reservation, a grudging kind of admiration, particularly among Caribbean critics. There are some who have been in many ways overtly or covertly really quite hostile. Now you find that there is much less written about *Masks* even though there is Maureen Warner-Lewis's special work on *Masks*. She digs into all the sources on what he has done, in fact I deliberately said in my study that I am not going to do that in *Masks* because it has already been done by Maureen.

The general reaction in the Caribbean is one of not really want-
ing to open themselves up to the African experience. The African
experience has been censored out of us, and we have learned to
censor ourselves. You say Africa, you say black, and the minute
you say those words, there is a sense of, why am I going on about
this? Or, why am I preoccupied with the past? These notions
immediately arise, and you feel that you shouldn't talk about it.
Not much was said about *Masks*. Almost nothing was said about
Islands; you can pick up ten articles but they don't say anything.
So here I was feeling that the poetry is gaining in dimension,
growing with every book. The words, the images and that the very
'superficiality' of which Eddy was overtly or covertly accused in
Rights of Passage, had disappeared by the time we got to *Islands*.
By that time the same people who might have criticised superficial-
ity were not prepared to go through the effort of discovery and
self discovery which was necessary if you were to come to grips
with the new dimensions in *Islands*.

It struck me that this was very typical of us, that there are
levels at which we are very superficial people. We talk about
writers without knowing the writers. I mean there is very little
autobiography in the West Indies. We literally talk about people
we don't know. It is something which we need to contemplate,
when we are contemplating this whole business about a biography
or autobiography in the Caribbean: the concealed self, the layers
and layers of *Masks*, or whatever that we create to protect us. Is
this the result of some strategy which we as a people designed
because our real selves were so frequently under attack? I mean
parents don't tell us about the past, they don't tell us about the
immediate family. You have no sense of the last generation. Our
writers have been preoccupied by history; they have been pre-
occupied by autobiography, maybe for that very reason, that this
was already an allusive thing. We grew up in the present moment,
without having been given this dimension, this sense of a linkage
with the past. I went into sketching the pattern of his ideas as he
had expressed them in his various non-poetic statements: in his
essays, in his reviews, in his articles, seeing how that mind was
developing before *Rights of Passage* had begun.

Nobody in the Caribbean wants to reassess the African pre-
sence, even those who talk about it. I mean if you go into the
libraries of our colleges, you'll see that the books on Africa are
largely unread. They don't know anything about it. The books
on India are also largely unread. The point about this is that where

knowing that past and knowing that self becomes hard work you're pretty certain that nobody wants to do it.

Islands has that dimension because having gone into Africa, Brathwaite gets a way out, he gets another eye. The eye was always there, but he didn't know. So another eye is opened. He can now, for example, approach an image from two cultural angles. So the cross becomes not only the Christian cross but the crossroad and an icon. If you look at my book *Pathfinder* you'll see that the cover is black, that black on the cover represents the black ground. The names are largely in white, that white represents the white language, which is an image taken from the book too, you see.

The ground is black, the ground of being is black. The language which has been imposed on you is white. You use that language but you are using it on a black ground, which is actually a total reversal of the European image of making black marks in the white snow.

Then you will see on the cover a circle cut by a cross. Now that represents the beginning, that is the central icon. Then there is the God, the crippled God, the old man who stands at the gate at the point of intersection of the crossroads. And he has to be invoked to open the barrier, to open the gate before you can begin anything. The circle is the central image in the sense of moving in four different directions, the sense of moving away from an origin or moving back to an origin if you like – everything there is icon.

Now if *Masks* projected us into the past, *Islands* is projecting us towards the future. Now the question of refashioning the future is fascinating because it suggests that the future has already been mapped out; we are already headed for something that needs to be changed, that needs to be refashioned. So, it's a concept again of the poets, the artists, a rule of constant redefinition, remaking. He's saying that unless we have an energy of consciousness which we inject into the present, we remain with a future which is already pre-determined for us. It's pre-determined for us by the people who have made us what we have been from the past. It is pre-determined for us by the moles, by the categories and prisons that they have created.

Before we look at the second Trilogy, let's look at what came in between. You had *Other Exiles* (1975), which is going back to some of his earlier work between 1948 or 1950, when he was at Cambridge. He has some interesting portraits of Europe and Europeans.

The poems which came out in *Black 'N' Blues* (1975) were written between 1969, 1970, 1971, and 1972. Now if you talk about a silence about *Islands*, there has been an almost total silence about *Black 'N' Blues*. Poems like 'Starvation', are severely focussed on the Kingston of the early 1970s. We are dealing with a phenomenon of terrifying violence. They are a response to the nakedness of now, the terror of now, with what we have become through the constant corrosion of being urban people in a ghetto, unemployed, and being in a sense trapped in that post-emancipation arrangement, by which we were not to be accommodated, by which we were never to possess the world into which we have supposedly been set free.

The dry season in the Caribbean is when the bushes burn. It's also when the hibiscus blooms. There are times when the place has been so dry, that the silver birch drops all of its leaves and you have this white skeleton of stems with a flower at the end of it. There's just not sufficient moisture to sustain the tree. That is the ambiguity running through *Black 'N' Blues*. The ambiguity of drought and a life which was there. The ambiguity of the bareness and bleakness.

Brathwaite spent his first extended stay in Barbados for nearly 20 years, in early 1975/76. What I think it did was to free him from the kind of mental oppression that is part of the Jamaican experience. Now I'm not saying this against Jamaica, but you live there in a society which is under pressure, under stress. The mid-70s was period of a lot of raping. The poem 'Spring Blades' is about raping, at least part of it is about that. It's a place that set fire to an old ladies home, a place which gunmen made children go back into. So that there is grimness there, which obviously is lifted off when you get to Barbados.

On the other hand, of course, I remember George Lamming saying that Barbados was stable – the stability of the cemetery. So that you can get the other sense in Barbados of the place being stable as well as static. I think though that what Barbados did was to give his mind an ease, and he began now to explore the Barbadian landscape.

Now, *Mother Poem* is autobiography. So is *Sun Poem*, and so to a certain extent is *X/Self*. The question is how do we see these three very different poems as part of a trilogy. If they are part of a trilogy, what kind of trilogy? They're certainly not the same kind of trilogy as *Rights of Passage*, *Masks*, and *Islands*. It is possible to see *Mother* and *Sun* poems as being two sides, two ways of looking at the Barbadian experience, *Mother Poem* being essentially the experience of the women, obviously as seen through the eyes of a man. Though the voices in *Mother Poem*, apart from the narrator's voice, are all those of women. *Sun Poem* is about the male experience. And, the images or central symbols are different. In *Mother Poem* you're dealing with the land, the women, and not so much the sea, you know, the sea becomes your existence towards the end, and I think there is a really marvellous poem about the sea towards the end of *Mother Poem*. Some of the best writing about the sea I know anywhere; where the actual pulse and rhythm of the poem is the long heave of the sea. Now we get hints of this early in the poem, like you know when you're in Barbados in the night and there is less traffic, and if you're close to the coast, you sometimes just hear the sea. And there is that poem about the land talking about what has happened to the consciousness of the ordinary Barbadian, who has been told to accommodate himself to tourism. And so he becomes maybe a beach-boy, or a bus-boy.

Although *Mother Poem* is autobiography, it is not autobiography in any simple way. There is a kind of process by which Brathwaite distances himself, but it is not autobiography for example in quite the same way as, say, Walcott's *Another Life*; even there there is distancing. The people who appear in *Mother Poem* are all voices for something much larger than themselves. They are voices for the landscape; they are voices for the whole historical process; they are voices of the psyche or consciousness, protesting at what is happening to it. And they are voices of the women coming into a consciousness of themselves, and into a kind of visibility which is quite similar to the apocalyptic movement in their arrivance. In other words in *Mother Poem* the women are moving from accepting their position in the room, you know, the domesticity to that voice in 'Cherries' which rebels.

These women are also located in history, because Brathwaite is very much aware that there was and is women's oppression. So that that passage at the centre of *Mother Poem* is historical; it deals with the confrontation of the plantation between the slave girl and the mistress. In other words it's not just simply that men oppress women, which is the formula we sometimes get. Oppression has got to be seen as part of a system, which includes women oppressing each other. So it includes a class dimension, a race dimension, as well as a gender dimension. *Mother Poem* I think is a very important poem.

Sun Poem is dealing with boyhood. It's more closely autobiographical. But the rituals are different. The rituals of the men are rituals of male confrontation, fighting on the beach, winning your spurs, and this kind of thing. That autobiographical strain is interrupted somewhere in the middle too, by a movement back to the past. Because Brathwaite is really interested in what has happened to the male archetype. Why is it that we don't have any heroes that look like ourselves? What was done to the male? What was destroyed when we destroyed the male archetypes in this society? He does this in the poem called 'Noon', in which he looks at the movement of the sun-god across the East Coast of Barbados. That East Coast is rugged; it's quite different from the other part of Barbados. He creates a myth, the dying of the god, but the dying of that god is also equated with the dying of Christ; the three hours of darkness, so that it is a dying of a male archetype.

The mother is not only a woman but the land, looking at the destruction of spirit and consciousness in her children, particularly in her sons. It is done in terms of the sea surging, that surge of the sea becomes more insistent. And then there is also the sense of trying to get the shape of the landscape in the movement of the verse, which is remarkable towards the end of *Mother Poem*. Barbados exists in terraces, the whole country can be seen as a series of steps, you move from one plateau right up to the other and then at the core of it there is this fairly hard rock, the rest of it is like stone.

There are all these caves because of the limestone, with water seeping through. Barbados is literally an island which has as its centre a womb of water. *Mother Poem* makes fantastic use of this geological fact. So the caves become wombs, become consciousness. The water is the fertility, the life, which is always springing there; but it's under the surface; you've got to get below these layers, you've got to get down into the caves before you discover Barbados. And that is seen as an almost archetypal female presence in the island. Mind you the real mother lives under a system of oppression, oppression on the job. Not only that, they are on the tail end of a system of oppression because when their man is oppressed they are oppressed too. And so at the beginning of *Mother Poem* you've got the monologue, there's a long monologue in which she is looking at her husband and what has happened to him. He has worked in a warehouse and it just mashes him up. But what is fascinating about that monologue is that it turns, it changes halfway through and she begins to contemplate that this is what my work has become. She's talking about what his work has done to him, and she's saying that that is all they give him, they didn't even give him a little gratuity, a little sense for all the work he had to do, in the morning. So that she is a rebel voice in the poem.

And of course there is the other archetypal thing of placing the poem in the framework of the sun, or of mythology. So that is the *Sun Poem*, but it ends, like *Mother Poem*, with a promise of rebirth: the sun goes down, the sun comes back up. So that cycle of death is also a movement towards rebirth. *Mother Poem* ends with the sea surging and the land is pulsating so that we get the sense that she isn't dead at all; she's become part of the process. So we get these two *Mother* and *Sun* poems becoming two ways of looking at Barbados. And there's a precision. Brathwaite tends to be geologically precise when he talks about the terraces and the steps and the movement up, they're there. So the thing is precise on a visual level, on a geographical level, as well as on a level of image and archetype.

In *X/Self*, what Brathwaite is doing and what links it with *Mother Poem* and *Sun Poem* is that it is his intellectual autobiography. In other words it is telling us that to understand where I am coming from you have to understand all of those things. So it is going to pose a lot of problems partly because the range and the scope of what it brings together is so wide. It has a lot to do with redefining the way in which we see. It is using the other eye to look at European history up to the point where Europe became involved with Africa creating the world we know today. So in a sense it is an autobiography of the mind, and of the development of the mind. But it is not done in an easy way. The eye for example is a Roman, an Emperor, or a Tribune. The eye is sometimes, just a black presence. And there is this sense of contrasts for example between Europe and Africa. *X/Self* is an attempt to explain why it is that Europe has been able to create the society it has created, and Africa has had a great deal of problems with the same thing. And what he is really saying is that Europe has done it because Europe has drained the resources of Africa. So that I think the central statement there is 'Rome burns and our slavery begins', because it begins to see the disintegration of the Roman Empire, particularly through the movement of Islam into the Iberian peninsula and into North Africa. He seems to see that as something which drove Europe back on itself which destroyed feudal Europe and created the Europe of the Compass, the Europe of Columbus, the Europe which moved out of Europe again in a sort of new wave of imperialism, which now included the 'dark continent'.

Now, saying that is one thing, but trying to look at how he worked that vision out in the poetry is another. I find a lot of the earlier European poetry that he wrote, some of which you get in *Other Exiles*, I find some of the style of that is there. A very relaxed style. At the same time I find this has added a kind of witty, almost comic style. I mean he's doing all sorts of things with words. He's laughing all the time. But it's a fun which tends to reduce the grandeur. A punning which reduces, which cuts down, which tries to see this thing in a new way.

The "X" is the unknown quantity, suggesting what you cannot contain in any single image or metaphor. The central vision is that of the confrontation between Europe and Africa, but not only Africa, it brings in a lot more of the new world, the American Indians; so it is really dealing with the frontier situation; with the question of conquest, and in its latter pages with apocalypse.

[1987]

Timehri

by EDWARD KAMAU BRATHWAITE
(extract)

I was born in Barbados, from an urban village background, of
parents with a "middle-class" orientation. I went to a secondary
school originally founded for children of the plantocracy and col-
onial civil servants and white professionals; [1] but by the time I
got there, the social revolution of the 30s was in full swing, and
I was able to make friends with boys of stubbornly non-middle-
class origin. I was fortunate, also, with my teachers. These were
(a) expatriate Englishmen; (b) local whites; (c) black disillusioned
classical scholars. They were (with two or three exceptions) hap-
pily inefficient as teachers, and none of them seemed to have a
stake or interest in our society. We were literally left alone. We
picked up what we could or what we wanted from each other and
from the few books prescribed like Holy Scripture. With the help
of my parents, I applied to do Modern Studies (History and Eng-
lish) in the sixth form. Since Modern Studies had never been
taught at this level before (1948), and there were no teachers to
teach it, I (with about four others) was allowed to study the subject
on my own with only token supervision and succeeded, to every-
one's surprise, in winning one of the Island Scholarships that
traditionally took the ex-planters' sons "home" to Oxbridge or
London.

The point I am making here is that my education and back-
ground, though nominally "middle-class", is, on examination, not
of this nature at all. I had spent most of my boyhood on the beach
and in the sea with "beach-boys", or in the country, at my grand-
father's with country boys and girls. I was therefore not in a
position to make any serious intellectual investment in West
Indian middle-class values. But since I was not then consciously
aware of any other West Indian alternative (though in fact I had
been *living* that alternative), I found and felt myself "rootless"
on arrival in England and like so many other West Indians of the
time, more than ready to accept and absorb the culture of the
Mother Country. I was, in other words, a potential Afro-Saxon.

But this didn't work out. When I saw my first snow-fall,[2] I felt
that I had come into my own; I had arrived; I was possessing the
landscape. But I turned to find that my "fellow Englishmen" were

not particularly prepossessed with me. It was the experience later
to be described by Mervyn Morris, Kenneth Ramchand and Elliot
Bastien in *Disappointed Guests* (Oxford University Press, 1965).
I reassured myself that it didn't matter. It made no difference if
I was black, or white, German, Japanese or Jew. All that mattered
was the ego-trip, the self-involving vision. I read Keats, Conrad,
Kafka. I was a man of Kulture. But the Cambridge magazines
didn't take my poems. Or rather, they only took those which had
a West Indian – to me, "exotic" – flavour.[3] I felt neglected and
misunderstood.

Then in 1953, George Lamming's *In the Castle of My Skin*
appeared and everything was transformed. Here breathing to me
from every pore of line and page, was the Barbados I had lived.
The words, the rhythms, the cadences, the scenes, the people,
their predicament. They all came back. They all were possible.
And all the more beautiful for having been published and praised
by London, mother of metropolises.

But by now this was the age of the Emigrant. The West Indies
could be written about and explored. But only from a point of
vantage outside the West Indies. It was no point going back. No
writer could live in the stifling atmosphere of middle-class
materialism and philistinism. It was Lamming again who gave
voice to the ambience in *The Emigrants* (1954), and in *The Plea-
sures of Exile* (1960). His friend Sam Selvon made a ballad about
it in *The Lonely Londoners* (1956), and Vidia Naipaul at the start
of his brilliant career could write (in *The Middle Passage*):

> I had never wanted to stay in Trinidad. When I was in the fourth form
> I wrote a vow on the endpaper of my Kennedy's *Revised Latin Primer*
> to leave within five years. I left after six; and for many years afterwards
> in England, falling asleep in bedsitters with the electric fire on, I had
> been awakened by the nightmare that I was back in tropical Trinidad . . .
> I knew [it] to be unimportant, uncreative, cynical . . .

For me, too, child and scion of this time, there was no going back.
Accepting my rootlessness, I applied for work in London, Cam-
bridge, Ceylon, New Delhi, Cairo, Kano, Khartoum, Sierra
Leone, Carcassone, a monastery in Jerusalem. I was a West
Indian, roofless man of the world. I could go, belong, everywhere
on the worldwide globe. I ended up in a village in Ghana. It was
my beginning.

Slowly, slowly, ever so slowly; obscurely, slowly but surely,
during the eight years that I lived there, I was coming to an aware-
ness and understanding of community, of cultural wholeness, of

the place of the individual within the tribe, in society. Slowly, slowly, ever so slowly, I came to a sense of identification of myself with these people, my living diviners. I came to connect my history with theirs, the bridge of my mind now linking Atlantic and ancestor, homeland and heartland. When I turned to leave, I was no longer a lonely individual talent; there was something wider, more subtle, more tentative: the self without ego, without I, without arrogance. And I came home to find that I had not really left. That it was still Africa; Africa in the Caribbean. The middle passage had now guessed its end. The connection between my lived, but unheeded non-middle class boyhood, and its Great Tradition on the eastern mainland had been made.

The problem now was how to relate this new awareness to the existing, inherited non-African consciousness of educated West Indian society. How does the artist work and function within a plurally fragmented world? How can a writer speak about "the people", when, as George Lamming dramatises in *In the Castle of My Skin*, those to whom he refers have no such concept of themselves?

'I like it,' I said. 'That was really very beautiful.'
'You know the voice?' Trumper asked. He was very serious now.
I tried to recall whether I might have heard it. I couldn't.
'Paul Robeson,' he said. 'One of the greatest o' my people.'
'What people?' I asked. I was a bit puzzled.
'My People,' said Trumper. His tone was insistent. Then he softened into a smile. I didn't know whether he was smiling at my ignorance, or whether he was smiling his satisfaction with the box and the voice and above all Paul Robeson.
'Who are your people?' I asked. It seemed a kind of huge joke.
'The Negro race,' said Trumper. The smile had left his face, and his manner had turned grave again...He knew I was puzzled...At first I thought he meant the village. This allegiance was something bigger. I wanted to understand it...

[1970]

NOTES:

1. See Austin Clarke, 'Harrison College and Me', *New World Quarterly*, Barbados Independence Issue (Bridgetown, 1966); Paule Marshall, *The Chosen Place, The Timeless People* (New York, 1969), p.61.
2. See 'The Day the First Snow Fell', *Caribbean Quarterly*, 5 no.3 (April 1958), p.128.
3. See 'A Caribbean Theme', *Poetry from Cambridge* (Cambridge, 1950).

Wings of a Dove

1
Brother Man the Rasta
man, beard full of lichens
brain full of lice
watched the mice
come up through the floor-
boards of his down-
town, shanty-town kitchen,
and smiled. Blessed are the poor
in health, he mumbled,
that they should inherit this
wealth. Blessed are the meek
hearted, he grumbled,
for theirs is this stealth.

Brother Man the Rasta
man, hair full of lichens
head hot as ice
watched the mice
walk into his poor
hole, reached for his peace
and the pipe of his ganja
and smiled how the mice
eyes, hot pumice
pieces, glowed into his room
like ruby, like rhinestone
and suddenly startled like
diamond.

And I
Rastafar-I
in Babylon's boom
town, crazed by the moon
and the peace of this chalice, I
prophet and singer, scourge
of the gutter, guardian

Trench Town, the Dungle and Young's
Town, rise and walk through the now silent
streets of affliction, hawk's eyes
hard with fear, with
affection, and hear my people
cry, my people
shout:

Down, down
white
man, con
man, brown
man, down
down full
man, frown-
ing fat
man, that
white black
man that
lives in
the town.

Rise rise
locks-
man, Solo-
man wise
man, rise
rise rise
leh we
laugh
dem, mock
dem, stop
dem, kill
dem an' go
back back
to the black
man, lan'
back back
to Af-
rica.

2

Them doan mean it, yuh know,
them cahn help it
but them clean-face browns in
Babylon town is who I most fear

an' who fears most I.
Watch de vulture dem a-fly-
in', hear de crow a-dem crow
see what them money a-buy?

Caw caw caw caw.
Ol' crow, ol' crow, cruel ol'
ol' crow, that's all them got
to show.

Crow fly flip flop
hip hop
pun de ground; na
feet feel firm

pun de firm stones; na
good pickney born
from de flesh
o' dem bones;

naw naw naw naw.

3

So beat dem drums
dem, spread

dem wings dem,
watch dem fly

dem, soar dem
high dem,

clear in the glory of the Lord.

Watch dem ship dem
come to town dem

full o' silk dem
full o' food dem

an' dem 'plane dem
come to groun' dem

full o' flash dem
full o' cash dem

silk dem food dem
shoe dem wine dem

that dem drink dem
an' consume dem

praisin' the glory of the Lord.

So beat dem burn
dem, learn

dem that dem
got dem nothin'

but dem
bright bright baubles

that will burst dem
when the flame dem

from on high dem
raze an' roar dem

an' de poor dem
rise an' rage dem

in de glory of the Lord.

Jah

Nairobi's male elephants uncurl
their trumpets to heaven
Toot-Toot takes it up
in Havana
in Harlem

bridges of sound curve
through the pale rigging
of saxophone stops
the ship sails, slips on banana
peel water, eating the dark men.

Has the quick drummer nerves
after the stink Sabbath's unleavened
cries in the hot hull? From the top
of the music, slack Bwana
Columbus rides out of the jungle's den.

With my blue note, my cracked note, full flatten-
ed fifth, my ten bebop fingers, my black bottom'd strut, Panama
worksong, my cabin, my hut,
my new frigged-up soul and God's heaven,
heaven, gonna walk all over God's heaven...

I furl
away from the trumpet
my bridge stops in the New York air
elevator speeds me to angels
heaven sways in the reinforced girders

God is glass with his type-
writer teeth, gospel
jumps and pings off the white
paper, higher and higher

the eagle's crook neck,
the vulture's talons clutching tight
as a blind baby's fist, still knows
the beat of the root blood
up through the rocks, up through the torn

hummingbird trees, guitar strings, eyrie;
the buffaloes' boom through the dust plains,
the antelope's sniff at the water, eland's sudden hurl
through the hurdle of fire, runnels upwards to them
through the hoof of the world.

But here God looks out over the river
yellow mix of the neon lights
high up over the crouching cotton-wool green
and we float, high up over the sighs of the city
like fish in a gold water world

we float round and round
in the bright bubbled bowl
without hope of the hook
of the fisherman's tugging-in root

eyes without bait, snout
without words, teeth with nothing to kill,
skill of fin for a child's wonder,
pale scales for collectors to sell

and God, big eyes bulging
his glass house aglobe
floating floating in heaven
without feet without wind

without wing without thunder
no stone under him
no sound to carry earth up to his fathoms
no ground to keep him down near the gods

Mont Blanc

Rome burns
and our slavery begins

in the alps
oven of europe

glacier of god
chads opposite

industry was envisioned here in the indomitable glitter
it out proportions the parthenon

the colosseum is not to be compared with it
nor dome nor london bridge bernini bronze nor donatello marble

there is more wealth here than with the bankers of amsterdam
more power than in any boulder dam of heaven

volt crackle and electricity it has invented
buchenwald nagasaki and napalm

it is the frozen first atomic bomb
its factories blaze forth bergs and avalanches

its unships sail down rhine down rhone down po down dan down
tiber

to the black sea dead to the world to the red sea of isaias

without it the sahara would have been water
latvium carthage tunis would have been dolphin towns

genoa would have become a finchal of the esquimaux
columbus would have sailed south along the congo's rivers

but being immobile here
more permanent than pope or charlemagne

it has burnt rome
but preserved europe

as it rises

chad sinks

sa
hara wakes out slowly

the dry snake of the harm
attan the harmattan reaches into our wells into our smiles in

to our cook
ing pot oil in

to the water re
flecting our walls in

to the bone
of the mutton in

to our dry
gully eyes

and the green brown dunn of sudan of bel uur of the niger
sa

hell

crumbles into these flickering miles miles silences of holes
of noon in our belly

narrow burning its protein to gravel
skin mouldered to ash

holocaust of dome
heads propped up on sticks of skeletones

ball headed children
naked of all else but large deep agate space age eyes

black bladders of dried milk hung haggard from my mannequin
flies dying into crevices of mouths from all the fertile places

with only memories of nipple suck suck suck
ing their blistered lips the flim crew cameras already closing in

like buzz like buzzards on this moonscape manscape in slow
motion

herdsmen becoming scarecrows
their howls of silent dust wheeling across the super

sands like paper
water in the shadow of this snow and ici/cle

this eye
less rise

ing gas
face mountain

Kingston in the kingdom of this world

The wind blows on the hillside
and i suffer the little children
i remember the lilies of the field
the fish swim in their shoals of silence
our flung nets are high wet clouds, drifting

with this reed i make music
with this pen i remember the word
with these lips i can remember the beginning of the world

between these bars is this sudden lock-up
where there is only the darkness of dog-bark
where i cannot make windmills of my hands
where i cannot run down the hill-path of faith
where i cannot suffer the little children

a man may have marched with armies
he may have crossed the jordan and the red sea
he may have stoned down the wells of jericho

here where the frogs creak where there is only the croak of starlight
he is reduced
he is reduced
he is reduced
            to a bundle of rags
            a broken stick
            that will never whistle through
            fingerstops into the music of flutes
            that will never fling nets white sails
            crossing

gospel was a great wind freedom of savannas
gospel was a great mouth telling thunder of heroes
gospel was a cool touch warm with the sunlight like water in claypots,
    healing

this reduction wilts the flower
    weakens the water
    coarsens the lips
fists at the bars, shake rattle and hammers at the locks

suffer the little children
suffer the rose gardens
suffer the dark clouds howling for bread
suffer the dead fish poisoned in the lake

my authority was sunlight: the man who arose from
    the dead called me saviour
      his eyes had known moons older than jupiters
my authority was windmills: choirs singing of the
    flowers of rivers

your authority is these chains that strangle my wrists
your authority is the red whip that circles my head
your authority is the white eye of interrogator's terror:
    siren price fix the law of undarkness

the dreadness of the avalanches of unjudgement

it is you who roll down boulders when I say the word
it is you who cry wolf when i offer the peace of wood-doves
it is you who offer up the silence of dead leaves

i would call out but the guards do not listen
i would call out but the dew out there on the grass cannot glisten
i would call out but my lost children cannot unshackle their shadows
    of silver

        here i am reduced to this hole of my head
        where i cannot cut wood where i cannot eat bread
        where i cannot break fish with the multitudes

my authority was foot stamp upon the ground
    the curves the palms the dancers
my authority was nyambura: inching closer
        embroideries of fingers silver earrings:
            balancers

and

i am reduced
i am reduced
i am reduced
to these black eyes
this beaten face
these bleaching lips blearing obscenities

i am reduced
i am reduced
i am reduced
to this damp
to this dark
to this driven rag

awaiting the water of sunlight
awaiting the lilies to spring up out of the iron
awaiting your eyes o my little children

awaiting

Horse weebles

Sellin biscuit an sawlfish in de plantation shop at pie
corner, was another good way of keepin she body an soul-seam
   together

she got she plot of cane, she cow, she fifteen pigeons in a coop,
razzle-neck fool-hens, a rhode islan' cocklin,
yam, pumpkin, okro, sweet
potato, green pea bush

there is lard ile in de larder
an shark ile for the children's colds
there is easin' ile for crusty locks
and castor oil with lime or salt or sugar for extreme
distress, and candle grease for sea-egg pricks an chiggoes

but she sells in the plantation shop at pie corner, hoping to make
   enns meet.

from she left school, taking up sewing since she was fourteen,
bringin forth myrtle, den eggbert, den
sammy an redsin de twin wuns

not a sarradee come you cahn fine she in there after 'leven o'clock
heat risin: smokin hi'sin' outside: blackbirds hidin from sun
white: weighin out flour, choppin up salt beef, countin out biscuit

shovellin
oat flake out o' de tin while she
frettin

evenin' miss
evvy, miss
maisie, miss
maud, olive

how you? how
you, eveie, chile?
you tek dat miraculous bush
fuh de trouble you tell me about?

de cornmeal flour is flow thru she fingers like time
self, me chile

the saltfish barrel is dark like a well an is broaden out to a lake at
   de bottom
where de swink is splash into slippery conger-eels

the crystal sugar is shine like stars that does twinkle into de dark
o' de akee tree

but you tek
it?

ev'ry night 'fore uh gets
into bed.

uh bet-
'cha feelin less
poorly a'ready!

i int know, pearlie,
man, any-
way, de body int dead.

no man, you even lookin
more hearty!

a'ready?
then all uh kin say
an uh say it agen:
we got to thank god
fuh small mercies

an she is dream of tears of stone
of dark meroë water lapping at the centre of the world

but then is cries an hungry faces: children
who can hardly shit: tin bones of ancient skeletones

the planter's robber's waggon wheels and whips
and she trapped in within her rusting canepiece plot.

so sar'dee nights when you hearin de shout
mister greedyman boltin he bars cross de gate
de pump-up glass lamp soon outin out

she is dust off she hanns
put back de rounn biscuit lid pun de barrel
help lock stock and socket de shop

collect what little they give she in small
change, handin back what she owe pun de frock

goin slowly down in de winks o de dark
to de half lot o' lann dat she callin a home

an not sayin a word to a soul what she see what she dream what she own

Stone
(for Mikey Smith)

When the stone fall that morning out of the johncrow sky
it was not dark at first . that opening on to the red sea sky
but something in my mouth like feathers . blue like bubbles and light
carrying signals & planets & the sliding curve of the world like a water
    picture
in a raindrop when the pressure drop

When the stone fall that morning i
couldn't cry out because my mouth was full of beast & plunder
as if i was gnashing badwords among tombstones
as if angry water was beating up against the curbstones of the
    palisadoes
as if that road up Stony Hill round the bend by the churchyard on the
    way to the

post office was a bad bad dream and the dream was on fire all the way
    past the
white houses higher up the hill and the ogogs bark
ing all teeth & furnace and my mother like she upside down up a
    tree like
she was screaming and nobody i could hear could hear a word i
    shouting
even though there were so many poems left and the tape was switched
    on & running
and the green light was red and they was standing up everywhere in
    London
& Amsterdam & at UNESCO in Paris & in West Berlin & clapping &
    clapping &
clapping & not a soul on Stony Hill to even say amen . and yet it was
    happening happening
the fences began to crack in my skull and there were loud *boodooooongs*
    like
guns going off them ole time magnums or like fireworks where I
    dreadlocks were in fire
and the gaps where the river coming down and the dry gully where
    my teeth used to be
smiling and my tuff gong tongue that used to press against them &
    parade pronounciation

now unannounce and like a black wick in i head & dead
and it was like a heavy heavy riddim low down in i belly bleeding dub
and there was like this heavy black dog thumping in i chest & pumping
        murdererrrrrrrr

and my throat like dem tie like dem tie a tight tie around it . twist
ing my neck quick crick quick crick and a never wear neck
tie yet and a laughing more blood and spittin out lawwwwwwwwwwwd
and i two eye lock to the sun and the two sun staring back bright from
        the grass and i

bline to de butterfly flittin . but i hear de tread of my heart
the heavy flux of the blood in my veins silver tambourines
closer & closer . st joseph band crashing &
closer & bom sicai sica boom ship bell &
closer & bom sicai sica boom ship bell &
when the saints...
        *

and it was like a wave on Stony Hill caught in a crust of sunlight
and it was like a broken schooner into harbour muffled in the silence
        of its wound
and it was like the blue of peace was filling up the heavens with its
        thunder
and it was like the wind was growing skin the skin had hard hairs
        hardering
it was like Marcus Garvey rising from his coin . stepping towards his
        people
crying dark . and every mighty word he trod the ground fell dark &
        hole behind
him like it was a scream i did not know and yet it was a scream . my
        ears were bleeding
sound . and i was quiet now because i had become that sound

the sunlit morning washed the coral limestone harsh against the soft
        volcanic ash
i was & it was slipping past me into water & it was slipping past me
        into root
i was & it was slipping past me into flower & it was ripping upward
        into shoot
while every tongue in town was lashing me with spit & cutrass wit &
        ivy whip &

wrinkle jumbimum . it was like warthog grunting in the ground . and
    children run
ning down the hill run right on through the splashes
that my breathing made when it was howl & red & bubble and sparrow

    twits pluck tic & tapeworm from the grass
as if i-man did never have no face as if i-man did never in this place

When the stone fell that morning out of the johncrow sky
i could not hold it back or black it   back or block it off or limp away
or roll it from me into memory or light or rock it steady into night be
cause it builds me now and fills my blood with deaf my bone with dumb &

lawwwwwwwwwwwwwwwwwwwwwwwwwwwwwwwwwwwwwwwwwd

i am the stone that kills me.

DENNIS SCOTT

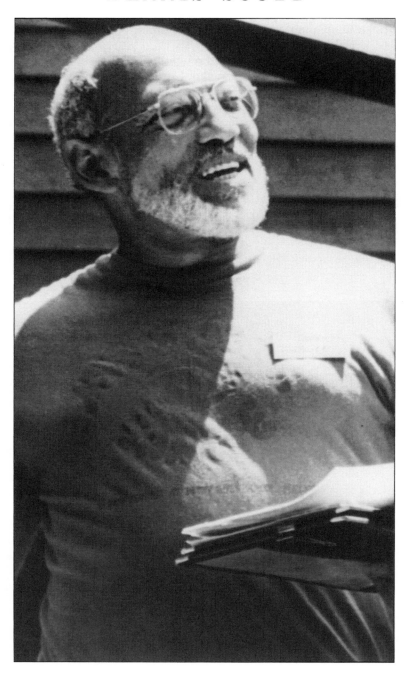

Dennis Scott was born in 1939 in Jamaica. He has had a profes-
sional career as a dancer, actor, theatre critic and director, as
well as being a playwright and poet. He is Principal of the Jamaica
School of Drama and Dean of the Four Schools (Art, Dance,
Drama and Music) of the Cultural Training Centre in Kingston.
He has also been editor of *Caribbean Quarterly*, and an Associate
Professor of Directing at Yale University. His plays include *An
Echo in the Bone* (1974), *Dog* (1981), and a verse adaptation of
the Middle English poem *Sir Gawain and the Green Knight*.

His collections of poetry are: *Journeys and Ceremonies* (Jamaica,
1969); *Uncle Time* (University of Pittsburgh Press, 1973), winner
of the Commonwealth Poetry Prize and the International Poetry
Forum Award; and *Dreadwalk* (New Beacon Books, London,
1982). He died in 1991.

Interview with Dennis Scott

by MERVYN MORRIS

MM: *I notice that in a recent conference paper Ian Smith quotes
you as saying that your poetry 'is far more political [now]...and
simultaneously far more personal'. What are we to make of that?
You called it a paradox.*
DS: Perhaps it's not a paradox at all. I think at one and the same
time my own sense of self and my sense of where that self is located
in terms of the society have been intensifying, getting clearer; to
me, at any rate. And therefore I feel much more comfortable
making statements about myself in the society, and therefore polit-
ical statements, than before when I was less concerned with, less
aware of, the relationship between self and society.
MM: *Isn't there a sense in which one of the things you're doing
is creating several different selves through different personae?
Or is there a consistent position which you think you are adopting,
politically, throughout the poetry?*
DS: No, I think that's absolutely accurate. The psycho-analytic
cliché that one in fact is several – that there are several parts to
one's self and that the healthy self is an integrated collection of
those various personae is absolutely right; and I find it useful as
a way of viewing people and behaviours. So that really each poem
is an attempt to come to terms with, to distinguish, define, and
locate a self in relationship to all the other selves and to the context
of each of the selves. One agglomerates, accumulates, statements
about the world. Hopefully, as each statement ties on to the next
few you develop a clearer sense, a clearer set of statements, about
the whole situation.
MM: *You've called your latest collection* Dreadwalk, *and the title
poem actually deals with an encounter between a Rastafarian and
a non-Rastafarian – a non-Rastafarian creator, perhaps poet. To
what extent do you find you are specially interested in Rastafa-
rians and for what purpose, really, in your work?*
DS: I'm interested in them because they seem to me one of the
healthiest phenomena that the New World has thrown up: healthy
in the sense of choosing a life-enhancing value system which
refuses to tolerate the destructiveness of most of the Western
civilisation's beliefs and practices; healthy also, in a sense,
because they are, so interestingly for me, a creole development –

a group, people, who can trace most of their roots to another continent, to other continents; have had to come to terms with an environment which is essentially strange to them – that is, we're not indigenous here – and to forge some kind of world-view. It seems to me (and to others, who are more qualified to talk about these things) that every time a New World man has chosen to swallow the value systems, the culture, wholesale of the Old World or – in the Caribbean – to take on the culture of the metropolitan areas of the New World we've gone awry, we've gone amiss. The Rastas seem to me to have opted – for good and bad reasons – for (logically, and irrationally, and a-rationally – a mixture of these things), for seeing themselves and seeing the world in a certain way which at least says we have to deal with ourselves, there's a possibility, a hope, of saving ourselves, no matter what. And this, I think, is a very important thing to have happened. In so doing they have manipulated, changed, influenced the culture around them to an amazing extent – particularly, of course, in language; which is what interests us, more, perhaps. And I'm intrigued, fascinated and excited by the kind of strategies – linguistic strategies – that they have used to redefine themselves in the world. So that they're one way of attempting to specify self. And since I regard art as a process of attempting to define, to specify, oneself in relationship to the world, then this strategy is particularly interesting to me and useful for my own work sometimes.

MM: *Could we extend a little bit that last remark? You 'regard art as...' What do you see as the function of the Jamaican or Caribbean poet?*

DS: The function for him (or her) self is to find out as much as he can about him (or her) self as possible and to record it, for his own – her own – self and for the entertainment and assistance of others. The function for the society is to provide information about the possibilities of being a human being in the society that other people may find interesting and/or useful.

MM: *In your first volume,* Uncle Time, *there seemed to many readers to be a predominant influence of theatre; a sense of persona that had a theatrical element in the way in which he presented himself. It seems to me that in* Dreadwalk *that element of theatricality has been somewhat diminished, and that one of the things very noticeable here – though there were bits of it in* Uncle Time *– is a greater interest in relating to the visual arts. Is there a development of that kind between these two books?*

DS: For one thing: during the period in which the poems of *Uncle*

Time was being written I was – far more than I have been since
then – a performer, literally on stage: a little bit as an actor, and
certainly as a dancer; and I'm sure that this influenced the way
in which I tended to express and, perhaps, see the world. Since
then I've been more a director and a playwright, so there is less
a sense of feeling and being on stage in the work. For another:
during that period in which *Uncle Time* poems were written I was
doing a lot of reviewing of the arts. I think that the pay-off to
some of that reviewing happens in *Dreadwalk* poems, in that there
is more a sense of the observer and less of the performer observing
himself. Also I think as my sense of where I am in the society and
where I choose to be in the society got stronger there was less felt
need to write about observing myself; I am much more comfortable
now simply existing there and observing the society itself. Also,
of course, the craft, I think, has been growing: I've been experi-
menting a lot with ways of drying out the lushness of some of the
earlier work, and I'm getting a crisp, cool, conversational style
in which images are shocking but you don't quite realise how
shocking they are until you think about the actual picture that
the words are making a second time. 'Apocalypse Dub', for
instance. Images of wounding, of body hurt, are being very much
underplayed now in the poems – increasingly so; even more so in
the new collection that's coming together.

MM: *You talked just now about shocking images and so on. Many
of these images seem, to some of us, surreal. Have you been influ-
enced by Surrealism?*

DS: One of the strong influences, I know, is science fiction, science
fantasy, the whole genre of literary fantasy – which I've always
enjoyed, purely as entertainment, and which I've learnt a lot
from, I think; which attracts me as a mode of describing reality.
The disjunction between practice and precept in the world as I
am growing older also, I think, jolts me into a sense of the strange-
ness of people's behaviour; and this maybe is a step-off point
towards creating stories – pictures and stories – in the work which
are very odd, which are (for want of a better term) surreal. I also
am very interested in the way in which stories can be told econom-
ically not by representationally chronicling the world but by
metaphors that function interestingly because of their strangeness
but also satisfyingly because of the way they echo and distort
reality. I'm not sure if that's not a circular definition, but never
mind.

MM: *One of the recurring metaphors in your work is bird. Would*

you say something about why the metaphor of bird recurs so often
in your work, and something about the multiple significances that
you are, at the moment, aware of?
DS: I don't know where that image started. It may have to do
with my sense of space. There definitely is a connection with
theatre, and probably also with dance, both of which (as far as
I'm concerned) are intimately concerned with telling stories that
happen in space and time. And there's a way in which, for me, a
bird – movement of birds – itself provides examples of a body
existing in space and time interestingly. It defies gravity, falls at
will. It refuses to fall. There's a sense of lightness combined with
mass, a sense of vulnerability combined with the possibility of the
kind of strength you get in birds of prey. They are very attractive
to me, in the same way as bodies moving in space are attractive,
because they are interesting to look at, and they tell stories,
whether they want to or not.

[1984]

Tricksong

Jukebox blue, he walks her home.
They drag the dark between them
like a skin, knotting their hands
into it. The music
scrawls after. It is thick
like new tar. Stone sucks at it,
the hungry trees twist their roots
out of the street, the dogs are slouching
that gutter full of shadows.
The moon worries their eyes.

A last lane turns to safety. In the stale room
when she hangs it on her cracking door
the key will turn like coins falling
the bed will scratch round, round,
the music will leak its dull pulse
down from the lintel.
And they won't bear the morning horns
or the jangle of the breadcart coming
never, never

Riversong

Sun up, she ben down
there, wash at the riverside
(ribber come far, ribber deep)
the boy a fish
and the man there bathing
(lang time, run hard,
ribber doan sleep).
The woman beating
the clothes like bread
for the dunny short
again this year

and the rock is hard
but a man must wear
clean, the boy have to show
good, bring up decent and straight, even
if him black.
(Wha de use? Wha him ketch?
Doan de line still slack?
All de same – check de man,
ketch him ead, look him back.
Im stan free. De wata like it
deliver him, dough it look like it move so slow;
de current strang.
Wait. Nat lang.)

A family man

At night when the ordinary loves have settled
like dust drifting a little in my son's cough, my wife's breath, my
        daughter's sigh,
I call them in. From the dark side of leaves,
from the countries of desire, from the cracks in the road,
from the places I went to and never gave back
at the border, the faces I wanted and never forgave
for dying, from the dark side of leaves, they come
softer than smoke, shadows on paper,
like dust drifting a little in my wife's cough, my son's sigh, my
        daughter's breath.
They make hoarse journeys in my head. They cry
at the lamp's white pain. I silence them.
They orbit, tongueless. They die like stars; they cool
to ash. I trace their stain on paper, and sign it. Watch them
wind my life down like small, burnt moons. Watch them fall
like dust drifting a little in my daughter's cough, my wife's sigh,
        my son's breath.

Weather report

That dumb bird knows enough to come in
out of the rain, shaking rhinestones over the
      cool porch,
watching the guttering afternoon
with one eye. The cat isn't sleeping at all.
It makes a river of muscle
into the air,
pouring
across the floor. That delicate umbrella opens
and closes.

What an unpleasant surprise.

Clearly the porch leaks.

Grampa

Look him. As quiet as a July river-
bed, asleep, an' trim' down like a tree.
Jesus! I never knew the Lord could
squeeze so dry. When I was four
foot small I used to say
Grampa, how come you t'in so?
an' him tell me, is so I stay
me chile, is so I stay
laughing, an' fine
emptying on me –

laughing? It running from him
like a flood, that old molasses
man. Lord, how I never see?
I never know a man could sweet so, cool
as rain; same way him laugh,

I cry now. Wash him. Lay him out.

I know the earth going burn
all him limb dem
as smooth as bone,
clean as a tree under the river
skin, an' gather us
beside that distant Shore
bright as a river stone.

Hatch: or, The revolution viewed as an exploding library

This is a stone.
These are men climbing it.
They eat their way up its face
spitting out bits of earth and blood. When they are tired
the stumps of their arms wedge
into cracks, they hang patiently till the next leg
of the journey can begin.
Nothing stops them. They come
like messages, poems, songs
about hunger.
Those words cannot run, or rub off.
Sometimes the rock shifts, scattering one
into the air. He falls
silently, over and over, too tired to shout.

They know what to do when they arrive.
The holes have been prepared
by time, pecked open
into honeycombs: a library of dreams.
They will place themselves, like documents.
Fused.
They will wait for the fist, and the fire.

That stone will open,
like a seed.

Time piece

There's a stone in my wrist
goes ticktocticktoc
it scares me sometimes, death,
I don't understand –
I mean the how
and the what,
but the why?
Ticktocticktoc.

The cells change completely
every seven years.
That's so your skin doesn't keep
the bruises
where people touch you
and hurt, you
can start again
fresh you see,
put them away
like old watches
you looked at a lot
(but the hands don't move
any more, or something)
and after a while you forget,
and forget, you see.
Ticktoc. Ticktoc.

Time-slip

He wore her extravagant laughter, and waved goodbye.

After the airport, at home,
tore the time of her holiday off. The calendar

bled moths. Nights, he heard them nibbling his clothes
and a goat munched at his dried groin.
That was a cold bed.

But every week he glued one more page back.
Moths grew drowsy. The nights healed a little, the goat
                    slept. Every week.
At last the clock stopped, the date on the wall
said 'today she is leaving'.

His wound hurt, scabbed over.
It was hard to stand. Naked,
he watched the plane
stab down again.

The infection

Something hurt inside.
He stripped down
but nothing showed.
He set off, running
to find it.

When he passed
they scored him
cutting the flesh with reluctant eyes, with sharp tongues.
That was all right. Only the muscle mattered,
the going to and fro,
the small movement inside that said, soon.

One day it worked itself out,
the colour of the moon,
he held it up triumphantly – see!

But the cop was frightened,
never having seen a man make a knife
out of moonlight and laughter.
So he shot him.

Now at night
he goes through the streets
touching his uniform secretly,
looking for what it is
that presses on the nerve so, that hurts

More poem

'No more poem!' he raged, eye red;
'A solitary voice is wrong,
Jericho shall fall, shall fall
at the People's song!'

So. Only I-tongue have the right
to reason, to that sense of dread.
Man must keep silence now, except
man without bread.

No. See the flesh? It is cave, it is
stone. Seals every I away from light.
Alone. Man must chant as Man can
gainst night.

Dreadwalk
for the Children

blackman came walking I
heard him sing his
voice was like sand
when the wind dries it

said sing for me dreamer
said blackman I cannot
the children are gone
like sand from the quarry

said are you afraid I
come closer said blackman
his teeth were like stone
where the pick cuts it

said do you remember
my mouth full of stones he said
give I the children
would not step aside

but you holding it wrong I
said love the fist opened
the knife fell away from
the raw hand middle

his voice was like wind
when the sea makes it salt
the sun turned a little
the shadows rolled flat
blowing closer afraid I
would not step aside

then he held me into
his patience   locked

one

now I sing for the children
like wind in the quarry
hear me now
by the wide torn places

I am walking

: for Joy

After all journeys, you. And in the centre
of a town where no one had invented trees
yet, I remember
a great kite stumbled
like some bird, sun-blind.
The houses spread out their sharp arms
the soiled windows shocked open
the hoardings cried out, the walls
sliced cold at the air with their edges
till it swung singing at last
aloft into the wind.
And the children floated
against that crooked street
silent as flowers.

So, constant, twine me
homes through waste, through wind
or hold me high –
I will hang simple as a child's toy, flying
my bones like bamboo
at your sky.

Sentry

It is forbidden to sleep on guard.
In the dreamshadow you can't see them limping along,
    covering their baskets like mouths.
Besides that, stone frosts and must be kept dry, or
    it shivers to sand,
things have a tendency to liquefy; become old
in the darkness of anger, running away into crevices.
Nobody explained this to me when I came.

Only I noticed the muscles softening, the flesh
    creased and ripened,
the young faces pinched
off at the base, breaking like shy stalks.
Since then I watch against reapers.

In the stone gardens of my mind
there are old men with fingers like scissors,
snip, snip. Harvesting heads.

Apocalypse Dub

At first, there's a thin, bright Rider –
he doesn't stop at the supermarket, the cool
red meats are not to his taste.
He steals from the tin on the tenement table,

he munches seed from the land
where no rain has fallen, he feeds
in the gutter behind my house.
The bread is covered with sores
when he eats it; the children
have painted his face on their bellies

The second rides slowly, is visiting, watch him, he smiles
through the holes in the roof
of the cardboard houses.
His exhaust sprays pus on the sheets,
he touches the women and teaches them
fever, he puts eggs under the skin –
in the hot days insects will hatch and hide
in the old men's mouths,
in the bones of the children

And always, behind them, the iceman, quick,
with his shades, the calm oil of his eyes –
when he throttles, the engine
grunts like a killer. I'm afraid,
you said. Then you closed the window
and turned up the radio, the DJ said greetings
to all you lovely people.
But in the street the children coughed like guns.

In the blueblack evenings
they cruise on the corner
giggling. Skenneng! Skenneng!

Uncle Time

Uncle Time is a ole, ole man...
All year long 'im wash 'im foot in de sea,
long, lazy years on de wet san'
an' shake de coconut tree dem
quiet-like wid 'im sea-win' laughter,
scraping away de lan'...

Uncle Time is a spider-man, cunnin' an' cool,
him tell yu: watch de hill an' yu se mi.
Huhn! Fe yu yi no quick enough fe si
how 'im move like mongoose; man, you tink 'im fool?

Me Uncle Time smile black as sorrow;
'im voice is sof' as bamboo leaf
but Lawd, me Uncle cruel.
When 'im play in de street
wid yu woman – watch 'im! By tomorrow
she dry as cane-fire, bitter as cassava;
an' when 'im teach yu son, long after
yu walk wid stranger, an' yu bread is grief.
Watch how 'im spin web roun' yu house, an' creep
inside; an' when 'im touch yu, weep...

Construction

Some time in de greathouse wall
is like a thumb mark de stone,
or a whole han.
Granny say is de work sign, she say
it favor when a man tackle de stone, an' mek
to tear it down, till de mortar tek de same shape
as him han. But I feel say
is like sumaddy push de wall up
an' hole it dere until de brick dem dry
out. Now dat is hard.

Guard-ring

Moon shadow burning,
Watch where I walking, Lord.
Make mi foot step hard
on the enemy's shadow
an hear me.

I wearing de ring dem tonight –
one gainst hate and de red pepper
tongue of malice, a snake-eye
bone-ring to touch
if I buck up de tempter,
one ring gainst love-me
an one gainst de finger of famine,
an one for the death by drowning,
an one from fire;
an a bright copper ring
that I fine in a fish belly,
tun me safe and salt
from de barracuta teet of desire.

But moon shadow falling.
I fraid for de shape of de winding –
de road too crooked,
it making a rope to twine me!
An Lord, I tired
to tell yu mi torment, but listen
an learn me, an reach me
to home. I believe
in de blessed ring, but Chris'
I praising yu candle also,
I raising mi heart like a smalls,
like a coal that outing
to light it –
            guard me asleep an awake!
De ring did bless in de balm yard
but Thee I praise.
I singing out loud
for de hill dem to hear me an tremble
De Lord is my Shepherd,
I shall not fear!
I singing so loud, down to de moon
going shake, I crying out,
Chris' yu hear!
An de moonshine wetting mi face up
like oil of plenty.

I going alone to mi house
wid de ring pon mi finger,
but walk wid me ever
an ever, tree score an ten,
an de moon shall wet me,
de ring shall praise Thee an heal me
an de mout shall bless Thee
for ever, amen
Amen.

Epitaph

They hanged him on a clement morning, swung
between the falling sunlight and the women's
breathing, like a black apostrophe to pain.
All morning while the children hushed
their hopscotch joy and the cane kept growing
he hung there sweet and low.
            At least that's how
they tell it. It was long ago
and what can we recall of a dead slave or two
except that when we punctuate our island tale
they swing like sighs across the brutal
sentences, and anger pauses
till they pass away.

MERVYN MORRIS

Mervyn Morris was born in 1937 in Kingston, Jamaica, and edu-
cated at Munro College, the University College of the West Indies,
and, as a Rhodes Scholar, at St Edmund Hall, Oxford. He teaches
in the Department of English at the Mona campus of the University
of the West Indies, where he is a Reader in West Indian Literature.
   In 1976 the Institute of Jamaica awarded him a Silver Musgrave
Medal for poetry. His books include *On Holy Week* (Kingston,
Jamaica, 1976), and three from New Beacon: *The Pond* (1973),
Shadowboxing (1979) and *Examination Centre* (1992).

Riding Pillion with the Poet

by MERVYN MORRIS

Vic Reid, the novelist – I remember – used to tell us: the artist who talks about his own work is like a window-cleaner stepping back to admire his accomplishment. A high risk activity indeed.

But I also recall – not without envy – that one of our Caribbean poets bolstered a small collection with his own detailed critical commentary, engendering perhaps in many readers a proper reverence for the poems. A real temptation.

The problem then: how to satisfy the editorial demand (for something 'on any aspect of [my] work or working, or any general notions about poetry or writing') without getting carried away?

The editor has preferred my earlier to my later published work – 13 poems of these 21 are from *The Pond* (1973), only three each from *On Holy Week* (1976) and *Shadowboxing* (1979). Of the two remaining poems, 'Literary Evening, Jamaica' is from the early 1960s, 'Peace-time' the early 1980s.

I don't know Archie Markham's reasons for the weighting of his selection. But I know there are readers who in the later poems miss, as one of my most generous critics says she misses, 'a palpable sense of the poet as guide: of pillion-riding the experience with your arms about his waist'.

Shadowboxing offers little comfort to the pillion-rider. There is warning in the title and its metaphoric extension in some of the poems – such as 'Working Out' (in which there is shadowboxing) and 'Interior' (with a shadow box revealing 'curiosa/ locked inside'). Very different from *The Pond*, in which the title poem ends, 'he saw his own face peering from the pool'. Yet even in *The Pond* there were hints that the apparent self-revelation may be largely a pretence. In 'Stripper', from that volume, a poet identifies with a stripper:

> She put on clothes to take them off, she wore
> performing pieces, such a fuss she made
> of skimpy little veils before
> her parts (which never were displayed).

Life is raw material. I don't believe that poems are a licence for indecent exposure, or for telling the world my personal business.

Data

facts lie
behind the poems
which are true
fictions

Poems such as 'Literary Evening, Jamaica' and 'Family Pictures'
give so much information that they perhaps encourage curiosity
about autobiographical sources. They are fiction all the same.
Wherever the poem may originate. I usually invent; and each
poem has, I hope, a logic, a direction, of its own. In talking with
people who are trying to write, I tend to stress that respect for
the original impulse can be an obstacle if it prevents the "author"
from seeing what the poem wants to be. I advocate a process Derek
Walcott has described:

He followed, that was all,
his mind, one step behind,
pacing the poem, going where it was going.

('Guyana')

Trying to see the emerging shape, I whittle away until what
remains is what I feel to be essential, as story, as metaphor. Pro-
vided the poems communicate something – a glance at love or time
or death perhaps, at moral tension, ironies of choice – the worlds
that they create need not direct us towards the author's life. Far
more important are the connections poems may make with the
lives of readers.

Three of the poems published here have been slightly revised
since their publication in *The Pond*.

In 'Stripper' I have altered the second line: I was too anxiously
pressing the central analogy. The poet was once 'pursuing mir-
rors'; which strikes me now as an unlikely reason for anybody,
even a poet, to be visiting a sleazy club. In 'Young Widow, Grave'
the first two lines have been revised, to remove a grammatical
error ('A wreath of mourners ring/ the grave') and to allow the
most common shape of a wreath to work without the redundancy
of 'ring'. I'm glad to find I have now done more with 'gapes': the
wreath gapes and the grave gapes.

In 'Nursery' the word 'white' has been replaced by 'little', which
I think improves the rhythm and the vowel patterns of the stanza,
and removes the over-emphatic opposition of 'colour' versus
'white'. The change also takes the poem further away from the
set of experiences out of which it originally emerged: of verbal

assaults in the early 1970s on Caribbean artists then deemed not "black" enough, considered pretentiously "autistic"/ "artistic", insufficiently involved in community. But what I hope remains are images, of embattled children playing at war, and of one child who, inhabiting a world the others do not know, is somewhat separate from their game but who, with all his problems (his little box of bricks), is holing on to something solid, more durable for construction, potentially more dangerous in conflict, than plastic building-blocks.

[1989]

Nursery

Everyone suddenly burst out screaming
and hurling plastic building-blocks;
the room was a riot of colour.

Did that autistic child have duller
things in mind, hugging his little box
of bricks and quietly beaming?

Greatest Show on Earth

The Great Majumboes
(to the noise of drums)
feign danger every show:
vivid above the safety nets
they swing.

The Mighty Marvo cracks the whip:
well-drugged tigers lumber into line.

Between the tigers and the acrobats
I do my act I
sit on chairs that aren't there
I play for time
(between the tigers and the acrobats)
a dwarf
who owns no whip
and will not leave this ground.

Case-History, Jamaica

In 19-something X was born
in Jubilee Hospital, howling, black.

In 19- (any date plus four)
X went out to school.
They showed him pretty pictures
of his Queen.

When he was 7, in elementary school,
he asked what naygas were.
In secondary school he knew.
He asked in History one day
where slaves came from.
'Oh, Africa,' the master said,
'Get on with your work.'

Up at the university he didn't find himself;
and, months before he finally dropped out,
would ramble round the campus late at night
and daub his blackness on the walls.

Stripper

At a sleazy club where strippers are on view
a weary poet stopped for wine
and song; but had to take the stripper too,
whose writhing seemed an image of his line.
She put on clothes to take them off, she wore
performing pieces, such a fuss she made
of skimpy little veils before
her parts (which never were displayed)!
Riddling hard to music, she performed
her teasing art, for which the patron paid.

Nice fleshy legs, gyrating hips that warmed
the watchers, sensuous lively educated tits.
The poet looked away, to check the eyes
of grim-faced lechers, soft men going to bits,
suckers deceived by lighting, sold on lies
(while there behind the smoke-dimmed crowd
the cunning pander lurked, a ponce on guard).
She took the last piece off the law allowed.
The poet felt his symbol growing hard.

The Pond

There was this pond in the village
and little boys, he heard till he was sick,
were not allowed too near.
Unfathomable pool, they said,
that swallowed men and animals just so;
and in its depths, old people said,
swam galliwasps and nameless horrors;
bright boys kept away.

Though drawn so hard by prohibitions,
the small boy, fixed in fear, kept off;
till one wet summer, grass growing lush,
paths muddy, slippery, he found himself
there at the fabled edge.

The brooding pond was dark.
Sudden, escaping cloud, the sun
came bright; and, shimmering in guilt,
he saw his own face peering from the pool.

Valley Prince
(for Don D.)

Me one, way out in the crowd,
I blow the sounds, the pain,
but not a soul
would come inside my world
or tell me how it true.
I love a melancholy baby,
sweet, with fire in her belly;
and like a spite
the woman turn a whore.
Cool and smooth around the beat
she wake the note inside me
and I blow me mind.

Inside here, me one
in the crowd again,
and plenty people
want me blow it straight.
But straight is not the way; my world
don' go do; that is lie.
Oonu gimme back me trombone, man:
is time to blow me mind.

Meeting

I

An unfamiliar bed
of radicals. And me
looking to root
out lies.

A nightmare –
comrade after comrade
springing
up to criticise!

I took
to planting
questions
in your eyes.

II
spuriously dry
we banter
knowing

something
critical
is growing
underground

a movement
threatening
solidarity

One, Two

I
Lying in the dark together
we
in wordless dialogue
defined community.

II
You switch the light on to inspect
an alien remark.
And now your body stutters.

No more lying in the dark.

Journey into the Interior

Stumbling down his own oesophagus
he thought he'd check his vitals out.
He found the entrails most illegible,
it wasn't clear what innards were about.

He opted to return to air and light
and certainty; but when he tried
he found the passage blocked; so now
he spends the long day groping there, inside.

Literary Evening, Jamaica

In a dusty old building just fit for rats
And much too large for precious poetry circles
The culture fans sat scattered in the first ten rows
Listening for English poetry.

Geoff read Larkin beautifully, Enright too,
And Michael Saunders talked between the poems:
'I don't say they are wonderful,' he said,
'And would not say that anybody says
They're great. I offer them
As two fair English poets writing nowadays.
They're anti-gesture, anti-flatulence,
They speak their quiet honesties without pretence.'

The longer section of the evening's programme
Was poems by the locals, undergraduates,
Some coarse, some wild, and many violent,
All bloody with the strains of rape and childbirth,
Screaming hot curses anti-slavery,
'Down with the limey bastards! Up the blacks!
Chr-rist! Let's tear the painted paper
Off all the blasted cracks!'

The more I heard the more it seemed
A pretty rotten choice to read us Larkin,
Dull-mannered, scared, regressive Phil,
Saying No to everything or Soon, Not yet.
So many bulging poets must have blushed
And wondered where the hell they'd ever get
With noisy poems, brash, self-conscious, colourful,
And feared that maybe they were born too crude.
Maybe they were; but it was bloody rude
Seeming to ask for things that don't belong out here
Where sun shines hot and love is plentiful.

For us standing here, a naked nation
Bracing ourselves for blows, what use
Is fearfulness and bland negation?
What now if honesty should choose
To say, in all this world's confusion
That we are still too young for disillusion?

The Early Rebels

Time and the changing passions played them tricks,
Killing the shop-soiled resolutions dead.
Gone are the early angry promises
Of rich men squeezed, of capitalists bled.
More adult honesties have straightened ties
And brushed the dinner-jackets clean,
Maturer minds have smelt out fallacies
And redefined what thinkers mean.

Hope drives a chromium symbol now
And smiles a toothpaste passion to the poor,
With colder eloquence explaining how
The young were foolish when they swore
They'd see those dunghills dank and dreary
All replaced by bright new flats:
Good sense was never youthful fury
And rash young promises by brats...

'Let's drink a loyal toast to dedication:
We mean the same but youth is past;
We are the fathers of our nation,
The thinking leaders come at last.
Cheers for the faith of simple minds,
Cheers for the love of humble friends;
Love does not alter when it finds
That we have redefined its ends.'

The House-Slave

A drum thumps, faraway;
around the lamp my tribe of blood
are singing brothers home.

But soon that central fire will rage
too harsh for relics of the whip:
they'll burn this building,
fire these books, this art.

And these are my rooms now:
my pallid masters fled,
freeing the only home I knew.
I'll stay another night,
sounding my tutored terror of the dark.

Young Widow, Grave

A wreath of mourners
at the grave. It gapes.
The people sing.
The service isn't meaning anything.

His secretary's legs look sleek in black.

The widow's looking farther back.
Across the gap, now flower-choked,
her swollen eyes have stumbled on
another man she lost; who poked
the fire, and when it stirred was gone.

That was another death.

Love Story

Love gave her eyes:
the tough man snatched,
locked them up tight.

Love gave her hand:
the tough man tickled it
early one night.

Love gave her tongue:
the tough man found
it tasted right.

Love gave her body:
the tough man smiled,
switched off the light.

Love gave her heart:
the tough man fled,
flaccid with fright.

Family Pictures

In spite of love
desire to be alone
haunts him like prophecy.

Observe: the baby chuckles,
gurgles his delight

that daddy-man is handy,
to be stared at, clawed at,
spitted-up upon;
the baby's elder brother
laughs, or hugs, and nags
for popcorn or a pencil
or a trip.

And see: the frazzled wife
who jealously
protects the idol infant
from the smallest chance
of harm, and anxious
in the middle of the night
wakes up to coughs; and checks,
and loves, and screams
her nerves; but loves him
patient still: the wife
who sweets the bigger boy
and teases him through homework,
bright as play.

But you may not observe
(it is a private sanctuary)
the steady glowing power
that makes a man feel loved,
feel needed, all of time;
yet frees him, king of her
emotions, jockey of her
flesh, to cherish
his own corner
of the cage.

In spite of love
this dream:
to go alone
to where
the fishing boats are empty
on the beach
and no one knows
which man is
father, husband, victim,
king, the master of one cage.

Peace-time

bomb-disposal
combed the area
and declared it clean

but love i cannot
guarantee
safe conduct

through the rubble
of my dreams –

i've read
too many people
blown to bits

by land mines
lying silent
in the dust

long after
all those bells
and all that joy

long after solemn treaties
had been signed and sealed

Terminal

She's withering
before our eyes

and no one
noticeably

cries
We do

the hopeful
ritual

each day
we bring

fresh fruit
we prattle

and we pray
for hours

Her room
is heavy

with the scent
of flowers

I Am the Man

I am the man that build his house on shit
I am the man that watched you bulldoze it
I am the man of no fixed address
Follow me now

I am the man that have no job
I am the man that have no vote
I am the man that have no choice
Hear me now

I am the man that have no name
I am the man that have no home
I am the man that have no hope
Nothing is mine

I am the man that file the knife
I am the man that make the bomb
I am the man that grab the gun
Study me now

From On Holy Week

A Priest

The chap's a madman rather than a liar:
I think he's quite convinced he's The Messiah!
But really! If this man were God,
God's choice of person still would strike me odd.
That God might be a carpenter! Absurd!
It's quite the silliest nonsense I have heard!
(You know my bias; but) a priest
– perhaps an elder, at the very least –
would seem to be more likely for the job
than some untutored Galilean yob!

Malefactor *(Left)*

So you is God?
Den teck wi down! Tiefin doan bad
like crucifyin!
Wha do you, man?
Save all a wi from dyin!

Malefactor *(Right)*

Doan bodder widdim, Master; him
must die;
but when you kingdom come, remember I.
When you sail across de sea,
O God of Judah, carry I wit dee.

JAMES BERRY

James Berry was born in 1924 in Jamaica, and has lived in Britain since 1948. He has a special interest in multicultural education and the development of Black British Literature. A popular performer, he has given numerous readings throughout Britain and overseas, as well as working on radio and television.

He won first prize in the Poetry Society's National Poetry Competition in 1981. He has published two seminal anthologies of Caribbean poetry, *Bluefoot Traveller* (1976) and *News for Babylon* (1984), the latter to be reissued by Bloodaxe in 1996 as a new anthology of Black British and Asian poets in Britain co-edited with Mahmood Jamal. His latest anthology is *Classic Poems to Read Aloud* (Kingfisher, 1995). His collections include *Fractured Circles* (1979), *Lucy's Letter and Loving* (1975 & 1982), *Chain of Days* (1985) and *Hot Earth Cold Earth* (Bloodaxe, 1995).

He has published ten books for children, including *When I Dance* (Hamish Hamilton, 1988), winner of the Signal Poetry Award, and most recently, *Celebration Song* (1994), *Playing a Dazzler* (1996) and *Don't Leave an Elephant to Chase a Bird* (1996). He was awarded the OBE in 1990.

Signpost of the Bluefoot Man

by JAMES BERRY

A person of a British Caribbean colony – fourth child and third son of both black Jamaicans – I was born in Boston, Jamaica, and brought up in another coastal village, Fair Prospect. Growing up there in sunny Jamaica of the 1930s I naturally spent my days mostly out of doors. Children helped parents with the growing of crops, the rearing of animals and the general fetching and carrying of food, wood, water – everything. Life was narrow and limited. We felt shut away from the world.

Active with brothers, sisters, cousins, friends in the usual ways, I had spells, alone in the fields, in the presence of animals, over-awed by nature. Other times I found myself confused in thought trying to work out the real meaning of different "bad" hints in school books, and in what people said, implying that the worst thing in the world was to be a black person.

I spent my late teens in America working, returned home and arrived in the bomb-battered and food-rationed London of the latter part of 1948.

I didn't have any address to come to in London. Walking with my suitcase I arrived in Brixton by accident and found a room to share with a fellow Westindian on the same day. Jobs were numerous but finding one wasn't easy. It was also practically impossible to find more suitable accommodation. Anyhow, I knew I was right for London and London was right for me. London had books and accessible libraries. Then, also, mysteriously, the hand of fate had played the main role in my coming to England. The war had dislocated Britain. Through that dislocation my chance opening to come to England as a settler appeared. White people went and settled where they liked – often with government assis-tance – not so for black people any of that. The British authorities would never have invited or assisted black people to come to Britain to settle. The tribal instinct would have always immediately rejected that as totally undesirable and unworkable!

In another way the authorities might well have suspected that a really noticeable black people's presence would have been too harshly and glaringly and embarrassingly educative for a big-boss "master" nation. In fact, as the years have rolled on, the way that the British people have had themselves reflected back through black people's eyes has often struck up bells of alarm nationwide. The consciousness-expansion process that black people's presence has set up in Britain is just about beginning to help the learners to feel that when they have calmed down they are bigger, deeper and more expansive human beings. I am really saying that for black people and their presence to have had the opportunity to activate their reverse missionary-role process on the natives of Britain, it had to happen through all the impact of surprise. And in all this – in the schools, in the art centres, at the festivals and conferences, etc – the active work of black poets has been reaching out in its new way.

I became a telegraphist with Post Office International Telegraphs (now British Telecom) from 1951 to 1977. Then, I began to write full-time. Awarded a C. Day Lewis Fellowship (1977-78), I worked as writer-in-residence in a London comprehensive school and developed a taste for multicultural education and tutoring of writers' workshops in classrooms and libraries.

Short stories were my first serious writing obsession. Poetry came unexpectedly and has continued relentlessly.

Perhaps because I was born under the blazing sun I particularly like to wake up under a snow-laden roof. But, a transplanted root, I need the right depth to survive – especially since I must always be discovering and be more and more celebrating the truth of myself relevant for survival. I like to think the way I use language in my poetry is connected with this.

Traditionally Caribbean writers *do* use their two-language heritage in their writing – Standard English and locally developed people's language. I am no exception here, though I try to do it in my own way.

Political Independence in the Caribbean ushered in a new recognition of the people's local language like a fanfare onto centre stage – alongside Standard English. Linked with identity, written use of the language has not merely increased its popularity but given it a special intensity. The process of independence brought new opportunity for the people to re-define themselves and re-discover who and what they really were. This is where I must say thanks to our poet and historian, Professor Edward Kamau Brathwaite, who cleared away a mighty lot of the wood which obscured appreciation of an aesthetic based on the culture of our African continuity. It's not surprising that in releasing of the people's language from the imprisoning dungeon of "dialect", Brathwaite came up with the new term – Nation Language –

"nation" identifies the language with its roots beginnings. Using Nation Language in my work, I celebrate echoes of those first sounds that made me know it was joyful to be alive.

A little bit about two or three of my poems in this anthology.

'Words of a Jamaican Laas Moment Them' is drawn from the last statements a cousin of mine made to his wife on his last morning just before he died, in his Jamaican village.

For me, 'Faces Around My Father' constitutes a process of "growing", of "maturing", from the earlier 'Thoughts on my Father', which uses my father as a target of rage. These poems record a conscious break with a past which showed him stamped, personifying a slavery-conditioned personality. The rage is against how he seemed finally won over by those insid ious dominating ways of slavery. And so he stays trapped, giving in to a less limited self, to a total forgetfulness, to not taking up the struggle to claim a new vision and reclaim himself. So there is no money in the family; slaves don't have money. There is no education and travel; slaves don't get education or permission to travel. Slaves have no power to see that their beautiful or ugly children are educated and helped to become beautiful or less ugly adults; slaves don't own themselves, don't own their children.

'Lucy's Letter' is the first of the "letter" poems. In this, like all the others, a Caribbean woman who came to England in the 50s writes letters back to her friend who has never left the village.

I grew up without books; now I feel impelled to write them. As a child at school I read nothing and was also taught nothing positive about my people; I go into schools now and read my own texts to teachers and pupils. In the world I grew up in, only people with a similar kind of face were respected and celebrated; my writing celebrates the excluded now.

I believe that poetry is not naturally and truly a minority interest. Poetry is language artistically arranged for everybody's enjoyment. I believe that a wide range of accessible poetry should be made available through the public media with a frequency that represents a favourable comparison with serious music. I have come to believe that exclusivity in poetry has been cultivated and simply proved successful in putting people off.

[1989]

Caribbean Proverbs Poems

3

'Good-boy' a fool nickname.
One-time fool noh fool;
two-time fool a the damn fool.
But – if fool dohn go markit
bad fruit dohn sell.
Fool drink soup with fork
and eat rice with pin.
Fool eat parch-corn dinner done,
fool lick him finger them.
Fool a 'hol-yah', 'carry-deh', 'bring-come'.
Follah fool yu turn fool.
Poun up fool in-a mortar
and tek fool out
him still same fool.

4

Stump-a-foot man cahn kick
with him good foot.

Tiger wahn to nyam a child, tiger sey
him could-a swear it woz puss.

5

Is a blessn me come me si yu.
Yeye-to-yeye joy is a love.

Is betta to walk fi notn
than si-down fi so-so.

A man with half-a-foot
mus dance near him door.

Good-friend yu cahn buy.
Cheap bargain tek money.

Betta to go heavn a pauper
than go hell a rector.

If ants waller too much in fat,
fat will drown ants.

Tretch yu hand and give,
it a God own grace.

hol-yah: hold here; helper who never develops to become skilled.
carry-deh: carry there; one who only carries things for others.
bring-come: one who only fetches things.
Stump-a-foot: stumpy or one-legged.
nyam: eat.
Yeye-to-yeye: eye to eye.
fi: for.
tretch: stretch.

Defendant in a Jamaican Court

Yes I did chop him, sar.
I chop him.
I woz full-full
of the vexation of spirit, sar.

I woz beyon all ow I know me, sar –
over the odda side cut off
from all mi goodness
and I couldn steady mi han firm, sar.

I chop him shoulder.
I let mi distric man blood stream down.

Him did storm up mi bad-bad waters
that I couldn settle –
that flood me, sar –
that mek one quick-quick terrible shut-eye
when all mi badness did rule.

Words of a Jamaican Laas Moment Them

When I dead
mek rain fall.
Mek the air wash.
Mek the lan wash good-good.
Mek dry course them run, and run.

As laas breath gone
mek rain burst –
hilltop them work
waterfall, and all
the gully them gargle fresh.

Mek breadfruit limb them drip,
mango limb them drip. Cow, hog, fowl
stan still, in the burst of clouds.
Poinciana bloom them soak off, clean-clean.
Grass go unda water.

Instant I gone
mek all the Island wash – wash away
the mess of my shortcomings –
all the brok-up things I did start.
Mi doings did fall short too much.
Mi ways did hurt mi wife too oftn.

What Is No Good?

I will stop
night's return,
stop dawn, stop dusk,
leave your eyes on
white dazzle of noon.

I will let sea rocks move
and fill in dark depths of oceans,

let storm clouds
and November be whitened,
leave you the glitter of space.

I will wash out
the brown of earth,
bleach out the tarmac of roads,
let gardens be white roses only,
leave you brilliant desert ways.

Sunlight's tanning
I will cancel,
leave you the show
of a tree
newly stripped of bark.

I will leave you time
with a dazzling face,
leave you a pale pale red
fixed on each other.
Would absence be abundance?

Ol Style Freedom

Darlin mi darlin
you lying down
all legs belly bosom face
quiet-quiet in room here
All of all so much –
street poverty can't touch me now
Hurts – threats – banished away

No pockets on me
I a millionaire
No test before me to fail me
I know I know everything

Darlin mi darlin
you the offerin with all things
   all of all so much
every tick of clock stopped
every traffic groan switched off
every peep of bird shut up
only sea waves risin risin

Hope she fixed sheself fo no-baby
I in a king time king time king time
   king time
      king time
         king time

Fractured Circles

my life once
a dancing leaf
took a blade through her stance

my life once
a seeking whale
spun it out in a bloody sea

my life once
a looking eagle
drifted in wing ensnared

my life once
a searching lion
flew when a shot turned her paws

my life once
a busy fox
rushed from the fangs of hounds

my life once
a hiding worm
leapt from flesh of fruit and jaws

> my life once
a hippopotamus
gave the gun stop a pale red lake

> my life once
a lamb
dealt a heart to cooking pots

> my life once
a green man
wandered from white sheets

> life I rage
in fractured circles
fill me a life

Lucy's Letter

Things harness me here. I long
for we labrish bad. Doors
not fixed open here.
No Leela either. No Cousin
Lil, Miss Lottie or Bro'-Uncle.
Dayclean doesn't have cockcrowin'.
Midmornin' doesn' bring
Cousin-Maa with her naseberry tray.
Afternoon doesn' give a ragged
Manwell, strung with fish
like bright leaves. Seven days
play same note in London, chile.
But Leela, money-rustle regular.

Mi dear, I don' laugh now,
not'n' like we thunder claps
in darkness on verandah.
I turned a battery hen
in 'lectric light, day an' night.

No mood can touch one
mango season back at Yard.
At least though I did start
evening school once.
An' doctors free, chile.

London isn't like we
village dirt road, you know
Leela: it a parish
of a pasture-lan' what
grown crisscross streets,
an' they lie down to my door.
But I lock myself in.
I carry keys everywhere.
Life here's no open summer,
girl. But Sat'day mornin' don'
find mi han' dry, don' find mi face
a heavy cloud over the man.

An' though he still have
a weekend mind for bat'n'ball
he wash a dirty dish now, mi dear.
It sweet him I on the Pill.

We get money for holidays.
But there's no sun-hot
to enjoy cool breeze.

Leela, I really a sponge
you know, for traffic noise,
for work noise, for halfway
intentions, for halfway smiles,
for clockwatchin' an' col' weather.
I hope you don' think I gone
too fat when we meet.
I booked up to come an' soak
the children in daylight.

labrish: to talk and to gossip without restraint.
naseberry tray: seller's tray of naseberries: roughish brown,
soft and sweet, Caribbean fruit about size of small apple.

Faces Around My Father

Hunger stormed my arrival.
I arrived needing.
I had need of older selves.
My mother's milk met
my parching. Streams were here
like stars and stones,
and a fatherhood compelling.

Fatherhood tailed a line
of fathers, we knew: a prehistory
book, a full season open all time,
a storehouse for emptying
for renewal, a marketing
of strength that stuffs away
richness of summers upon summers.

I'd work up a clean slate full.
Crafts and arts would engage me,
my urgent hands would grow
in homely voices,
the land would amaze
my roaming eyes,
incite my impulses.

Head striped, sir, with sounds
of birds in the hills,
sweat smells in clothes stuck
with soil and sun, you come
into the house at evening
like a piece of hillside.
I wait to take your drinking mug.

A silence surrounds your eating.
The dog catches and gulps
pieces of food you pitch
that somehow cut your distance.
A son washes your feet.
Another brings glowing firewood:
you light up your pipe.

Your incidental money getting
not believed, a child asks for cash
for boots or book.
Our words are stones
tossed on a genial guest.
You vanish into twilight.
A sleeping house receives you back.

And father is a scripture
lesson. Father knows
blueprints of seeds in the moon,
knows place of a cockerel's
testicles, knows coins
in minutes. His body sets
defences, set boundaries.

Yet strong hints had soaked us:
we are not beautiful,
we are a cancellation
of abundance and sharing.
I am charged with unmanageable
hunger. I am trumpeted
for ungettable distances.

I must cross our moat of sea,
and I have no way. I must list
lost tracks, must write
my scanning of time, must plant
hot words in ministers like cool
communion bread. Yet I should drown
in language of our lanes.

In and about your preclusion, sir,
dead footsteps entrapped me.
You chopped wood and sang,
I listened behind a wall.
In hot field of pineapples
fermenting, I watched you
dreaming: I walked away.

Your tool's edge touched work
barely, and you resharpened.
Sir, in fresh sunny magnitude,
your dramatic grind of machete
should flatten forests. Yet
you left for work looking,
'What boss shall I serve today?'

Were you being your father
or just a loser's son? Sir,
did old scars warn you to yield
and hide? Were you strangely
full of a friendly enemy
voice? Did you feel
your movements failure fixed?

Schemed in your steady
good health, we were placed
to proliferate loneliness,
birthdays of lacks,
trouble growing in our flesh,
lips moved by ventriloquists,
beginnings with approaches of daggers.

We needed that safety, sir,
that wonderment of caressing eye,
that steadiness that allows
strongest and sweetest voice,
that sanctioned contentment
that walked bright
in the constellation of children.

Our voices deepened,
our limbs emulated trees,
our appetites expanded,
our silence encircled you
like strangers with killer plans.
I disowned you to come to know
thanks to connection that someone may feel.

I saw your body full
and fit and free, ready
in the sun's recycle,
never the husbandman
of exalted acclamations.
I saw you die, sir,
well bluffed by subjugation.

The Coming of Yams and Mangoes
and Mountain Honey

Handfuls hold hidden sunset
stuffing up bags
and filling up the London baskets.
Caribbean hills have moved and come.

Sun's alphabet drops out of branches.
Coconuts are big brown Os,
pimentoberries little ones.
Open up papaw like pumpkin you get
the brightness of macaw.

Breadfruit a green football,
congo-peas like tawny pearls,
mango soaked in sunrise,
avocado is a fleshy green.

Colours of sun, stalled in groups,
make market a busy meeting.
The sweetnesses of summer settle smells.

Mints and onions quarrel.
Nutmeg and orange and cinnamon hug
themselves in sun-perfume.

Some of the round bodies shown off
have grown into long shapes.
Others grew fisty and knobbled.
Jars hold black molasses like honey.

And yams the loaves
of earth's big bellies and sun,
plantains too huge to be bananas,
melons too smooth to be pineapples –
chocho, okra, sweetsop, soursop, sorrel –
all are sun flavoured geniuses.

Nights once lit the growing lots
with fields of squinting kitibus.
Winds polished some of the skins cool but warm
when sun drew stripes on fish.

But, here, you won't have a topseat cooing
in peppers, won't hear the nightingale's
notes mixed with lime juice.

Red buses pass for donkeys now.
Posters of pop stars hang by.

Caribbean hills have moved
and come to London
with whole words of the elements.
Just take them and give them
to children, to parents and the old folks.

kitibu: the click-beetle, or firefly, with two luminous spots
that squint light in the dark.

Fantasy of an African Boy

Such a peculiar lot
we are, we people
without money, in daylong
yearlong sunlight, knowing
money is somewhere, somewhere.

Everybody says it's a big
bigger brain bother now,
money. Such millions and millions
of us don't manage at all
without it, like war going on.

And we can't eat it. Yet
without it our heads alone
stay big, as lots and lots do,
coming from nowhere joyful,
going nowhere happy.

We can't drink it up. Yet
without it we shrivel when small
and stop forever
where we stopped,
as lots and lots do.

We can't read money for books.
Yet without it we don't
read, don't write numbers,
don't open gates in other countries,
as lots and lots never do.

We can't use money to bandage
sores, can't pound it
to powder for sick eyes
and sick bellies. Yet without
it, flesh melts from our bones.

Such walled-round gentlemen
overseas minding money! Such
bigtime gentlemen, body guarded
because of too much respect
and too many wishes on them.

too many wishes, everywhere,
wanting them to let go
magic of money, and let it fly
away, everywhere, day and night,
just like dropped leaves in wind!

E.A. MARKHAM

E.A. Markham was born in 1939 in Montserrat, and moved to Britain in 1956. He read English & Philosophy at the University of Wales (Lampeter) and taught in London in the late 1960s (Kilburn Polytechnic). He then directed the Caribbean Theatre Workshop in the West Indies (1970-71); built houses with the Cooperative Ouvrière du Batiment in the Alpes Maritimes, France (1972-74), and from 1983 to 1985 worked as a media coordinator in Papua New Guinea.

He has edited several magazines, including *Artrage* (1985-87), and has held writing fellowships at Hull College of Higher Education (1978-79), Brent, London (C. Day Lewis Fellowship, 1979-80), Ipswich (1986), and the University of Ulster (1988-91).

His Selected Poems, *Human Rites* (Anvil Press, 1984), contains work from several previous collections, ranging from *Crossfire* (1972) to *Family Matters* (1984), and including three published under the name Paul St Vincent: *Lambchops*, *Lambchops in Disguise* and *Philpot in the City*. His subsequent collections are: *Lambchops in Papua New Guinea* (IPNG Studies, 1985), *Living in Disguise* (Anvil Press, 1986), *Towards the End of a Century* (Anvil, 1989), *Letter from Ulster and The Hugo Poems* (Arc, 1993) and *Misapprehensions* (Anvil, 1995). His book of short stories, *Something Unusual*, was published by Ambit in 1986.

Many Voices, Many Lives

by E.A. MARKHAM

In the early 1960s, while still at University, my main artistic outlet seemed to be the theatre – a platonic piece of mine, *The Master-piece* – being mounted, in Lampeter, in 1963 or '64. Later, in London, I was part of various semi-professional troupes – in Shepherds Bush, and at the City Lit and the Marylebone Institutes – which led sometimes to individual, sometimes to group productions. Towards the end of 1969 I formed the Caribbean Theatre Workshop to explore certain "non-naturalistic" ways of writing and playing; and, in 1970-71, toured the Eastern Caribbean staging plays in St Vincent and Montserrat, and lecturing/rehearsing groups elsewhere. My interest in theatre remains strong, my most recent play, *The Rainbow Arts Factory* – about Black Arts in London – going into production in the autumn (1989).

Though our focus here is poetry, I find it useful to mention the theatre work and also my prose fiction. The interest in form – fascination with ways of telling the story – and 'a tendency towards the surreal' which some people find in later work, might well be traced back to the plays. Also, the relative absence of nation-language in the poems might be because nation-language is so overwhelmingly part of the plays – as well as featuring in the stories – that the voices I find when I dredge for the poems, come through this time with all those "dramatic" and "prose" registers informing their tone and stress, rather than their idiom. The linguistic continuum (to use that much abused word) must be seen across *genre*. Careless critical opinion of Caribbean poetry has tended to concentrate on the more and not the less obvious manifestations of nation-language; and as such, has encouraged literalness in many writers and complacency in both reader and audience.

The main lesson learnt from the Caribbean Theatre Workshop tour was that it wasn't enough to be a practitioner in the arts if one was to have more than a marginal impact; one had also to be involved in administration. So back in Britain, when I turned increasingly to poetry, I took stock of the context within which it was going to be received; joined a performing troupe (The Bluefoot Travellers); and involved myself in administrative labour – serving on the General Council of the Poetry Society (1976-77); the

Poetry Book Society (1987-89); for some years, the GLA New
Writing Committee, as well as being part of the editorial team of
Ambit magazine. But most crucially, I've been involved in MAAS
(the Minorities' Arts Advisory Service) and, from 1985 to 1987,
edited its magazine, *Artrage*.

The dramatic revelation that poets (like dramatists and
novelists before them) in and from the Caribbean had two voices
– nation-language and Standard English – released many energies;
but we had to be sure that this wasn't to be interpreted that we
had *only* two voices, *only* two modes of expression: for this might
gel into two modes of perception, the one antagonistic to the other;
the debate internal; the possibilities of a different mode
unexplored.

I was interested in testing the whole range of voices (experience
in the theatre and on the poetry-reading circuit might be a factor
here) that were possibly real for me. I experimented with per-
sonae: three pamphlets were conceived in this way, had an iden-
tifiable personality, a logic of place, and marketed under the name
Paul St Vincent. It was only after the poems ceased being written
– the Lambchops, Philpot and Maureen poems – that I claimed
them for *E.A. Markham* in reprints. E.A. Markham was, I hope,
enlarged – not just by being added to – by the parallel process of
discovery. Later, the Sally Goodman poems (some of which have
been reprinted in *Living in Disguise*) extended the search in
another direction. Paul St Vincent is young, black and concerned
with survival in inner-city London; Sally Goodman is feminist,
non-black: the test was to force their creator to accommodate
types of consciousness which, at the very least, served to enlarge
one area of Westindianness. The *personae* have served their pur-
pose; their territory, hopefully, has been absorbed.

If I had an image for my life (and, hence, one that informed
my work) I suppose it would be 'Pioneer'. I was an immigrant in
the literal sense of going to live in a country in which I was not
born; but that was a relatively small part of my self-definition
(and others, too, who have followed this route, have felt this).
While admiring the effectiveness of Walcott's image of the *Casta-
way* and Brathwaite's wandering, rootless 'Tom', my own literary
fantasy is nearer to the resourceful traveller having something to
offer to the host society. This is the spirit in which I now approach
England; Papua New Guinea; the North of Ireland.

This is one man's form of survival. There is urgency but, I
hope, not desperation. What feeds all this is partly the place where

I happen to be, but what contributes to the perspective are a few things which won't go away – a grandmother presiding over the household in Montserrat; the battle of wills between grandmother and grandson – she aged 80, he 10 – the space, the physical space accorded them all week to rehearse their drama till the weekend came, and the performance could be played out to the rest of the family: mother *plus* elder brothers and sister back from the town, from the Grammar School. That house, that childhood environment which seems to grow richer and more bizarre over the years – returning in poems, stories, radio talks, plays – the grandmother long dead, the house now a ruin, is an important part of my London/Ulster/Stockholm/Port Moresby reality.

I distrust the exclusivity of the British *versus* Caribbean cultural debate. Britain for me is part only – though, an important part – of a European experience (I've worked in Sweden, Germany, France – the last in which I sometimes live): at times it's useful to identify this Europe as the old colonising power or as the new rich "North"; more often just as the "other" to the majority of black and blackish people in the world. Sometimes I think of nation-language and Standard English as the two languages in which my life *must* be lived; sometimes I think of Melanesian pidgin and French as two languages in which my life *might* be lived. It's an exciting prospect, not an anxiety-making one.

A question which engages me now is how to protect (first of all) and then to extend what we might call our living spaces, both public and private. I'm not going to deal here with the public spaces. Both nationally and internationally, we are beginning to find at least the rhetoric to convey the tone of urgency necessary to restoration of global *greenness*; dismantlement of patriarchy; denuclearisation; the cessation of war etc. But I'm thinking now of certain cultural/spiritual spaces (linked, of course, to those mentioned above): how not to be limited, how not to be ghettorised; how not to collude with corrupting self-censorship? (One of our national theatres in Britain has informed me that my "West Indian" characters in a play are not like West Indians because, it seems, they betray a degree of self-consciousness about their condition that people who go to the Royal Shakespeare productions at the Aldwych would fail to recognise as *their* West Indians; I am told by another – reputable – publisher that my stories are too "difficult" for a West Indian readership (surely, West Indian readers would take action if they knew that a specially segregated diet of stories which failed to stimulate their interest in – among

other things – how stories might be told, is being prepared, per-
petually, for them). Strangest of all, I am told that someone in
academic power in Barbados has denied my right to be a West
Indian writer, and has denied a student her (perhaps academic,
perhaps human) right to investigate the possibility that I might
be such an animal. These are, indeed, strange times.

These "aliens" all collude to limit your space. Naturally, you
can only continue to deny them by being as fully human as you
can. It's fun, you know – and who's to say you won't succeed?

[1989]

The Boy of the House

The ruin of the house, he lies on his stomach, womanless.
The boy is in water, frog-like, his mouth tastes of sea-weed.
He is looking at the rose-garden, it's not there
No longer at the front of the house –
Of what used to be the house...

The rose-garden is now at the bottom of the sea
And the boy throws a line, then another
To prevent more of the house drifting away.
He does this instead of growing into middle-age, or going abroad:
The boy is a great source of worry.

This England?

...guests at midnight
                          stopping
outside the house. The one
without the gun demands

her name and (through
an interpreter) tells Mammie

she's got nothing to fear
if she's legal.

Grandmotherpoem
(for grandmother, Margaret – 'Miss Dovey', 1865-1954)

thinking many things, grandmother
I can't trap the memory, itself like a kite
to blanket us without coarsening our pact:
it is not cold climate, not famine relief that triggers this need.

Though more than the annual hat of fashion must clothe us in words.
So I put it off, more and more play the errant;
with dissenting verbs occupy this or that high table where the world
    lies bloated.

You must be asking when this apprenticeship will end?
Running & jumping, ball-games, preaching and Latin were early
    fantasies.
Now, wandering in a garden far from us, I step
on the wrong end of a rake
and crack my skull: the yellow scream of grandmother burns the
    head.
Surprise, a hint of things malordained, skids me past *us*
till embarrassment makes it safe: this is an accident.
A third time I step on the rake: *this is god!* 'Boy, wha happenin?'
I am at risk in the world. This is no accident.
Something leaking through my head has value.
It wines, it lusts, it fills empties fills my space.
Its logic meanders like a stone too heavy for the stream.
It heaves sense against sense cascading down the boneface
while the wet of mothermother drips into thimble: my bucket, my
    ocean.
And the kite is a cloud of badness dribbling, drizzling a parable.
From somewhere maleness spits defiance to hold soft matter in its
    rock of stubbornness

from the wreck, debris of grandmotherpoem
and a thing not recognised as fear of rakes.
Bits of me, long abandoned, floating past
jostle one another like strangers on a march.
The voice which breaks from its full set of teeth
comes like a uniform, polished: we are at risk.
Grandmother, grandmother, her bath over, smelling of bay rum &
    bible
knows how bad habits, like long years abroad, and the profession of
    maleness,
lead to ugly bumps on the head. So men must cover theirs.
In my hat, in a foreign garden, when the leaf is about to fall from its
    tree,
grandmother appears to speak to me:

Two Haiku

Third-World War

The beach, walking off
inland, dragging its bed of
sand. And look, no guns!

Food-Chain

The feeding over:
one eye hard and accusing –
fish out of water.

The Sea

It used to be at the bottom of the hill
and brought white ships and news
of a far land where half my life
was scheduled to be lived.

That was at least half a life ago
of managing without maps, plans, permanence
of a dozen or more addresses
of riding the trains like a vagrant.

Today, I have visitors. They come
long distances overland. They will be uneasy
and console me for loss of the sea.
I will discourage them.

A Mugger's Game
(a Lambchops poem)

Chase him down the alley
put him behind bars

in a basement and charge him rent.

Lambchops has potential
for violence. He's faking

says the Pig in the wig

make him an example
of our collective self-defence.

Black them here stop them there

before they get too cheeky
too second-generation aware

and ape us overtake us

queuing up for houses
they claim their fathers built.

They're a problem so he's a problem

a potential mugger
on a quiet English street

so smash him smash him

or soon he'll flash an education
and leave you crumpled in a heap.

Conversation Across Water
(a Sally Goodman poem)

I outstare the pond
and imagine you wet with effort. But now
all is clear water innocent of us.

The ocean between forbidding in a new way
censures thought of self-destruction:
it's as pure as your first promises.

I wait and wait for all the drowned things to surface.
At the house, your present arrives as promised –
a book, delivered with its back broken.

A Good Life Sonnet

And all in all it's been a good life
(Not just to have outlived the sane, clever people)
But to have settled down finally with someone else's wife.
In the fog, we stood waiting for the bus
(I know, in Venice it would be on water)
But Archway in January was romantic enough for us.
She slipped her fortunes through my arm
Scarved herself to yashmak lest the harm

Of seeing too soon what the fog concealed
Prevent what proximity would soon have sealed.
So we stayed loyal to the fancy that brought us together
And released stray families from their vows of forever.
And all in all it's been a good life
To have brought my bad taste home to someone else's wife.

Rendezvous

And she must dress carefully, dress well
For this encounter with a stranger; the children
Will be fed, put to bed: someone will read them stories.
At home they say she has a lover.
She goes past shrines where the faithful stand
And wait – for a Mandela, for news of a family,
In respect for those freakishly dead –
In spite of the logic of men in uniform.
She goes past them, keeps going, refusing to think
How few things can be accomplished in one life
As lived by her; composing
In her mind letters to some who must doubt
Her love. And, beyond that, more...
Is this where it happens? She is not unnerved by her affliction.
Today, she is *taken* with her consent.
Back home, there is no complaint. The children
Are fed, she is put, gratefully, to bed.
How clever of others to live her life, take the stress?
...And now again we see her dressing carefully,
Dressing well for a rendezvous.

Love in the Hospital

She slaps him; feels a twinge:
and now he won't hit back. Too weak
to stamp hot anger on her face
he heaves, heaves. She slaps him
perhaps to hurt
more than pride: through blood
and memory he sees her peeling
cardigans, wife-flesh collapsing
heaps in front of strangers.
The shame of it. Nurse. Nurse!

She struggles to remove shirt and trousers
skinning him naked in reproach.
There is no blood. Nurse holds the eye
of an ancient ally, draws back, colludes.
In seconds she has banished
old age, marriage, from her plans.
The other has not lived for this:
this is no payment for life's
submission – though she must return
compliments she was never meant to have.
She slaps him not for the ward's
benefit; and there, damp soft
clay she can't quite mould
through years of fingers going stiff;
and it hurts, the pressure hurts.

The Mother's Tale

So many terrible people are people still
GAVIN EWART

Goodness, she said:
Unless you eat this,
Unless you get to bed

The black man
Will get you
And that's worse than

Being dead.
You're all at sea now
In above your head:

The grasping hand
Reaching out to you
From land

Is folly. Just realise
I didn't make you try that one
For size.

He's everything
I promised
Though he won't sing

And dance.
And if he doesn't beat you, well
That's by chance.

I'm truly sorry for being right
Though we must take
Delight

In the buff-
Coloured darlings. Yes,
It's been rough

For all of us,
Determined to meet this setback
Without fuss.

We've been here before
With the Wars and bullies:
It's just a bore

In a home like this
To have brought on
With the bedtime kiss

When this game began
Something rather worse
Than the stock policeman.

A Date on the Calendar

The days come and go.
I lurch this way and that
through my Amazonian
exile, dripping

hallucinating. I get up,
peel away nightrags,
find something dry,
uncontaminated

and collapse again.
Dreams come in shoals,
jealous of body's treat
to something special;

or to collude with brain
that minutes not days
break these spasms
of measurement.

I dream a man
remote from us –
a white farmer, say,
somewhere in Africa,

or Wyoming –
calls on a lady
of my acquaintance. She buys
(or sells or declines)

a ticket for a function.
She marks the date
on the calendar. Ah,
the rest is forgotten.

I am travelling down
'Oronoko', hacking through
Yanomami country. Centuries
or inches. Time to take stock.

Bodyrags cling to me.
How could you sieve
so much sludge
through unbroken skin

and be repelled
by a life of slime?
You grasp a bramble:
African farmer

and Wyoming lady
resolve their bet.
One wins. The other chooses
a date on the calendar

to oppress me. Us.
And here I am
becoming fish.
Here I am

Letting old rivers
of salt bed me,
unable to change
for the wedding.

Letter to Kate

*When imprisoned in 1979 for 'incitement and obstruction', i.e. for
having been a founder member of Charter 77, Vaclav Havel was
allowed to write one four-page letter to his wife, Olga [his only wife]
under the following restrictions: 'No crossings out or corrections were
allowed; no quotation marks, no underlinings or foreign expressions.
"We could only write about 'family matters'. Humour was banned
as well: punishment is a serious business, after all, and jokes would
have undermined the gravity."'*

I reach for your name and then think
Better of it, but I'm not allowed
Crossings-out, so you must stand, my love.
Let me explain, not who I am –

For this being a family letter,
You must know me – but why you have been
Reacquainted with this lover. I am,
As they say, distanced from a more familiar
Kate – not her name, you understand –
And must not use life's mishap to deny
Things their consequences: you cannot recouple
For a jailor's convenience. Kate, the name,
Is less foreign than Medbh or Tracy; sufficiently
Far from earlier family and not likely
To be suspected as a joke. Dear Kate,
Though apart, we must thank our luck
To be living at the same time in history,
And as one of us is not attuned to jokes,
The ban on this right, sorry, rite (emphasised
Not underlined) is not, indeed, onerous.
There are games that we like, separately,
And by rehearsing play at times fixed
By some public clock – a cockerel crowing-in
The day, or a blackout where I live –
We might win safe conduct for this letter.
Or the next. Carnal matters I dare not
Hint at publicly. I should lose you then,
And be claimed by some professional wife
With your name. My love, I count your lashes –
Sorry, no private joke of bedrooms,
Just the miniature fans that frame your eyes;
And no hint, truly, of the days crossed off my back.

Long Lines from the Island

He was of a certain age, the dad, convicted with due cause to his room.
(Unlike an animal tied somewhere and fretting, he was contented
          with his lot.)
She was in another world where hopes which flew high as aeroplanes
          were not supposed to crash –
though she knew better, Mimijune, Julieblossom, with brothers to
          protect her, and a green skirt trailing like a target.

On the island he stopped and started disciplines, families, shopped
    around like a spendthrift seeking value.
And she was giddy in the air, on the ground, trailing her green skirt
    like a banner.

He was the old house, the island, hanging learning up to dry like
    Nellie's sheets free of salt;
hanging facts and logic on any old dog or cat, draping philosophies
    on the passing stranger
(rewriting the history of the world, renaming the children, the
    presidents & the gods).
She was separated from partners, each fighting his battle: the tripping
    up in London, the slight in Rome, stale bagels in New
    York.
She was there, where a telephone to report the crash didn't work:
    it was here.
And she is found staggering from a National Park in the cause of
    elephant and rhino.

There were those who saw her, green skirt above her head like the
    heroine of an Australian film stopping the traffic;
the same skirt trapped in the door of the car, cruising (and her
    brothers, the Generals and Marshals reverting to type).
Then she was a silver train serving passengers as they wished; some
    who saw the mistake
and were patient, read by her light as they entered the tunnel which
    echoed:
*Why are the faces of animals expressionless as riddles? Where is there fresh
    government of bagels?*
And back on the island she would confront an inmate who still refused
    to be bought off with god knows what degrees and
    victories.

Hinterland

The dreams are wet. Tonight rain
In Portrush, home of two months. I wake
To seagulls, accept the logic

Of dream and unpack the cases: life
Will be here near Malin Head –
Like Rockall, an outpost on the weathermap.
I rehearse a prayer to my travelling
Relic, a grandmother sure to exact,
Like other gods, penance for this blasphemy.
The first wet dream was not the joke
Schoolboys brag about, but fear
Of stretching out a foot from Montserrat
And falling into sea. In France, in Germany,
In spray-white Sweden the first stumble
Across a street turned ground to water
With waves of language rearing up
To lift you out of depth. Lucky
You didn't unpack – though the cases now
Are full, wares and gifts outdated,
And your fresh discoveries changing shape
And colour like your photograph.
Another day in Portrush: wind and rain.
There is security in this, part
Of the hinterland of an experience
Still to be reclaimed. New Guinea
Was too fabled, generous in its reprieve:
A threat – its gift too close to dreams
For waking comfort. London was like a parents'
Home from which to rebel. Now here, on the edge
Of the edge, the sea hurling defiance
At old, at new gods, I pray to the familiar
In my suitcase, in my head: I have
Explored the world, tasted its strangeness,
Resisted and colluded out of strength,
Out of weakness, failed to colonise it
With family tongue or name. Are you pleased
Secretly, with a frown pulling down on relief?
The treasures I carry in my head fail
To match the refuse in my case.
But it will do, and the dreams tonight
To douse a fear, will perhaps be wet.

OLIVE SENIOR

Olive Senior was born in 1943 in Jamaica. She has worked in journalism in Jamaica and Canada, and divides her time between the two countries. She is currently Visiting Professor of Creative Writing at St Lawrence University, USA.

She has published two books of poems, *Talking of Trees* (Calabash, Jamaica, 1985) and *Gardening in the Tropics* (McClelland & Stewart, Canada, 1994; Bloodaxe Books, UK, 1995); and three collections of short stories: *Summer Lightning* (1986), winner of the Commonwealth Writers Prize; *Arrival of the Snake-Woman* (1989); and *The Discerner of Hearts* (1995). Her non-fiction works include *The Message Is Change* (1972), *A-Z of Jamaican Heritage* (1984) and *Working Miracles: Women's Lives in the English-Speaking Caribbean* (1991).

Interview with Olive Senior

by ANNA RUTHERFORD

(extract)

AR: *How isolated was the world in which you grew up?*
OS: Very. We were isolated even from the nearest town. The village I grew up in had no running water, no electricity, one or two people might have had a radio. There was only a dirt road and even a trip to the nearest town was a considerable undertaking. There was virtually no transportation. The train was our main means of communication and then you had to get the mail van to the railway station which was about twelve miles away. So even the rest of Jamaica seemed very far away. People think of us islanders as all living by the sea. I grew up in the mountains. I never saw the sea until I was pretty old. It was a very isolated kind of existence.

Funnily enough the kind of metropolitan contacts that a lot of us had was with Latin America because a lot of people in my background had been emigrants to Panama, to Costa Rica and the United States. They had been among the wave of migrants who had left the Caribbean in the late 19th to early 20th centuries. In fact my adopted family, my great uncle and my great aunts had gone to Panama during the time of the building of the Panama Canal and had later gone to the United States. So in a sense the contact with the outside world was a contact with the Americas though we were socialised to revere 'Mother England', 'Missis Queen' and all things British.

AR: *How did you come to write yourself?*
OS: As a small child I first wanted to be an artist and I'm still interested in drawing and painting though I have never pursued Art seriously. Then at a very early age, for some strange reason, I decided I was going to be a journalist. I'm not even sure I knew what a journalist was, but I knew that writing was somewhere in my future. I used to write things as a child – poems, stories, and at school I used to win prizes for all kinds of things, essays, poetry, but I only started to write seriously when I was at university in Canada. That for me represented a period when my own identity crisis came to a head and I started writing as a means of trying to integrate myself, trying to make a whole person out of a very fragmented part; so writing served a largely therapeutic function at that stage. I started to write *out* some of the things that had

been hurtful and painful to me. I have gradually moved from that early, highly subjective stage to a more conscious objective pursuit of writing as a craft.

AR: *You commented the other day on forms of oppression and it would appear from your comments and your work that you found the oppression of the church particularly damaging. Is that so?*

OS: Yes. I felt more oppressed by religion as a child than I did by anything else. A very restricted, narrow kind of Christianity combined with poverty is, I think, a ruthless combination, in that they both attack the spirit, they are both anti-life, they are both anti-freedom, soul-destroying as far as I am concerned. My whole childhood, adolescence, early adulthood were spent – wasted, I feel – trying to transcend these.

AR: *Do women have a particularly rough deal in Caribbean society?*

OS: Caribbean women have had to be very strong because they have had to assume the role of both mother and father, because the father is usually absent for one reason or other. There are a lot of contradictions in her situation. The myth of the black matriarch projects an image of the Caribbean woman as strong and powerful, and she does play a powerful role in the family, even though that role might be forced on her because of an absence of male support. But the myth disguises the fact of her powerlessness in the wider society. The majority of working women are in low-paid, low-status jobs such as domestic service, and women, especially young women, experience the highest rates of unemployment. Women have little share in the formal power structures although they are the ones who are the domestic managers. Caribbean women shoulder the most tremendous burdens. There is something sacrificial yet noble about the lives of poor women especially because they end up investing everything in their children. But there is now growing a new generation of well educated, upwardly mobile young women, so maybe this will herald a change in women's attitudes and status.

Caribbean women are powerful in the sense that they are positive for the most part, which doesn't mean they don't allow themselves to be exploited by the system or by men, which is in fact the paradox about them: that they are often very weak in their relationships with men but very strong otherwise.

AR: *Do you have any theories about why they are weak in their relationships with men?*

OS: Part of it has to do with the fact that the "powerful" Caribbean woman is still socialised according to traditional lines – to defer to men, to accept patriarchic structures and values, even though she might be entirely independent of male support. Our socialisation still continues to reinforce the stereotyped female image which girls still internalise but which might be at odds with the reality of women's lives in the Caribbean. Women are still trapped in the thinking of their mothers and grandmothers and somehow haven't yet been able to develop a sense of their own self-worth in their relationships with men. That is a very personal opinion and is only a small part of the story...

I am writing a book on the roles and status of Caribbean women in which I am attempting to examine some of these issues. The book will be largely based on the research findings from a three-year multi-disciplinary Women in the Caribbean Research Project which operated from the University of the West Indies in Barbados. In fact some of the findings of this research is now being published by the Institute of Social and Economic Research and it is important because this is the first extensive woman-centred piece of research from the English-speaking Caribbean. I think it will contribute greatly to a better understanding of the Caribbean woman – including her relationships with men.

AR: *In your talk at the conference [Caribbean Writers' Conference, Commonwealth Institute, London, October 1986] you said that you had very little reading material as a child. But still most writers have some other writers who have influenced them. Are there any you could mention?*

OS: Well, I'm not conscious of whatever influences there might have been before my early teens. I went to high school in the town of Montego Bay and there was a library there and I started doing a lot of reading, and of course at school English literature was an important area of study. But the earliest writers that impressed me greatly that I can remember are the writers who are now referred to as the 'Southern Gothic School', people like Flannery O'Connor, Carson McCullers, Truman Capote. I distinctly remember when I read their works how moved I was because for the first time I realised there were people like myself; because they do write of young people who are at odds with the world around them, and they write of societies that are constricting and narrow, so I identified very strongly with a lot of their characters and with a lot of what was happening in their world. Those writers represent for me my earliest identifiable influences. Later on there

were many other influences from English and American literature.
I was exposed to Caribbean literature at a much later date
because when I went to school we weren't taught Caribbean liter-
ature or Caribbean history. This was in the closing days of the
colonial era, so I came very late to reading Caribbean writers. I
did read Vic Reid's *New Day* when I was at school and I think
that had a profound impact on all of us, on my generation. And
of course we all recited Louise Bennett's poetry, but we did not
recognise Louise Bennett's work as "literature". It wasn't until
Mervyn Morris wrote his seminal essay 'On Reading Louise Ben-
nett Seriously', which was published in *Jamaica Journal* [Vol. 1,
December 1967], that people began to consider that Louise Ben-
nett who was writing in dialect which we were taught was "bad
talking" was writing "literature". I came to Caribbean literature
very late. In fact up to when I started to write in Canada I had
read very little Caribbean material.

AR: *You said there were very few books, newspapers or radios
in the village in which you grew up. Does that mean that perhaps
your strongest influence at that time was the oral tradition?*

OS: I think that the oral tradition has profoundly influenced me
as a writer because I grew up in a society where the spoken word
was important. We created our own entertainment, every night
as a child living in the village I remember an adult told us stories
– Duppy stories, Anancy stories, or whatever, or we told each
other stories. There was also something dramatic in the quality
of real life, people would narrate everyday events in a very drama-
tic way. As a child I didn't talk much, but I listened a lot and I
think the results of that listening have come out in my work. To
me the sound of the voice is extremely important. I try to utilise
the voice a great deal in my work and more and more find that
what is happening is that the voice is taking over. In other words,
I am more and more concerned that my characters should speak
directly to the reader and therefore I am dealing almost purely
in narrative, in letting people tell their own story. I suppose fun-
damentally I'm a story teller and I attribute that to my early
experience of growing up in an oral culture. [OS was talking here
about her stories.]

AR: *I've been teaching a course on Caribbean literature in
Denmark. One feature that struck my Danish students when read-
ing Caribbean writing was the prevalence of physical violence.*

OS: I think we do live in a violent society. It starts with domestic
violence, it starts with violence against the child. Children are

raised very very strictly and are beaten, though not so much as
they used to be. There is a certain amount of brutality directed
at children. A lot of it is unintentional. People are just perpetuat-
ing the way they themselves were raised. And then there's also a
lot of violence in the home; not necessarily physical violence,
though there is that too. People are very aggressive in the language
they employ and in the way they deal with one another. And of
course then it goes out into the street. We all grew up with this
sense of one group of people threatening another; there is a whole
manipulation of the weaker people by the more powerful, and in
our society a lot of the powerful people in the domestic situation
are the men. I grew up with a great consciousness of this, with
people being aggressive towards one another. In a way of course
it's a reflection of the social structures in which people find them-
selves, because if a man is unable to support his family because
he can't get work, he's going to come home and take it out on his
wife. The economic conditions contribute to a lot of what happens
in the home and ultimately on the street. And yet, having said all
this, I also feel – and I believe that this also comes out in my work
– that there is in our society still a great deal of love, of caring,
of good fellowship, of kinship and friendship bonds which are
strong and lasting. Jamaica is still a society of great spirituality,
of great psychic energy. A lot of creative artists feel this – and
this is probably why we stay.

AR: *You've had a book of poetry and a collection of stories pub-
lished. Do you have a preference for either genre?*

OS: I write prose or poetry as the material dictates, though what
I feel is happening now is that my prose and poetry are getting
closer together. I'm not a prolific writer, I don't really have the
time to devote to writing, but what I'm working on now are nar-
ratives. Some are long, so they are stories; some are short, in
poetic form, so they are poems.

[1986]

Birdshooting Season

Birdshooting season the men
make marriages with their guns
My father's house turns macho
as from far the hunters gather

All night long contentless women
stir their brews: hot coffee
chocolata, cerassie
wrap pone and tie-leaf
for tomorrow's sport. Tonight
the men drink white rum neat.

In darkness shouldering
their packs, their guns, they leave

We stand quietly on the
doorstep shivering. Little boys
longing to grow up birdhunters too
Little girls whispering:
Fly Birds Fly.

Cockpit Country Dreams

I

In Cockpit Country
the hours form slowly like stalagmites
a bird sings
pure note
I-hold-my-breath
the world turns and
turns

I mountain goat plunged
headlong into this world
with eyes wide open
(dreaming so)
blinded by flame trees
and sunlight on river

green nurtured me

till mules turned circles round the mill
and large dark wings
like War

– Planes bringing bombs, said my father

– Babies, said my mother

(Portents of a split future).

II
Our road led to places on maps
places that travelled people
knew. Our river, undocumented
was mystery.

My father said: lines on paper
cannot deny something that *is*.
(My mother said: such a wasted life
is his).

III
Listen child, said my mother
whose hands plundered photo albums
of all black ancestors: Herein
your ancestry, your imagery, your pride.
Choose *this* river, *this* rhythm, *this* road.
Walk good in the footsteps of *these* fathers.

(Yet she could no more stop my mind slipping
those well-worn grooves of piety, work, praise
than rivers cease flowing).

Listen child, said my father
from the quicksand of his life:
Study rivers. Learn everything.
Rivers may find beginnings
in the clefts of separate mountains
Yet all find their true homes
in the salt of one sea.

IV

Now my disorder of ancestry
proves as stable as the many rivers
flowing round me. Undocumented
I drown in the other's history.

V

I had thought of walking far from the terrible
                                        knowledge
of flames. Spathodea. From ghost-ridden
Trumpet Tree. From personal
disaster. God's blinding judgement. Drunken mystery

And wisps of smoke from cockpits crying lonely
                                        lonely

But walking in the woods alternating dark with
                                        sunshine I knew
nothing then of cities or the killing of children

in their dancing time.

Epitaph

Last year the child died
we didn't mourn long
and cedar's plentiful

but that was the one
whose navel-string
we buried
beneath the tree of life

lord, old superstitions
are such lies.

Childhood

Rivers flow red and swollen with the clay
of upstream mountains where the
rains fall. Mockingbirds call
in the woods from the roseapple tree
echo the cry of crazy-lost children
and the bird-filled hills fear still
sudden death. By slingshot.

The dead in a certain graveyard
cannot rest again after a long ago
awakening when Sunday School childen
hunted cashew nuts on the way to church
and wept over penny-for-the-collection-plate
lost in the crack of the tombs.

At the river Job's Tears wait still
eager hands seeking treasure
for stringing and logwood blossom boats
float far as Falmouth – or China – bringing
a fleet of magical ships to all
lingering downstream. The day
could turn magic. From the river
tables rise and rivermaids comb
their hair golden in the afternoon
singing.

Hill Country

The sun etches out the minutes of my days
under my dark eyes. The train, our only
regulation, shakes down the hours stakes out
the limits of our lives
on this, my harsh and gentle island.

My ring finger tingles as my machete
flints on a stone. From far
hear my wife pounding cassava
in a cracked mortar singing
a cracked tune O
              the futility
of crop cultivation in this place
the census takers never come. To whom
shall I marry my daughter?

Sons, too young to help, too old
to be not-born, too precious
to have seedlings feeding on your dreams
Fist this red clay in your hands
hold the red gold, I tell them.
But I look into their eyes
and no gold comes, no dreams
arise and I know
this is merely the red clay
of a broken hillside and the parakeets
sit on the cedar stump waiting
for the young corn to ripen.

The sun cuts an arc on the housetop
the day goes by
my thoughts tremble on the edge
of something undesirable
my wife sings still
the sunbaked questions
of our lives...

The sun marks the minutes, the train
the hours. Among the yam vines
and the trumpet trees we need
no clocks, no timepieces, no time

for the hunger in our bellies tells us
which way a clock's hands should go.

The train pulls home the day
draws it into citylight on two
black parallels. Later
when my sons discover the agonies
of leached hillsides
it will draw them too
        O weigh
down these memories
with a stone.

One Night, the Father

One night
the father
split
a house
in two
one side
the only
sound the
mother
weeping
weeping
the other
ricochet
of bullets
butchering
banana leaves.

One night
the father
held them
in a state
of siege.
Furniture
loomed
barricades

against
the door
as in
war lore
each child
thought:
this bullet
is meant
for me.

One night
the neighbours
said a
drunken brawl
is all
the mother
shouted
an obstinate
No.

When the father
spent the bullets
for them he'd
also spent
himself.
Came
like a dried
canestalk
trashed
by hooves
of obstinate
mules
turning
the cane mill
round
round
till the day
the father
finally
broken
became
part of
that ground.

X

December that year started out
all right though I knew
my heart could tear easily
as tinsel.

On King Street watching the legless
beggar on wheels I
counted my fortunes.

But what's the use of legs if you're
burdened with a mind
rushing headlong into dark
endings said the shadow

That night exorcising terror I
offered you love you
called me jailor

The season prematurely ended.

Up north Christmas trees
quietly retreated to the
dark forests and the
long awaited baby

never came.

City Poem

I

Now the afternoon crossing of back streets
brings the call of voices: *hello hello. miss. psst psst.*
but I cannot answer: The Age of Anxiety
alas, is still very much alive.

(And if you taught me to speak
with your words would I touch
could I reach beyond the collapse
of garbage cans in hungry streets?)

II

Wen de bulldoza come a back-a-wall
we jus pick up all we have an all
we have is chilren an we leave
Mavis doan wan leave Mavis aksin
why why why A seh Mavis
move fus aks question las
de ting out dere biggern yu
an it caan talk
so Mavis move to but is like
she leave all sense behin. Fram dat
all Mavis good fah is aksin
why.

III

Why
did you damage
the statue
of the National Hero?

– Because I have plenty damage
inside me.
You want to see
my scar?

IV

Halfblue childhood shocks but these
didn't matter. All roads
led outwards and Home
was Mother. Then afternoons
went dark. Hunger
became Brother. The hazy future
shadowed the roads. Failure
was Father. A night flashed
steel cold, your life
went dark six feet under.
The only road led back home
where, I do not remember.

r
a
i
n


```
rain          viet                              hiro
fall          nam                     shima's children
scatters      ese                        also    played
the           bamboo                     until   white
playing       trees                        r     c
children      provide                      a     a
with          frail                        i     m
the           cover                        n     e
cutting       from
edge          the
of            breeze
r             from
 a            the
  i           green
   n          r          trench town      children play
    d          a         trench town      children play
     r          i
      o          n          bullets hail down
       p                    bullets hail down
        s                   bullets hail down
```


The Victim

Bobby Curren alias Festus alias Gre Gre
never come home last night

Bobby Curren
tie up tight

in crocus bag

two fingernail
and him eyelid gone
Bobby Curren wont
walk again
without toes

but who need that
or head

when you dead?

The Lady

At 12 Daimler Close Kingston 6 Armour Heights/
Mistress Marshall wakes late with a headache/ the
light hurts her eyes/ what with pills and the whiskey/
her mouth tastes like death

She must go to the gym/to keep fit and trim/for
her husband who's cheating with a girl/ who's not
slim

Mistress Marshall calls Eunice/ bring tea and the
papers/ no one dead no one born/that she knows of/
but she turns to page eight/ and it's just as she feared/
for the columnists say that the p.m. is failing/ the
country is falling/ the party is foundering/ the
people are restless/ and the prophets of doom are
predicting a crash/ you see what I mean Mistress
Marshall doesn't know/ why her husband so worthless/
to stay on in this place/ every night the black people/
just waiting to break in/ to rob kill and worse/ but
he'd have to shoot first/ no black man will get in/
except that time there/ before she knew better/
before Mister Marshall start courting/
big family and all/ his hair was so curly /
his skin almost white/ not like
hers/ but it improve now she stop stand in sun
at the bus stop/ at the seaside she cover
with kaftan and hat/ say her skin is so delicate/ it

peels if the sun rests lightly on it/ everybody
wonder how naseberry/ so easy to peel/ but they
dont wonder long/ her jewels are real

Mistress Marshall want to go/ every day there she
nagging/ want to go to Miami where everyone gone/
for her skin would improve so/ and in climate that
cool so/ her hair would grow straight/ and the shops
are so full with strawberries and crystal/ caviar and
silver/ real silks and satin/ ryvita and salmon/
mushrooms and gammon/ in short everything that a
human could need

and the damn servant classes/ dem all is a crosses/
where the hell is Eunice?

Drought

This is no place for a
Christian man to
live in   the house
to a slight wind's tap
will give in

and tonight
the moon has a circle
round its eye the old
men say hard rain
will fall   let
the hard rain fall
if my fields go under I
will not surrender
in this place tender
shoots may yet arise

(and O bear this my
heart dont weep if
land is dear rum's
still cheap).

LORNA GOODISON

Lorna Goodison was born in 1947 in Kingston, Jamaica. She studied art at the Jamaica School of Art and at the School of the Art Students' League in New York, and has worked professionally as an artist, designer, painter and illustrator. Her poems have been published in Jamaican newspapers and magazines for over 20 years, since she was a schoolgirl. She has been writer-in-residence at the University of the West Indies and (1986-87) at Radcliffe College, USA, and is now a freelance writer in Kingston. In 1987 she received a Musgrave Medal in Jamaica for her contribution to poetry.

Her books are: *Tamarind Season* (Institute of Jamaica, 1980); *I Am Becoming My Mother* (New Beacon Books, London, 1986; also on cassette), winner of the Americas section of the Commonwealth Poetry Prize; and *Heartease* (New Beacon Books, 1989).

A Far-Reaching Voice

by ANNE WALMSLEY

'One good thing about living in Jamaica, in the Caribbean, is that you can't go for a day without remembering that there are hungry people and people who don't live anywhere.' Lorna Goodison made this comment even before Hurricane Gilbert had ravaged her home island in September 1988. 'This is a hymn' in her latest collection of poems, *Heartease*, expresses her sense of awareness, of kinship, with the hungry and homeless, with the dispossessed of the world:

> This hymn
> is for the must-be-blessed
> the victims of the world
> who know salt best
> the world tribe
> of the dispossessed
> outside the halls of plenty
> looking in
> this is a benediction
> this is a hymn.

It is deliberately 'a hymn': 'may it renew/what passes for your heart'. Her sense of the religious properties of poetry is strong and compelling, especially of poetry when read aloud.

Another poem in this collection, 'An Airport Waiting Room', ends with repetition of the name 'Azania', which she explains thus: 'I think that to repeat something has great power. And I want to say that the place is called Azania, not South Africa. The more times more people say "Azania", the more Azania will come into being eventually. You first envision something, and then you speak it and then it will *be*, you know.' Goodison's poetry combines wide sympathies with a sense of her own specific placing. She speaks always as a Jamaican woman and as a person of the Third World. Such sympathies and self-awareness, and the lyrical, at times incantatory, quality of her writing, combine to make hers one of the most effective new voices in contemporary poetry.

Lorna Goodison trained professionally, and worked first, as a visual artist. 'I started out painting, and I always said that a lot of my poems were left over from ideas for paintings in that I get possessed or obsessed with an idea and I paint it. And then when it still won't go away, I turn out writing it.' Her poems convey the

specifically personal and broader references through sharply
remembered or visualised images. Those in 'Bedspread', from her
second collection, *I Am Becoming My Mother*, were prompted by
a newspaper cutting about the confiscation by the South African
authorities of a bedspread woven in the ANC colours for Winnie
Mandela:

> They wove the bedspread
> and knotted notes of hope
> in each strand
> and selvedged the edges with
> ancient blessings
> older than any white man's coming.

She recalls how her first awareness of herself as a person with
African ancestry, with a collective memory of Africa, was through
painting. 'I was at primary school, about 7 or 8, and sad to say
in those days Jamaican children used to do drawings and paintings
of people and they were all white people. I remember doing this
painting of a lady sitting down, reading a book or something. I
remember mixing red and yellow and black together and I painted
this lady a very dark brown. The children laughed and they said,
"You've painted an African lady." And the teacher said to them,
"But you know, that's really ridiculous, because a lot of you look
like that lady." She put the painting up, and it was up there for
a long time. It just affirmed something for me very much in my
head.' Likewise, she claims that her close feeling for Egypt stems
from her childhood attraction to its art. 'The wonder of the sym-
metry of the friezes, the figures in profile. I've always felt this
very strong connection with Egypt, Egypt being part of Africa.'
The covers of all three of her books feature her own paintings.
Others have been used on books by Jamaican fellow writers:
Edward Baugh, Hazel Campbell, Mervyn Morris.

Goodison is generous in acknowledging the help that she has
received from these writers in terms of constructive criticism, and
equally her debt to Louise Bennett, until recently marginalised
as a writer of "dialect verse", described by Goodison as 'mother
of the Jamaican language'. She never underestimates the long,
demanding work involved in crafting her poems. 'Poetry is very
hard work and the effects of hard work show, although sometimes
the results can look frighteningly simple. But you can know when
somebody has worked at something and it comes out, it's right,
it's whole. I don't like sloppiness in poetry.' She is equally clear
about her uppermost criticism of a good poem. 'My measure for

when a poem is a good poem is when it doesn't sound as if the person was talking as opposed to listening. I don't know of a good poet who is not a listener. I can't deal with poetry which sounds as if someone was consciously pontificating.' In the past, she confesses, 'I have tried consciously not to write poetry because I find it very burdensome, it can be very consuming. I used to spend a lot of time saying, "I don't want to write poetry any more."' But with more publication, more demands for readings, the response to her work and awards for it, has come acceptance, embrace even, of what she sees as her calling as a poet.

For Goodison combines an unfamiliarly old-fashioned respect for such a calling with an unashamed recognition of what she calls her 'mystic side'. In one of the 'Heartease' series of poems:

> For my mission this last life is certainly this
> to be the sojourner poet carolling for peace
> calling lost souls to the way of Heartease.

Her first collection, *Tamarind Season*, was, she says, 'a sort of Tagore. Rabindranath Tagore speaks about a soul trying to strive for wholeness and there's a process where it's almost like a crying out which takes place within you.' Of her latest, *Heartease*, 'It's a sort of continuing. I think it's my personal, internal journey.' She lists some of her recent reading: '*Chasm of Fire* by a woman who studied under a Sufi master in India; *Abandonment to Divine Providence*, a very small book written by a French monk in the 18th century', books which have, she explains, developed her interest in mysticism. 'I think a lot of it comes out in the third collection.' There is certainly more of the mystic, more references to her search for light, for change and renewal. 'I think I'm concerned more with re-unification than anything else. I really feel that is the paramount task of humanity: things have to be re-unified.' The mysticism, the religious awareness, is firmly anchored in the here and now. 'I love the literal meaning of the word "religious" which is realignment, being re-bound to the source, being connected again. Whatever is going to reconnect me to the source is fine, so, yes, I'm a religious person in a very big sense.'

She is a wide but selective reader, deliberately following her interests and sympathies. 'I read a lot of Ngugi wa Thiong'o and Chinua Achebe, and I loved that Buchi Emecheta, *The Bride Price*, a terrific book... I re-read books by Toni Morrison, and I like Toni Cade Bambara – *The Salt Eaters*, and her short stories. Very often I find that I will read through a book and sometimes I'm

wondering why am I ploughing through this book? But it's usually
because there's something in there which is very important to me:
just one passage which becomes the nucleus of a poem.' She is
consciously a 'book person'. 'My Will', from her second collection,
is addressed to her son:

> May you like me earn good
> friends
> but just to be sure
> love books.
> When bindings fall apart
> they can be fixed
> you will find
> that is not always so
> with friendships.

Goodison is amazed that poems about herself, a Jamaican
woman – as granddaughter, daughter and mother, as lover and
friend – are identified with by audiences not only in Jamaica, but
also in the United States and Britain. 'I started off thinking that
a lot of the things I write about are personal and original. And
they're not: they tend to transcend all sorts of barriers which I'd
no idea they would.' She tells how, after reading the poem, 'For
My Mother (May I Inherit Half Her Strength)', a young man in
the audience came up to her and said, 'But that is my parents'
story, how did you know it?' Her poems especially speak for and
strengthen other women: from the realism of 'We are the women'
and other poems in *I Am Becoming My Mother*:

> We are the women
> who ban our bellies
> with strips from the full moon
> our nerves made keen
> from hard grieving
> worn thin like
> silver sixpences

to the similarly rooted but transcended reality of poems in *Heart-
ease*, like this from one of the title series:

> If we mix a solution
> from some wild bees honey
> and some search-mi-heart extract
> better than red conscience money
> and we boil it in a bun-pan
> over a sweet wood fire
> make the soft smell of healing
> melt hard hearts and bare wire.

The voice is unmistakably Jamaican, but reaches far.

For My Mother
(May I Inherit Half Her Strength)

My mother loved my father
I write this as an absolute
in this my thirtieth year
the year to discard absolutes

he appeared, her fate disguised,
as a sunday player in a cricket match,
he had ridden from a country
one hundred miles south of hers.

She tells he dressed the part,
visiting dandy, maroon blazer
cream serge pants, seam like razor,
and the beret and the two-tone shoes.

My father stopped to speak to her sister,
till he looked and saw her by the oleander,
sure in the kingdom of my blue-eyed grandmother.
He never played the cricket match that day.

He wooed her with words and he won her.
He had nothing but words to woo her,
On a visit to distant Kingston he wrote,

'I stood on the corner of King Street and looked,
and not one woman in that town was lovely as you'.

My mother was a child of the petite bourgeoisie
studying to be a teacher, she oiled her hands
to hold pens.
My father barely knew his father, his mother died young,
he was a boy who grew with his granny.

My mother's trousseau came by steamer through the snows
of Montreal
where her sisters Albertha of the cheekbones and the
perennial Rose, combed Jewlit backstreets with French-
turned names for Doris' wedding things.

Such a wedding Harvey River, Hanover, had never seen
Who anywhere had seen a veil fifteen chantilly yards long?
and a crepe de chine dress with inlets of silk godettes
and a neck-line clasped with jewelled pins!

And on her wedding day she wept. For it was a brazen bride in those
        days
who smiled.
and her bouquet looked for the world like a sheaf of wheat
against the unknown of her belly,
a sheaf of wheat backed by maidenhair fern, representing Harvey
        River
her face washed by something other than river water.

My father made one assertive move, he took the imported cherub
        down
from the heights of the cake and dropped it in the soft territory
between her breasts...and she cried.

When I came to know my mother many years later, I knew her as the
        figure
who sat at the first thing I learned to read: 'SINGER', and she
        breast-fed
my brother while she sewed; and she taught us to read while she
        sewed and
she sat in judgement over all our disputes as she sewed.

She could work miracles, she would make a garment from a square
        of cloth
in a span that defied time. Or feed twenty people on a stew made from
fallen-from-the-head cabbage leaves and a carrot and a cho-cho and
        a palmful
of meat.

And she rose early and sent us clean into the world and she went to
        bed in
the dark, for my father came in always last.

There is a place somewhere where my mother never took the younger
    ones
a country where my father with the always smile
my father whom all women loved, who had the perpetual quality of
    wonder
given only to a child...hurt his bride.

Even at his death there was this 'Friend' who stood at her side,
but my mother is adamant that that has no place in the memory of
my father.

When he died, she sewed dark dresses for the women amongst us
and she summoned that walk, straight-backed, that she gave to us
and buried him dry-eyed.

Just that morning, weeks after
she stood delivering bananas from their skin
singing in that flat hill country voice

she fell down a note to the realisation that she did
not have to be brave, just this once
and she cried.

For her hands grown coarse with raising nine children
for her body for twenty years permanently fat
for the time she pawned her machine for my sister's
Senior Cambridge fees
and for the pain she bore with the eyes of a queen

and she cried also because she loved him.

The Mulatta as Penelope

Tonight I'll pull your limbs through small
soft garments
Your head will part my breasts
and you will hear a different heartbeat.
Today we said the real goodbye, he and I
but this time
I will not sit and spin and spin
the door open to let the madness in
till the sailor finally weary
of the sea
returns with tin souvenirs and a claim
to me.
True, I returned from the quayside
my eyes full of sand
and his salt leaving smell
fresh on my hands
But, you're my anchor awhile now
and that goes deep,
I'll sit in the sun and dry my hair
while you sleep.

On Becoming a Mermaid

Watching the underlife idle by
you think drowning must be easy death
just let go and let the water carry you
away and under
the current pulls your bathing-plaits loose
your hair floats out straightened by the water
your legs close together fuse all the length down
your feet now one broad foot
the toes spread into
a fish-tail, fan-like
your sex locked under
mother-of-pearl scales

you're a nixie now, a mermaid
a green tinged fish / fleshed woman / thing
who swims with thrashing movements
and stands upended on the sea floor
breasts full and floating buoyed by the salt
and the space between your arms now always
filled and your sex sealed forever under
mother-of-pearl scale / locks closes finally
on itself like some close-mouthed oyster.

The Mulatta and the Minotaur

And shall I tell you what the minotaur said to me
as we dined by the Nile on almond eyes and tea?
No, I shall not reveal that yet.
Here, I'll record just how we met.
We faced each other and a bystander said,
'Shield your eyes, he's wearing God's head'
but it was already turbulent and deeply stained
with the merciless indigo of hell's rain.
And I, delaying my dying, hung my innocence high
and it glowed pale and waterwash against the sky.
And we met, but he was on his way
So he marked my left breast with this stain
which is indelible till we meet again.
And our lives rocketed through separate centuries
and we gave life to sons in sevens
and I was suckled of a great love or two
split not all the way asunder
and stuck together with glue.
And he wed the faultless wind
and wrestled with phantasms
and fantastic djinn
and came through the other side whole and alone
with a countenance clear as wind-worried bones
and the seal of a serpent engorged by a dove
imprinted on marching orders for love.

And I was suckled of a great love or two
split not all the way asunder
and stuck together with glue.
For the Queen of Sheba had willed me
her bloodstone ring,
and flight of phoenix feathers
and her looser black things.
So,
Minotaur;
God's-head wearer
Galileo
Conqueror-of-Paris
Someone I don't know
There will be a next time
Centuries ago.

Keith Jarrett — Rainmaker

Piano man
my roots are african
I dwell in the centre of the sun.
I am used to its warmth
I am used to its heat
I am seared by its vengeance
(it has a vengeful streak)

So my prayers are usually
for rain.
My people are farmers
and artists
and sometimes the lines
blur
so a painting becomes a
december of sorrel
a carving heaps like a yam hill
or a song of redemption wings
like the petals of resurrection
lilies — all these require rain.

So this sunday
when my walk misses
my son's balance on my hips
I'll be all right if you pull down
for me
waterfalls of rain.
I never thought a piano
could divine
but I'm hearing you this morning
and right on time
its drizzling now
I'll open the curtains and
watch the lightning conduct
your hands.

'Mine, O Thou Lord of Life, send my roots rain'

GERARD MANLEY HOPKINS

For I've been planted long
in a sere dry place
watered only occasionally
with odd overflows
from a passing cloud's face.
In my morning
I imitated the bougainvillea
(in appearances
I'm hybrid)
I gave forth defiant alleluias
of flowering
covered my aridity with
red petalled blisters
grouped close, from far
they were a borealis of
save-face flowers.
In the middle of my
life span
my trunk's not so limber
my sap flows thicker

my region has posted signs
that speak of scarce water.
At night God, I feel
my feet powder.
Lord let the preying worms
wait to feast in vain.
In this noon of my orchard
send me deep rain.

I Am Becoming My Mother

Yellow/brown woman
fingers smelling always of onions

My mother raises rare blooms
and waters them with tea
her birth waters sang like rivers
my mother is now me

My mother had a linen dress
the colour of the sky
and stored lace and damask
tablecloths
to pull shame out of her eye.

I am becoming my mother
brown/yellow woman
fingers smelling always of onions.

Nanny

My womb was sealed
with molten wax
of killer bees

for nothing should enter
nothing should leave
the state of perpetual siege
the condition of the warrior.

From then my whole body would quicken
at the birth of everyone of my people's children.
I was schooled in the green-giving ways
of the roots and vines
made accomplice to the healing acts
of Chainey root, fever grass & vervain.

My breasts flattened
settled unmoving against my chest
my movements ran equal
to the rhythms of the forest.

I could sense and sift
the footfall of men
from the animals
and smell danger
death's odour
in the wind's shift.

When my eyes rendered
light from the dark
my battle song opened
into a solitaire's moan
I became most knowing
and forever alone.

And when my training was over
they circled my waist with pumpkin seeds
and dried okra, a traveller's jigida
and sold me to the traders
all my weapons within me.
I was sent, tell that to history.

When your sorrow obscures the skies
other women like me will rise.

For Rosa Parks

And how was this soft woman to know
that this 'No'
in answer to the command to rise
would signal the beginning
of the time of walking?
Soft the word
like the closing of some aweful book
a too-long story
with no pauses for reason
but yes, an ending
and the signal to begin the walking.
But the people had walked before
in yoked formations down to Calabar
into the belly of close-ribbed whales
sealed for seasons
and unloaded to walk again
alongside cane stalks tall as men.
No, walking was not new to them.
Saw a woman tie rags to her feet
running red, burnishing the pavements,
a man with no forty acres
just a mule
riding towards Jerusalem
And the children small somnambulists
moving in the before day morning
And the woman who never raised her voice
never lowered her eyes
just kept walking
leading us towards sunrise.

Bedspread

Sometimes in the still
unchanging afternoons
when the memories crowded
hot and hopeless against
her brow

she would seek its cool colours
and signal him to lie down
in his cell.
It is three in the afternoon Nelson
let us rest here together
upon this bank draped in freedom
colour.
It was woven by women with slender
capable hands
accustomed to binding wounds
hands that closed the eyes of
dead children,
that fought for the right to
speak in their own tongues
in their own land
in their own schools.
They wove the bedspread
and knotted notes of hope
in each strand
and selvedged the edges with
ancient blessings
older than any white man's coming.
So in the afternoons lying on this
bright bank of blessing
Nelson my husband I meet you in dreams
my beloved much of the world too is
asleep blind to the tyranny and evil
devouring our people.
But, Mandela, you are rock on this sand
harder than any metal
mined in the bowels of this land
you are purer than any
gold tempered by fire
shall we lie here wrapped
in the colours of our free Azania?
They arrested the bedspread.
They and their friends are working
to arrest the dreams in our heads
and the women, accustomed to closing
the eyes of the dead
are weaving cloths still brighter
to drape us in glory in a Free
Azania.

Heartease (I)

We with the straight eyes
and no talent for cartography
always asking
'How far is it to Heartease?'
and they say,
'Just round the corner.'

But that being the spider's direction
means each day finds us further away.
Dem stick wi up
dem jook wi down
and when dem no find
what dem come fi find
them blood we and say
'walk wid more next time'.

So, take up divining again
and go inna interpretation
and believe the flat truth
left to dry on our tongues.
Truth say,
Heartease distance
cannot hold in a measure
it say
travel light
you are the treasure.
It say
you can read map
even if you born
a Jubilee
and grow with your granny
and eat crackers for your tea.
It say
you can get licence
to navigate
from sail board horse
in the sea's gully.

Believe, believe
and believe this
the eye know how far
Heartease is.

A Rosary of Your Names (II)

The Merciful
The Peace
The Source
The Hidden
The All Strivings Cease.
The One
The First
The Bridge
The Last
The Height
The Ocean
The Promise come to pass
The Blessing
The Beloved
most Beloved
In whose eyes worlds live
The Everlasting
The First Song
The Maker of Mountains
The Give
The Most Blessed
The Belong
The Architect of Planets
The One in Charge
Superior
Almighty
All Knowing
Large
There is no God But God
He lit the First Flame
Orchestrator of Dawns and Sunsets
chant a rosary of His Names
Painter of limitless palette
Harpmaker, song giver
Light which takes wings
God is
God is
Infinity
Blessings.

LINTON KWESI JOHNSON

Linton Kwesi Johnson was born in 1952 in Chapeltown, a small town in the rural parish of Clarendon, Jamaica. He came to London in 1963, went to a Brixton comprehensive, and later studied sociology at Goldsmiths' College (University of London).

After leaving school, he joined the Black Panthers, helped organise a poetry workshop within the movement, and developed his work with a group of poets and drummers called Rasta Love. In 1977 he was awarded a C. Day Lewis Fellowship as a writer-in-residence in the London Borough of Lambeth; later he worked at the Keskidee Arts Centre as a Library Resources and Education Officer.

His poems first appeared in the journal *Race Today*, and in 1974 Race Today Publications brought out his first collection, *Voices of the Living and the Dead*. *Dread Beat An' Blood* (Bogle-L'Ouverture, London, 1975) was his second book of poems, and also the title of his first LP record, released by Virgin in 1978. A third book followed, *Inglan is a Bitch* (Race Today, 1980), and three more records on the Island label: *Forces of Victory* (1979), *Bass Culture* (1980) and *Making History* (1984). His latest book is *Tings an Times: Selected Poems* (Bloodaxe Books/LKJ Music Publishers, 1991).

Interview with Linton Kwesi Johnson

by MERVYN MORRIS

(extract)

MM: *At eleven, when you left Jamaica, where did you go to in England?*

LKJ: My mother was living at the time off Acre Lane which is just on the outskirts of Brixton, or part of Brixton if you like. There were a lot of Jamaicans around. In Brixton market you could see yam, banana, all the things that you were familiar with in Jamaica, you could still hear people talking in the Jamaican way, the Jamaican language. And at school there were a lot of boys who had just come up like myself from the West Indies, so it was very easy to settle down. But I found a lot of things quite shocking. For example, when I saw the English houses at first I thought they were all factories because they had these big chimneys on them, you know, and they looked ugly. And another thing I found surprising was to see a white man sweeping the streets. All the white people I saw in Jamaica drove fish-tail cars and smoked cigars. So when I saw someone, a white person, actually sweeping the streets it was a bit of a revelation.

At school it was, to begin with, a very traumatic experience, because you were called 'black bastard' by the white kids, all kinds of racist names, and told 'you live in trees' and 'you eat monkeys', and all kinds of things. The teachers would behave not so drastically but in a similar way. For example, if you were noisy in the class they would ask you where did you think you were, Brixton market on a Saturday afternoon? Once I was running along the corridor – I was late for a lesson – and a teacher jumped out of his room, grabbed me by the collar, dragged me into his room, gave me two strokes of the cane, and asked me if I thought I was in a jungle, and I should learn to walk and not run. And you had these experiences with teachers from time to time. Quite a lot of teachers were physically assaulted by black pupils because of the way they treated us.

MM: *At what stage did you start writing fairly seriously?*

LKJ: I began writing when I was about seventeen. I was still at school and I was in the Panthers, the Panthers' youth section.

MM: *What year was that?*

LKJ: About '69, '70, I began writing poetry. And how I began, it was this book I came across in the library – the Black Panthers had a black literature library and for me it was a new thing, you know, I didn't know there was such a thing as black literature, I mean I thought books were only written by Europeans – and I came across this book and began reading it, by W.E.B. Dubois, called *The Souls of Black Folk*. I mean, I've never been through such a deep emotional experience with any other piece of work of art by anybody. And I just felt like I wanted to write too, to express and say something about what was going on in England with young people, and how black people were being treated, and so on.

MM: *At what stage did you join* Race Today?

LKJ: I joined *Race Today* in 1976, but I have always been associated with it from its very inception.

MM: *Which was when? Its inception was when, about?*

LKJ: 1973. *Race Today* existed before then, as something else. The only continuity with the past is the name *Race Today*. *Race Today* was, basically, a race relations rag of the Institute of Race Relations, set up by business interests and academic interests to study the natives, so to speak.

Darcus Howe, who had been in the Black Panther movement with me, was offered the editorship. He took it, and promptly, with the connivance of John La Rose and other people, hijacked *Race Today* – literally, physically, hijacked the magazine, typesetter and everything, and went to an old house in Brixton and squatted, and built an organisation around the journal, transforming the journal, from a rag of the Institute of Race Relations, into a political weapon, which could be used to inform and to mobilise people around struggles of blacks and Asians in Britain and the world over.

MM: *What does the Race Today Collective do, beyond producing the journal?*

LKJ: Well, we're involved in the black movement. We're involved in building mass organisations, or mass-based organisations, and assisting others in that process. For example, the George Lindo Action Committee, which was an organisation of working-class blacks, formed to free a man who was wrongfully put in prison – *Race Today* was central to the organising of that. We're actively involved in the campaign to keep carnival on the streets of London, because, you know, at one time the government wanted to ban it. We're involved in organisations like the New Cross Massacre Action Committee. And we work in close alliance with the Black Parents' Movement (which is an organisation of parents) and the

Black Youth Movement (an organisation of youth) which work together. We're collectively known as The Alliance.

We have a little section of the organisation, it's more or less independent of *Race Today*, but we can't really separate them. It's called Creation for Liberation. That came into being around 1978. I was trying to mobilise fellow artists like myself, whether they be involved in performing poetry or music or painting or whatever, to have a group of people who would be committed to doing public performances to raise money for struggles, or for campaigns, and also to foster the development of the creative expression in Britain among the black artists. And to that end we have sponsored tours for Oku Onuora and Michael Smith in Britain; we've tried to publish unknown writers in *Race Today*, and we've put on various poetry recitals and variety concerts and music concerts with rock groups as well as reggae groups.

MM: *Now Linton, can we return specifically to your poetry and when it started in the early 1970s? Of the poems which have been published, can you remember which is the very earliest in composition?*

LKJ: The earliest in composition, of the ones which have been published, is 'Two Sides of Science' – I wrote that in 1972, followed by 'Five Nights of Bleeding', 'Doun de Road', 'Yout Scene' (in fact 'Yout Scene' is the first poem I wrote in the Jamaican language, the very first one), and 'Double Scank'. They came out of a thing that I was doing an experiment with, called 'Notes on Brixton'.

The poem 'Di Black Petty-Booshwah' – it's the first poem I ever wrote where the music was there first before the words. I was messing around with the bass guitar – cos I'm not really a musician – I was sitting down with my little bass guitar that I work out my bass line with, and messing around, and just going up and down the A string and I found this combination of notes (da-da-da-da-da-da-di-di-di-di-di-di-di...) and after I worked it out the words just came, the words just suggested themselves.

MM: *Your poetry has been very firmly concerned with political action and with helping to further that. But you began in the early 1970s writing poems which to many listeners suggested what was in fact the case, that you were intimate with Jamaican popular music. Would you say something about the connection between your interest in popular music and your beginnings in writing poetry?*

LKJ: Well, from a boy here in Jamaica I'd always loved music.

As a little boy I'd make bamboo fife and make, you know – what time of the year was it? I can't remember if it was Easter or Jonkonnu time or whatever, a certain time of the year we'd go down to the river, get an old butter pan and get a piece of old khaki and get some mud and bush and cord it, and I used to make that and play fife and drum and I've always been interested in music and loved music. And when I entered adolescence I began buying records, and I used to fancy myself as a singer. I always used to, when the records were playing, close my eyes and pretend that I was singing the song and all this kind of thing. And then I became interested in the music because I found that, growing up in England, you're listening to all kinds of music – you're listening to American music, British pop, all kinds of music, middle of the road music – but reggae music stood out. Number one, it was very danceable. And number two, there seems to be a great social focus on the part of lyricists: they were always singing about whatever was happening in a society at a particular time; and I found this fascinating. And I found the style and the nature of our music also fascinating, and I became a student of it.

So when I began to write poetry... When I began to write, in fact, I had no poetic models to draw from because I wasn't very much into poetry at school. I remember I quite enjoyed it when I was out here in Jamaica, but in those days they taught you parrot fashion and you just learnt everything and the whole class said it. 'O wind a-blowing all day long,/O wind that sings so loud a song...' But I was very much into the poetry of the Old Testament. I used to read to my grandmother (who was illiterate) at nights; and she used to love the Psalms, the Proverbs, Songs of Solomon, Ecclesiastes. And I used to love that kind of poetry; and when I began to write I used to write a lot of 'thou' and 'thy' and all this kind of thing – that was my poetic model. And then I found that what I wanted to say could have been much more easily and more appropriately expressed in the Jamaican language. And I don't know how or why it happened, but from the moment I began to write in the Jamaican language music entered the poetry. There was always a beat, or a bass line, going on at the back of my head with the words. And so I developed this style of writing – always with music in mind, always hearing music when I'm composing my poetry, or writing my poetry. And it was only the logical development, I suppose, of it, to bring out the music at another stage which was inherent in the poetry. Quite a few of the poems in *Dread Beat an' Blood* came out of my experiences with that workshop situation with Rasta Love. I would do my poetry and they would give me the drum accompaniment, I used to play funde myself in fact in the group, and they would do their Rasta chants and sing their Rasta songs. So it was like a poetry and Rasta music thing. And then everywhere I read people kept on saying, 'Oh, your poetry sounds so musical, you can hear the reggae beat in it, why don't you put it to music?' So that is what eventually happened, when I was working at Virgin Records. I worked there as a freelance copywriter when I was still at college. Virgin Records is an English record company, and they had just become involved in reggae at that time. When I was there I used to write biographies on the artistes...

MM: *This would have been when?*

LKJ: About '77. This is after *Dread Beat an' Blood* had been published. I did radio ads for them. And I was just earning pocket money. And being there I naturally put to them — I put the idea to a friend called John Varmon, an English fellow who was doing most of the marketing, and he put it to the directors and they said yes, and I did 'All Wi Doin Is Defending', which was very poorly recorded, and sounded awful, but they were satisfied with the returns they got from that, they were confident enough of the returns they got from that, to do an album, and that's how I made my first album, *Dread Beat an' Blood*, which was made over a weekend in fact. We laid down the tracks on the Friday night, we overdubbed on voice on the Saturday night, and mixed on the Sunday.

MM: *Are there problems in having actual music behind the voice?*

LKJ: Yes, there are a number of problems. Firstly, when you're beginning to do the thing it's a problem with the musicians, of them understanding exactly what you're trying to do, and being sensitive enough to it, to realise that what you're doing is poetry and not just straight pop music or straight regular reggae music, and that there's a difference. There's always a danger of people mistaking what you do for just reggae, and accepting it on the level that they might accept a deejay or a singer. There's also the danger of the music overwhelming the word so that the word becomes just a little additive to the music, you know. And one has to guard very carefully in the actual recording and the actual mixing to make sure that the voice is heard. That is the greatest danger, I believe.

MM: *I think even now, although your records are on sale and have been bought, you sometimes perform items without music.*

How does that tend to go?
LKJ: Oh, it goes very well. I always insist, if I'm performing in
a music context – that is, at a music venue where people go for
musical entertainment – if I'm performing with tapes which I used
to do I don't do that anymore because I work with a band now –
I always do a couple of poems, two or three poems, always, without
musical accompaniment, to remind my audience that that is what
I'm about: poetry, you know. And in fact most of the work I do
is just poetry recitals. I do far more poetry recitals than I do
musical performances. And recently I toured Scandinavia with a
band called Dennis Bovell Dub Band – excellent musicians from
London – and it was a good tour and we got a tremendous response.
It was the first time that I had done it with a band, because I
normally used to do it with a tape – you know, mix down my music
on tape and just recite the poetry on top of it. That was rewarding,
but I still find I get much more out of reciting to a small group of
maybe 300 people in a room, just doing the words, it's much more
intimate, you get much more feedback and you pick up the vibes
from the audience and it's a much richer and deeper experience.
MM: *When you're performing with a band, are you conscious of
the band's performance varying in the same sort of way your own
reading of a poem would vary from performance to performance?*
LKJ: Oh yes. Sometimes the band is tighter than other times, you
know. Occasionally a musician might play a bad note, or an instru-
ment might be too loud. But at the same time it's easier for me as
a performer. The musicians they take a lot of the strain off of
you, because the audience is watching them as well; it's not just
you there. So in that sense it's easier, yes. But to get back to the
music. After a while I became actively interested in studying the
music, and I used to go out an buy records and listen and copy
down the words and analyse the words, listen to the different
beats and compare different style of approach, different studios,
different producers, and then I began to do some freelance writ-
ing.
    When I began to do the poetry with the music and people were
looking for a bag to put it in, to describe it, I said "reggae poetry".
I said "reggae poetry", but I realised soon after that it was a
mistake, because one is looking for a way of describing a particular
style, and I suppose it's accurate in so far as there's a thing like
jazz poetry, you know – you have "reggae poetry" because it's
largely connected to the reggae music tradition.
    I also coined the phrase "dub poetry", but I was doing that as

a student of reggae music. I did that as early as 1974. I came up
with the term "dub poetry" and "dub lyricism" as a way of talking
about the deejays, the reggae deejays, because at that time I tried
to see them, and tried to argue that what they were doing was
really poetry, and that it had a lot in common with traditional
African poetry in so far as it was spontaneous, improvisatory and
had a musical base. I was surprised a few years later to see the
term "dub poetry" applied as an umbrella term to describe what
people like Oku Onuora, Michael Smith, Brian Meeks, Mutaba-
ruka, myself and others were doing. I think Oku Onuora's theory
goes a little bit too far, because if it's by definition something
connected to music and to the reggae tradition, then I don't see
how he would locate Miss Lou [Louise Bennett] in that. If any-
thing, Miss Lou is working in a mento tradition rather than a dub
tradition. And since I myself, and Oku Onuora himself and
Michael Smith are using original music, which comes out of the
poetry that we write, to call it "dub poetry", I think, is a little
misguided, because "dub poetry" implies that you get a piece of
dub music and put some poetry to it – which is what the deejays
do. They get a piece of instrumental music or a song with the
lyrics taken out, and improvise spontaneous lyricism describing
everyday happenings and events. And that is what I was trying
to get at when I wrote this thing about "dub poetry".

MM: *Where did you write it, Linton?*

LKJ: I think you'll find it in an article I wrote in *Race and Class*
called 'Jamaican Rebel Music', published in June '76. And I think
it also appeared in an article I did on the Jamaican deejay called
'I-Roy' which was published in either '75 or '76 in the *New Musical
Express*.

MM: *Mind you, the fact that the term is in origin slightly mislead-
ing need not be a problem for long once people have adapted the
term to applying to a group of people that they more or less know
they mean. I wonder if you'd say a little bit about how you would
see the distinction between what the so-called dub poets are doing
– people like Oku and Mikey and Muta and so on – and what the
deejay performers are doing.*

LKJ: The deejays, obviously they have a history and tradition
which has evolved since the early talking tunes of Prince Buster
in the sixties and the rhythmic mouthings of people like King Stitt
and Count Machuki over the shuffle rhythms of the ska, to the
stage where people began to actually come up with lyrics, to evolve
a lyricism. It's rooted in the sound system culture, and it's functional

in so far as the whole idea behind it is to liven up the dance, and to "nice up the dance", and to get people involved in the music. So in that way it's by nature different from so-called dub poetry, because dub poetry functions on another level.

MM: *On what level?*

LKJ: As something within its own right: as poetry, it functions as poetry to be recited to poetry-listening audiences, something separate from the sound system tradition. Where the overlap comes is that we, all of us, I think, have been inspired, and have been impressed, by the deejays. I myself particularly by people like Big Youth, U-Roy, I-Roy, Prince Jazzbo, King Stitt, and I was also influenced, I believe, by Prince Buster's talking tunes and Lee Perry's talking tunes, things like 'Ten Commandments of Man' and 'Judge Dread' and 'The Lecture' and 'Kimble the Nimble' and all these things by Lee Perry. Another difference is that the whole nature of the composition is different: you sit down and you compose a poem, you write a poem, always with music in mind; the deejay now he begins with music, he begins with a piece of pre-recorded music to which he improvises lyrics. The nature of this art is closer to the African oral poets in so far as it's spontaneous, and there's not that element of spontaneity in dub poetry – you sit down and you work it out and you write it and you compose it and you change this word and that word. But the lyricism of people like Michigan and Smiley, for example, the odd Yellow Man, the odd Brigadier Jerry, or even some of the things by Big Youth, could stand in their own right without the music, as poetry. Again, to repeat what I said before. I tried to argue that what they were doing was in fact poetry – hence the term dub poetry, you see. There is that overlap.

MM: *What do you see as the future of dub poetry? Do you think the better poets will simply emerge, write some things that are dub and some things that are not? Or do you see it as a kind of trend that might continue? I ask this partly because one of the key things about dub poetry is that it has widened the audience. The only poet in the Jamaican context that had an audience as wide as the dub poets would be Louise Bennett.*

LKJ: Yes, I think it's a very interesting trend and development, and I think the more the merrier for the time being, and obviously the wheat will sort itself out from the tares. The good ones will, hopefully, progress and go on to writing different kinds of poetry and deepening their knowledge and their experience of poetry *per se*; and the charlatans and the pretenders will probably disappear off the scene. When something new starts everybody jumps on the bandwagon; there are some people who obviously are talented, like Michael Smith and Oku Onuora and Muta and so on, and there are others who are not. I think we'll have to wait and see who are the real talents and who are just riding on the bandwagon. But I think it's a healthy development. My only caution is that I think people should remember that poetry is much wider than dub poetry. To talk dub poetry alone or to call yourself a dub poet is a limitation, you know, it's putting yourself in a bag and it's a dangerous business. I think when asked how would you describe yourself you should say that you're a poet and you write a style of poetry which could be described as dub poetry among other things, because to just say I write dub poetry is to limit yourself.

MM: *Yes.*

LKJ: And to add – it's something that's not particular to Jamaica, it's something that's developing throughout the Caribbean. They generally tend to call it "rhythm poetry". But it's a trend, it's a modern day trend in the entire Caribbean. There's Abdul Malik from Trinidad; there's a group there called Network who do what they call Rapso, like a rap poetry with calypso rhythms, and they incorporate mime and dance with it on the stage – very good performers. There are quite a few other people. There's this fellow in Barbados.

MM: *Bruce St John?*

LKJ: Bruce St John, of course. But I'm thinking of this Rasta poet from Barbados. Michael Rasheed Foster. There's a whole lot of them. Since the poetry is oral it would be very difficult for music not to creep into it, and I think the most sensible vehicle for the dissemination of that kind of poetry is the record.

MM: *What do you find takes most of your time at the moment, and how much time are you finding for actually writing new poems?*

LKJ: Most of my time is taken up with earning a living, Mervyn; which means actually going out and performing poetry, going and performing at music venues, doing tours in Europe, and then doing my freelance journalism. The rest of my time is taken up with my political work. It's very hard to work out a balance, because sometimes I feel I should be doing more political work, but then I have to be out of the country for quite a lot of the time. And sometimes I think that I'm performing too much and I need more time to actually sit down and write. I don't really find the time – I've gotten so many ideas for poems which have just vanished into thin air really, simply because I haven't had a chance to sit down and let them germinate in my mind and so on. But I'm working on some new poems. I think I've got enough material together now for a new album which I intend to make next year.

MM: *Nearly all your published or recorded poetry in recent years has been very firmly political. One of the exceptions I can think of is the poem 'Lorraine'. Do you write a number of poems which might be broadly considered a- or non-political? Or you just don't now?*

LKJ: I never have. From the time I began writing, my initial inspiration came from the general conditions that black people were living under and what we were experiencing in British society. And that has been the mainstay of my creative source . . . like I'm a one theme writer, I suppose . . .

MM: *What about 'Lorraine'? That seems to open up a whole range of possibilities which you have not really been doing much with recently.*

LKJ: From time to time I get tempted to write light-hearted little things like that. But, tell you the truth about that poem: it's just simply that I got fed up of people saying to me, you're always writing about the ugly things in life, why can't you write about love and all this kind of business. And I said, well, I'm going to show people that I have a sense of humour, so I just sat down and wrote this poem. But funnily enough I've had experiences where I've recited that poem and people take it seriously and ask me 'Oh, did that really happen to you?'

MM: *Have you thought about the title of your next record?*

LKJ: Yes. Provisionally it's called *Making History*. It's the title of one of the new poems that I wrote, dealing with basically what has happened over the last five years, with the riots and the responses of official society to it – things like the New Cross Massacre, where thirteen young children were murdered by fascists who threw an incendiary device into a sixteenth birthnight party, killing thirteen children, injuring twenty-seven. You know, what is happening in the world generally – what is going on in Poland, and you know, what's going on in England now at the moment, really, Scarman and all that. I mean, official society seemed to be surprised when the Asians fought off the fascists in Southall in 1979, they seemed to be surprised when young blacks insurrected in Bristol in 1980, surprised when the whole country was in insurrection in 1981. And the poem 'Making History' simply says, well, it's not no great mystery, you know, we just simply making history – we making history in Britain now.

MM: *There has been news in Jamaica that you have recently given your "farewell concert" in London. When was that concert, and what exactly did you mean by "farewell concert"?*

LKJ: The concert was the 7th or the 8th of December, 1985 at the Camden Centre in London. What I mean by "farewell concert" is that I am taking my leave from the stage as a reggae performer.

When I began to write poetry at first it was simply a need I had as a young black person growing up in England to express my ideas about how I felt about our experiences there, and I just chose poetry as a means of doing that. Then I got involved in recording, and through making records I've been able to take my poems to a much much wider audience than I could have ever dreamed of reaching through poetry alone in book form. But that has its own drawbacks, because although I've performed in about twenty-one countries – played to hundreds of thousands of people, sold hundreds of thousands of records, I've realised over the last few years that my poetry has suffered as a consequence.

MM: *In what sense has your poetry suffered?*

LKJ: It's suffered in terms of the craft of poetry. The kind of poetry I was writing, that I am known for, at least, would be written in a way that a poetic idea would come to me as a musical one. The two would be the same thing – a musical idea or a poetic idea. I can't find any better way of putting it. But eventually I found that I was getting drawn closer to the music, and trying to write within the strict parameters of the reggae form which is very limiting. You're not conscious of it at the time, but you get drawn closer and closer and closer to the music until in the end what you're doing is basically making reggae songs or composing reggae music. Basically, I think I've been able to sustain my popularity over the years because of the strength of the music, number one, and because people generally identified with the sentiments of what I was saying. In a sense I have consciously seen it as my function to document the experiences and highlight the moments of the history of blacks in Britain, and that is what I've been using my poetry to do over the last few years. But to go back to the original question about why I'm withdrawing from public performances on the stage...

MM: *On the stage with music...*

LKJ: On the stage with music, yes. I mean, I'll still do the odd poetry reading. And I don't know, I mean, if somebody makes me an offer that I can't refuse – to go somewhere that I've never been with the band before, I will, because that's how I've been earning my living over the years. But another reason why I've stopped – I've stopped because I want to give myself some time to write some better poems and I want to stop because I feel that I've been very very very lucky indeed and I don't want to push my luck too far. Also, I don't think I have anything more to say which I haven't said, or which other people aren't saying, as effectively or even more effectively. There are a lot of powerful voices around the place now. And dub poetry is very much alive. If I have achieved anything, I feel that what I have achieved, in Britain at least, is to show the black youth of England or young black people in England that you don't have to be immersed in classical literature or to have been to a university to be able to write poetry that strikes a common chord of response among your peer group.

MM: *Is there a particular activity that you may be involved in which will keep you going on a regular basis in terms of income?*

LKJ: No. It's a big step I've taken. I have a little savings that could tide me over for a couple of months. After that I don't know where I'm going to earn my bread and butter from, but I'll have to find something. And I'm not a proud fellow, I can do anything.

[1982/86]

Reggae Sounds

Shock-black bubble-doun-beat bouncing
rock-wise tumble-doun sound music;
foot-drop find drum, blood story,
bass history is a moving
            is a hurting black story.

Thunda from a bass drum sounding
lightening from a trumpet and a organ,
bass and rhythm and trumpet double-up,
team up with drums for a deep doun searching.

Rhythm of a tropical electrical storm
(cooled doun to the pace of the struggle),
flame-rhythm of historically yearning
flame-rhythm of the time of turning,
measuring the time for bombs and for burning.

Slow drop. make stop. move forward.
dig doun to the root of the pain;
shape it into violence for the people,
they will know what to do, they will do it.

Shock-black bubble-doun-beat bouncing
rock-wise tumble-doun sound music;
foot-drop find drum, blood story,
bass history is a moving
            is a hurting black story.

Dread Beat an' Blood

brothers and sisters rocking
a dread beat pulse fire, burning:

chocolate hour and darkness creeping night.

black veiled night is weeping,
electric lights consoling, night.

a small hall, soaked in smoke:
a house of ganja mist.

music blazing, sounding, thumping fire, blood.
brothers and sisters rocking, stopping, rocking;
music breaking out, bleeding out, thumping out fire: burning

electric hour of the red bulb
staining the brain with a blood flow
and a bad bad thing is brewing.

ganja crawling, creeping to the brain;
cold lights hurting, breaking, hurting;
fire in the head an a dread beat bleeding, heating fire: dread.

rocks rolling over hearts leaping wild,
rage rising out of the heat of the hurt;
and a fist curled in anger reaches a her,
then flash of a blade from another to a him,
leaps out for a dig of a flesh of a piece of skin.
and blood, bitterness, exploding fire, wailing blood,
                                                and bleeding.

Bass Culture
(for Big Yout)

muzik of blood
black reared
pain rooted
heart geared;

all tensed up
in the bubble and the bounce
an the leap an the weight-drop.

it is the beat of the heart,
this pulsing of blood
that is a bubblin bass,
a bad bad beat

pushin gainst the wall
whey bar black blood.

an is a whole heappa
passion a gather
like a frightful form
like a righteous harm
giving off wild like is madness.

Five Nights of Bleeding
(for Leroy Harris)

I

madness...madness...
madness tight on the heads of the rebels;
the bitterness erupts like a hot-blast.
                broke glass.
rituals of blood on the burning
served by a cruel in-fighting;
five nights of horror and of bleeding,
                broke glass,
cold blades as sharp as the eyes of hate.
                and the stabbings.
it's war amongst the rebels:
madness, madness, war.

II

night number one was in BRIXTON:
SOFRANO B sound system
was a beating out a rhythm with a fire
coming down his reggae reggae wire.
it was a sound shaking down your spinal column,
a bad music tearing up your flesh;
and the rebels them start a fighting
the youth them just turn wild.
it's war amongst the rebels;
madness, madness, war.

III

night number two down at SHEPHERD'S,
right up RAILTON ROAD:
it was a night named friday
when everyone was high on brew,
or drew a pound or two worth of kally;
sound coming down NEVILLE KING's music iron;
the rhythm just bubbling and back firing,
raging and rising, when suddenly the music cut:
steel blade drinking blood in darkness.
it's war amongst the rebels;
madness, madness, war.

IV

night number three
over the river
right outside the RAINBOW.
inside JAMES BROWN was screaming soul
outside the rebels were freezing cold.
babylonian tyrants descended
pounced on the brothers who were bold;
so with a flick
of the wrist,
a jab and a stab,
the song of blades was sounded,
the bile of oppression was vomited
and two policemen wounded.
righteous, righteous, war.

V

night number four at a blues dance.
               a blues dance:
two rooms packed and the pressure pushing up.
hot. hot heads. ritual of blood in a blues dance.
               broke glass,
splintering fire, axes, blades, brain blast;
rebellion rushing down the wrong road,
storm blowing down the wrong trees.
so LEROY bleeds near death on the fourth night,
               in a blues dance,
on a Black rebellious night.
it's war amongst the rebels:
madness, madness, war.

VII

night number five at the TELEGRAPH:
vengeance walked through the doors
so slow
so smooth
so tight and ripe and smash!
　　　　　　　broke glass;
a bottle finds a head
and the shell of the fire-hurt cracks;
the victim feels fear
　　　　　　finds hands
　　　　　　holds knife
　　　　　　finds throat
o the stabbings and the bleeding and the blood.
it's war amongst the rebels:
madness, madness, war.

Reggae fi Dada

galang dada
galang gwaan yaw sah
yu nevah ad noh life fi live
jus di wan life fi give
yu did yu time pan ert
yu nevah get yu jus dizert
galang goh smile inna di sun
galang goh satta inna di palace af peace

o di waatah
it soh deep
di waatah
it soh daak
an it full a hawbah shaak

di lan is like a rack
slowly shattahrin to san
sinkin in a sea of calimity
where fear breed shadows

dat lurks in di daak
where people fraid fi waak
fraid fi tink fraid fi taak
where di present is haunted by di paas

a deh soh mi bawn
get fi know bout staam
learn fi cling to di dawn
an wen mi hear mi daddy sick
mi quickly pack mi grip an tek a trip

mi nevah have noh time
wen mi reach
fi si noh sunny beach
wen mi reach
jus people a live in shack
people livin back-to-back
mongst cackroach an rat
mongst dirt an dizeez
subjek to terrorist attack
political intrigue
kanstant grief
an noh sign af relief

o di grass
turn brown
soh many trees
cut doun
an di lan is ovahgrown

fram country to town
is jus thistle an tawn
inna di woun a di poor
is a miracle ow dem endure

di pain nite an day
di stench af decay
di glarin sights
di guarded affluence
di arrogant vices
cole eyes af kantemp
di mackin symbals af independence

a deh soh mi bawn
get fi know bout staam
learn fi cling to di dawn
an wen di news reach mi
seh mi wan daddy ded
mi ketch a plane quick

an wen mi reach mi sunny isle
it woz di same ole style
di money well dry
di bullits dem a fly
plenty innocent a die
many rivahs run dry
ganja plane flyin high
di poor man im a try
yu tink a lickle try im try
holdin awn bye an bye
wen a dallah cant buy
a lickle dinnah fi a fly

galang dada
galang gwaan yaw sah
yu nevah ad noh life fi live
jus di wan life fi give
yu did yu time pan ert
yu nevah get yu jus dizert
galang goh smile inna di sun
galang goh satta inna di palace af peace

mi knows yu couldn tek it dada
di anguish an di pain
di suffahrin di prablems di strain
di strugglin in vain
fi mek two ens meet
soh dat dem pickney coulda get
a lickle someting fi eat
fi put cloaz pan dem back
fi put shoes pan dem feet
wen a dallah cant buy
a lickle dinnah fi a fly

mi know yu try dada
yu fite a good fite
but di dice dem did loaded
an di card pack fix
yet still yu reach fifty-six
before yu lose yu leg wicket
'a noh yu bawn grung here'
soh wi bury yu a Stranger's Burying Groun
near to mhum an cousin Daris
nat far fram di quarry
doun a August Town

Di Black Petty-Booshwah
(for Railton Youth Club members)

dem wi' gi' whey dem talent to di State
an' di black workin' class andahrate
dem wi' side wid oppressah
w'en di goin' get ruff
side wid aggressah
w'en di goin' get tuff

dem a black petty-booshwah
dem full a flaw
an' dem a black petty-booshwah
dem full a flaw

tru dem seh dem edicate dem a gwaan irate
true dem seh dem edicate dem a seek tap rate
dem a seek posishan
aaf di backs af blacks
seek promoshan
aaf di backs of blacks

dem a black petty-booshwah
dem full a flaw
an' dem a black petty-booshwah
dem full a flaw

dem a run-up dem mout' an' a shout all about
tru dem have a lat a dou't 'bout di stren't af blacks
dem a run-up dem mout'
an' a shout all about
but w'en wi launch wi attack
dem wi' haffi dress back

dem a black petty-booshwah
dem full a flaw
an' dem a black petty-booshwah
dem full a flaw!

Song of Rising
(for Sista Vi who knows why)

> 'dere'ill be peace / in da valley / some day' – ROMAN STEWART

dere'ill be peace
in da valley
some day.

yu got to do as de say;
yu got to find a way;
swing wid de swing;
risehup de sway!
let all man say:
risehup de sway!

dere'ill be love
in da valley
some day.

yu got to fite
fe yu rite
wid yu mite
fe yu life
fe suvvive
an be wise
an strive

in peace
wid love
den...

dere'ill be peace
in da valley
forever

dere'ill be love / in da valley / forever

Di Great Insohreckshan

it woz in April nineteen eighty-wan
doun inna di ghetto af Brixtan
dat di babylan dem cause such a frickshan
an it bring about a great insohreckshan
an it spread all ovah di naeshan
it woz truly an histarical okayjan

it woz event af di year
an I wish I ad been dere
wen wi run riot all ovah Brixtan
wen wi mash-up plenty police van
wen wi mash-up di wicked wan plan
wen we mash-up di Swamp Eighty-wan
fi wha?
fi mek di rulah dem andahstan
dat wi naw tek noh more a dem oppreshan

an wen mi check out
di ghetto grapevine
fi fine out all I coulda fine
evry rebel jussa revel in dem story
dem a taak bout di powah an di glory
dem a taak bout di burnin an di lootin
dem a taak bout smashin an di grabbin
dem a tell mi bout di vanquish an di victri

dem seh: di babylan dem went too far
soh wha?
wi ad woz fi bun two kyar
an wan an two innocent get mar
but wha?
noh soh it goh sometime inna war
een star
noh soh it goh sometime inna war?

dem seh? win bun dung di George
wi coulda bun di lanlaad
wi bun dung di George
wi nevah bun di lanlaad
wen wi run riot all ovah Brixtan
wen wi mash-up plenty police van
wen wi mash-up di wicked wan plan
wen we mash-up di Swamp Eighty-wan

dem seh: wi commandeer kyar
an wi ghaddah aminishan
wi buil wi barricade
an di wicked ketch afraid
wi sen out wi scout
fi goh fine dem whereabout
den wi faam-up wi passi
an wi mek wi raid

now dem run gaan
goh plan countah-hackshan
but di plastic bullit
an di waatah cannon
will bring a blam-blam
will bring a blam-blam
nevah mine Scarman
will bring a blam-blam

MICHAEL SMITH

Michael Smith was born in 1954 in Kingston, Jamaica. On 17
August 1983 he was stoned to death by four men at Stony Hill,
St Andrew, Jamaica, during the election campaign. When they
stopped him in the street, he told his attackers: 'I-man free to
walk anywhere in this land.'

His father was a mason, his mother a factory worker. While
claiming he'd picked up most of his education on the street, he
nevertheless enrolled at the Jamaica School of Drama, and by
the time he graduated in 1980, he had become a popular performer
of his poetry in Jamaica.

Before taking Britain and Europe by storm in 1982, he had
appeared on a BBC *Arena* film of Carifesta in Barbados in 1981
reciting his celebrated poem 'Me Cyaan Believe It'. He made one
record (single) in Jamaica, *Word* (Light of Saba, Kingston, 1978);
two further singles followed in 1980 on Linton Kwesi Johnson's
LKJ label, *Me Cyaan Believe It* and *Roots*. In 1982 his LP record
Me Cyaan Believe It (produced by Dennis Bovell and Linton Kwesi
Johnson) was released by Island, and he went on a tour of music
venues with reggae singer Gregory Isaacs.

His only book, *It A Come*, was published in 1986, and received
a Poetry Book Society Recommendation. He had worked on some
of the poem texts with Mervyn Morris, who edited the book for
Race Today.

Interview with Michael Smith

by MERVYN MORRIS
(*extract*)

Michael Smith was interviewed on 27 May 1981.

MM: *Mikey, when did you start writing?*
MS: Me can't remember the year. But me know is a good time. Me kind of did get discourage one of the time, because me did write a whole exercise book a thing and show the old man, and him never really too check of it, cause him did seh well right now you can't make you living by that, so him jus bun it up.
MM: *You mean, literally burnt it up?*
MS: Mmhm. Him burn it up. An then me just cool off. And then me meet in a accident and when me deh pon the hospital now me seh, 'Cho, me jus a go write again.'
MM: *What was the accident? How did it happen?*
MS: Me fall off a tree when time me a youth, and...
MM: *Fall off a what?*
MS: Tree. A mango tree. And bruck me two hand. Two wrist-dem. And me lick out me knee and lick up the head and the hip.
MM: *How old were you at that time?*
MS: About 14.
MM: *Is that why you limp?*
MS: Mmhm. Not gunshot, as some people think.
MM: *I don't know who thinks that. Where did you go to school?*
MS: Oh. School. Well, most of the thing what me learn, you know, a pon the street still. Me go a whole heap of school. Me never too love school, still. Me go a Jones Town Primary School, me go a Denham Town, me go a KC Extension, me go a St George's, me go Lincoln College; but one of the thing what firm me up still was drama school. But me really did learn more mongst me and me brethren-dem because we used to sit in and we used to reason and me used to read whole heap, whole heap, whole heap from me did small.
MM: *What sort of thing did you like to read?*
MS: History, you know. History me used to penetrate.
MM: *What do you read now? Do you read much now?*
MS: Yeh, man. As a writer you can't stop read, you know. The more you read the more you know and the more you consciousness build. Me is a man read all kind a literature. Sometime me read

little comic, you know, but me read. If a one come to me and seh, 'Boy, a think you should read this book', me go inna it. Me no really have no biasness as such. Whe knowledge is concern one fi just go out deh and get it and see wha a gwaan. Me really believe seh you have fi learn the ABC of Babylon fi destroy them. So you know you haffi really have a sense of awareness of what's happening around, so you can explain to people wha a gwaan.

MM: *You said the School of Drama helped in your development. What did you get from the drama school?*

MS: Well, me get a insight and awareness of your whole structure – your body as such, how fi use it, how fi use your voice, how to lay out a show, how to direct a show. Me get a whole heap of artistic training, and me can express it now. First time me couldn't express it. And it make me much more stronger and much more confident. As both a writer and a performer. And you find that sometimes it even create conflict within me, because sometime you want specialise and you seh, 'Cho, better you just direct and just cool.' And you seh, 'Cho, better you just act and just cool out.' And you seh 'Cho, better you just write and just cool.' You know. Well, is just fi mesh the whole thing what you can do. It develop a whole heap of my talent. Other areas what I never know seh I coulda do.

MM: *Do you have a priority now? In what order would you rate your interest in acting, writing and directing?*

MS: Me a one writer first, me a one actor second, and me a one director third.

MM: *Can you recall your first big success?*

MS: As a writer?

MM: *Yes. As a writer. You know: as somebody who was writing but was also writing for performance in many cases, and performing what he wrote.*

MS: The first big thing for me, still, was when people start listen to me. That was the first big thing. That time you know seh you a seh something important. And it was at the community level. When you read a poem pon a youth club show and them listen, and them seh them want more. That was the first big thing for me. Major thing for me. Me read a whole heap a youth club, you know. Whole heap a youth club. But I think the first reading take place right down in Golden Spring. Down a Golden Spring Community Centre. And, yeh, it was some poem about Ian Smith. One morning me did get up and just see Smith seh no to black majority rule, and me just write a poem, and jus go down, and them have a function and me just read it. And them just love it. And just respond to it.

MM: *Many of us first became aware of your talent and the strength of it when we heard 'Me Seh Me Cyaan Believe It'. When did you write that, and when did you first perform it before any large gathering?*

MS: Me no remember the year, you know. Me no remember the year.

MM: *Tell me something about how you view your role as a poet. What are you trying to do?*

MS: Really just try fi make people aware, you know, of certain things. I have fi really try fi educate a lot of people out inna earth, because, Jamaica how it rest ya now, a whole heap of we can't read and write, you know. And we seem to rally round the spoken word very nice; and politician have it pat, if you want a good demonstration of that. So when I write now I just want them fi understand wha I a deal with: describe the condition which them live in but to also say, 'Boy, don't submerge yourself under the pressure. You can do better, and if you organise yourself and you make demands on who there is to make demands on then you will achieve your objective. And just break up the little dependency attitude that is so characteristic of J.A.' Poetry as a vehicle of giving hope. As a means of building them awareness as such. Poetry is a part of the whole process of the whole liberation of the people.

MM: *So you see your poetry as, in the broadest sense, political?*

MS: It political. More than political, still, you know. It more than political. It, it written out of a political experience of political and social environment. And as such it transmit that message, but it also is not within a partisan politician sense, partisan politics. It also have its international arena to stand up in, and it also seh to people, 'Look, not you suffering here alone. There is other people far out – Britain, wherever it is. So you know, you have to link your experience and don't make them limit your percep-tions to only here, and you only think with your belly and can't use your head. And just see the wider what-is-happening, and have a more broader perspective of global international and social politics and how it affect your life, and know it affect you.

MM: *Yes. Have you ever been conscious of having offended people by poems that you wrote and recited?*

MS: Me have a funny way, you know. Me can offend people and them still like it.

MM: *But I remember being present at a performance where one of your poems which was, I think, being critical of people who were pretending to be Rasta but presumably were not authentic – where that poem clearly caused offence among some brethren who called out loudly, 'What about the baldhead? What about the baldhead?'*

MS: Yeh. Me remember that now. Yes. Me remember that night-deh. Me naw apologise for it. A just some of the contradiction that is inherent in certain things that, you know, you just have fi point out and seh, 'What happen to that? What you a deal with?' So if them want balance it off with 'What happen to the bald-heads?' well, me lick out gainst baldhead too. Me no partial. Me no sectarian inna my view. Me lick out gainst baldhead, PNP, JLP, any one of them P-deh.

MM: *Yes. But have you ever felt any pressure to conform to a particular party line or ideological view?*

MS: Yes, sometime me feel that way-deh. Yeh. One and one come to me and seh, 'Boy, if you do this . . .' But sometime me have a anarchist tendency, which part me can listen to you sometime and then me just bus out and just seh 'Go weh!', and me just no deal with you, and me just go do what me want to do. Me have an attitude, me know, of not caring sometime. So regardless of how you come and tell me seh, 'Boy, you no fi do this, and you do that, and you do that . . .' – the devil know what – and sometimes is really fi divert your energies, you know. You have to always be aware. A no everyone who come to you an give you advice really mean you good, you know. Some of them really come fi destroy you. And me no inna that. Well, so me feel pressures. Me feel pressures. One come to me and them talk to me, but, you know, me make them know how me feel.

MM: *Yes. Do you write many poems that you would consider personal? Or are the poems all of them very much community based and community directed?*

MS: Well, me check seh anyhow me feel, other people feel it too. So me just no seh, 'Well, a me one a feel da-way-yah. Me feel seh anything me feel, everybody feel it too, so when time me write it me just no write it fi how me feel. Me write it fi other people. So it encompass other people's feeling. Cause if me feel hungry tonight, me know seh a next man out there a feel hungry tonight. So me just write. So anytime me seh, 'Boy, me hungry', me know seh another out deh a feel it, for me a feel it too.

MM: *Have you written love poems, for example? Or poems about*

the death of a relative or friend?
MS: Well, you see, anytime you dead, you dead. There is work
to be done and the living have fi do it, so the living have fi carry
it on. So although it is good to mention those that is past – right?
– me can't get bogged down into lamentation all day long. You
know. So you have work fi go on, so me just deal with it. People
deh really a feel the pinch, so you deal with it. Me can't bother
go talk bout auntie and all uncle who pass away, and school teacher
or something.
MM: *What about love? For example, in the work of Oku Onuora
and Mutabaruka and many other poets people would find it
natural to compare you with, there are praise poems or love
poems, which seem to be more or less absent from your work.*
MS: Love inna my work, still. All a my works-dem have love inna
it; because the love fi a people, that's what me a write about –
them things-deh, you know. Is a love fi them, and is a determina-
tion fi see that whatever exploitation is being meted out to them
is not being perpetrated; so is a passion that drive me to them.
But if you talk bout lovey-lovey stuff...
MM: *You know, like Oku's poem, 'I exclaim inly/ in wonderment/
at your sight'. I mean that kind of thing.*
MS: No, me no reach deh-so yet. Me just probably don't reach
there yet.
MM: *Now tell me something about the way in which you compose.
How do you go about composing these poems? I'm talking now
about the more or less physical process. What do you do? Do you
make it up in your head and keep it for several days until you
have sorted it out, or do you tend to write it down and change it
up? How do you go about it?*
MS: Well, you see, it come – it all come, first and foremost, from
a process of observation. Me is a man walk whole heap a street.
Me walk all hours a night. And practically walk go anywhere too.
And it seems to me that what happen is that I observe a lot, and
I listen a whole heap, so I will all go stand up at a bus stop and
spend all two hours, no because me a wait pon bus or so, but
because me waan hear wha them a seh. Just basically waan hear
what people seh and how them talk and the phrases, you know.
A man seh, 'Boy, me can't believe it, that the thing gone up, you
know.' Me seh 'Rahtid, a it that, you know! We can't believe it.
And when you can't believe it and you look and you see the things
that you can't believe!' And then me go home now and me seh,
'Yeh. Poem now. I waan get a poem. "Cyaan believe it". That's

the poem I want.' And then it slowly evolve. It might work out. You might jot it down – line, piece a line – and you go weh and you leave it, and then you come back and you build on it. Or it might come 'roops', right out. The whole intensity just come right out and you just really – it release. Or sometimes a rhythm come to me first. You know, is a rhythm, and me seh, 'Dah rhythm-ya feel nice, you know, feel nice.' And then me try remember the rhythm. And when time me go home me seh, 'Boy! "Can't take it inna Babylon, da, da, da/ Can't take it inna Babylon, da, da, da".' And if that is the line what I going ride now, I seh, 'Yeh. "Da, da, da/ Can't take it i…"'', and then I build under that, build up under that. Build under that and catch me breaks and the bridges. Just like how a musician a work out. Cause I very close to musicians. And so I really pay a lot of attention how musician work out.

MM: *What do you mean by, 'I'm very close to musicians'? Do you yourself play music, or have you been a listener for many years, or are you a close friend of musicians?*

MS: Well, me listen to music fi a number of years, cause me used to love dance, and me still love dance, and me still go dance and listen DJ and all them thing-deh. And out that, you know, man get fi start know the musician-dem now wha actually play the music, and me start go mongst them and rest mongst them; and some a them me and them a friend, you know, very good friends. When them a rehearse, you know, me sit down deh. Me can't play any instrument, still. Me only can probably keep a little drum beat, you know. Congo drum beat. Me sit down there, and me listen to them, and me see how them work out. See how them work out. And me seh, 'Yeh!' Or might seh, 'Well, that no sound good. If him did do that and that, it woulda come out much better.' But me is a man who have built-in rhythms inna my head. And me can hear them. And built-in sounds in my head. And sometime when time me even work out with a musician, although I can't work out the music structurally, I say it. I tell them I hear this and them must try hear that too. And we don't stop rehearse until him get out wha inna my head. So I carry it in my head. I can hear it. I can carry it. I know I do that, you know.

MM: *Right. In addition to hearing the music rhythms or hearing rhythms you are clear about and want to follow through, do you like saying your poems to the accompaniment of music?*

MS: Yes, sometimes. But, you see, musician is a very funny set of people-dem. Sometime them ego get big, you know; them ego

get big and them want outshine you, or them want outplay you.
Or them get carried away. To me, to work with a musician me
have fi know the musician-dem. Me have fi know them very close.
Me have fi know them very good. So that me can seh to them seh,
'Well, watch-ya. Don't bother go, you know; don't bother go inna
it too hard! And just cool out. And just know how you a run it.'
And then now we can work and we ketch the vibes, and then we
go properly. But me love work out with musicians. But man who
and me close. Me no like work with you until me know you. Me
like to feel very close to man and man wha me work with. More
like you feel a oneness. So me couldn't really go work with any
and any musician, you know.

MM: *The name "dub poetry" has been applied to some of the
poetry with which you are associated. Can you tell me how the
name arose?*

MS: You see "dub poetry" now? Dub poetry come out a argument,
you know. One argument wha surround Orlando Wong – formerly
Orlando Wong, wha name Oku Onuora – Noel Walcott and myself.
We just deh a reason. And it just come out. We identify the same
thing we find run through Langston Hughes poems. Langston
Hughes have a blues mood go through it, and we just feel seh,
well, we have something, and we seh boy it was the beat. And we
realise now that because we is a people who we go whole heap a
dance and different, we influence by that sound system. Sound
system. And is it we carry with we. And the DJ, the DJ twisting
and turning. Still, I-man was hit first, I was fascinated first by
the storeman-dem down a Orange Street. Little pink and black
store, Orange Street. The man used to seh, 'Come-een, come-een,
come-buy-up, buy-up. But no come-een, come-een, come tief-up,
tief-up, cause we wi beat-up, beat-up!' A so them used to advertise
them little thing, and me did just fascinated by that little rhythms,
you know. And then me just feel seh me coulda do one too and
do it better. So, you know, the whole thing start, and you just
start to find different analogy. But dub poetry? Dub going to be
the future, you know, a reggae music. A deh-so it a go go. It a go
dub-wise. It haffi go dub-wise.

MM: *Do you think your poetry would be widely accepted in book
form? Or does it depend so much on performance that it really
ought to be on records or presented in performance?*

MS: Both of them go together. It's very good for documentational
purposes to have it in book form, but also to hear it is another
experience.

*　　*　　*

MM: *By readings 'far out' you mean readings internationally?*
MS: Yes.
MM: *Is your work understood by people who are not close to Jamaican language and culture?*
MS: You can feel it. If you can't understand some of it, you can feel it. Which is a nice little thing wha I probably bless with, you know. Me have a way of just going in and be transformed, totally be transformed, that bridge the gap, you know. Me always seem to be able fi do it, you know, so there is no problem as such. There is no problem. We haffi really look into the whole thing of the language thing, because sometime it is used in a negative sense as a hindrance to your progress, and people think seh, 'Boy, why don't you communicate in Standard English?' Standard English is good to be communicated in what you also comfortable in. And what is widely being used by your own people from which you draw these source. So that's why me communicate da-way-deh. And if me can really spend some time fi try learn the Englishman language and so, the Englishman can spend some time fi learn wha me seh too, you know – or the American, fi that matter, any one a them, it no really matter. Them can really spend some time and understand. That's the only way them can get over some of them romanticism that them have bout Jamaica and Jamaican people, especially Rasta. You know, spend some time and really get a good grasp of the whole cultural expression and the cultural movements as such.
MM: *What exactly do you mean by 'romanticism about Rasta'?*
MS: Whole heap a people come and extract the symbols of Rastafari. Them feel seh if them put on a red, green and gold belt or them have a badge wha mark 'Ites A Lion' them just automatically become Rasta. And is really just extracting symbols and spouting mock rituals of poverty or some religious chat which really – Rasta don't stop at that, you know. Rasta go further than that. And them people-deh really just come fi divert people's energy and attention, and really get people captivate into all kinds of foolishness, you know. Them do more harm to the movement than anything else. But through some a we so steep inna we ignorance now, and feel seh anything wha white is right we just lock them up and just embrace them. Still, some a the time a fool we a fool them still, because we a master at the Anancy deception game at times.
MM: *Tell me something about your own relation to Rasta. Are*

you Rasta? How would you describe your relation to Rasta?
MS: Me is very close to Rasta, you know. Very, very close. In that a lot a things inna Rasta me can understand, and me can identify with. A that really make me very close. Some Rastaman would seh me is Rasta already, because me talk of the things of Rasta and my expression is of Rasta. Me no want too comment pon da question-yah, still, because it use fi divide up, divide we up; and me no too really want go inna it, you know. Me just seh me is very close to Rasta.
MM: *Rastas have described you as seeming like Rasta, but you are not describing yourself as Rasta.*
MS: Rastaman seh from you born and you come to a certain consciousness bout you people and them livity and which part them supposed to be heading as a people, you is Rasta. So a baldhead can be a Rasta. Him no have fi have locks. You understand? A just that me have fi seh pon the whole thing a Rasta, you know.

*   *   *

Me Cyaan Believe It

Me seh me cyaan believe it
me seh me cyaan believe it

Room dem a rent
me apply widin
but as me go een
cockroach rat an scorpion
also come een

Waan good
nose haffi run
but me naw go siddung pon high wall
like Humpty Dumpty
me a face me reality

One little bwoy come blow im horn
an me look pon im wid scorn
an me realise how me five bwoy-picni
was a victim of de trick
dem call partisan politricks

an me ban me belly
an me bawl
an me ban me belly
an me bawl
Lawd
me cyaan believe it
me seh me cyaan believe it

Me daughter bwoy-frien name Sailor
an im pass through de port like a ship
more gran-picni fi feed
an de whole a we in need
what a night what a plight
an we cyaan get a bite
me life is a stiff fight
an me cyaan believe it
me seh me cyaan believe it

Sittin on de corner wid me frien
talkin bout tings an time
me hear one voice seh
'Who dat?'
Me seh 'A who dat?'
'A who a seh who dat
when me a seh who dat?'

When yuh teck a stock
dem lick we dung flat
teet start fly
an big man start cry
me seh me cyaan believe it
me seh me cyaan believe it

De odder day
me a pass one yard pon de hill
When me teck a stock me hear
'Hey, bwoy!'
'Yes, mam?'
'Hey, bwoy!'
'Yes, mam!'
'Yuh clean up de dawg shit?'
'Yes, mam.'

An me cyaan believe it
me seh me cyaan believe it

Doris is modder of four
get a wuk as a domestic
Boss man move een
an bap si kaisico she pregnant again
bap si kaisico she pregnant again
an me cyaan believe it
me seh me cyaan believe it

Deh a yard de odder night
when me hear 'Fire! Fire!'
'Fire, to plate claat!'
Who dead? You dead!
Who dead? Me dead!
Who dead? Harry dead!
Who dead? Eleven dead!
Woeeeeeeee
Orange Street fire
deh pon me head
an me cyaan believe it
me seh me cyaan believe it

Lawd
me see some blackbud
livin inna one buildin
but no rent no pay
so dem cyaan stay
Lawd
de oppress an de dispossess
cyaan get no res

Wha nex?

Teck a trip from Kingston
to Jamaica
Teck twelve from a dozen
an me see me mumma in heaven
Madhouse! Madhouse!

Me seh me cyaan believe it
me seh me cyaan believe it

Yuh believe it?
How yuh fi believe it
when yuh laugh
an yuh blind yuh eye to it?

But me know yuh believe it
Lawwwwwwwwwd
me know yuh believe it

I An I Alone

I an I alone
a trod through creation.
Babylon on I right, Babylon on I lef,
Babylon in front of I an Babylon behind I,
an I an I alone in the middle
like a Goliath wid a sling-shot.

'Ten cent a bundle fi me calaloo!
Yuh a buy calaloo, dread? Ten cent.'

Everybody a try fi sell someting,
everybody a try fi grab someting,
everybody a try fi hustle someting,
everybody a try fi kill someting,

but ting an ting mus ring,
an only a few can sing
cause dem naw face de same sinting.

(Sung) *It's a hard road to travel*
An a mighty long way to go.
Jesus, me blessed Saviour,
will meet us on the journey home.

'Shoppin bag! Shoppin bag! Five cent fi one!'
'Green pepper! Thyme! Skellion an pimento!'
'Remember de Sabbath day, to keep it holy!
Six days shalt thou labour,
but on the seventh day shalt thou rest.'
'Hi, mam, how much fi dah piece a yam deh?'
'No, no dat; dat! Yes; dat!'
'Three dollars a poun, nice gentleman.'
'Clear out! Oonoo country people too damn tief!'
'Like yuh mumma!'
'Fi-me mumma? Wha yuh know bout me mumma?'
'Look ya, a might push dis inna yuh!'
'Yuh lie! A woulda collar yuh!'
'Bruck it up! But, dread, cool down!'
'All right, cool down. Rastafari!'

De people-dem a teck everyting meck a muckle.
Dem a try fi hustle down de price
fi meck two ends meet,
de odder one a try fi push up de price
fi meck de picni backbone get sinting fi eat.
But two teet meet an dem a bark,
dem cyaan stan de pressure,
dem tired fi compete wid hog an dawg,
but dem mus aspire fi someting better
although dem dungle-heap ketch a fire.

Cyaan meck blood outa stone,
an cow never know de use a im tail
till fly teck it, but from dem born
dem a fan de fly of poverty from dem ass
for dem never have a tail fi cover it.

'Watch me, watch me, watch me!' 'Hey, handcart-bwoy,
mind yuh lick dung me picni-dem, yuh know!'
'Tief! Tief! Tief!' 'Whe im deh?
Look out, meck a bruck im friggin neck!'
'Im a one a de P-dem!'

Yuh see it? Zacky was me frien
but look how im life a go end?
Party politics play de trick
an it lick im dung
wid de big coocoomacca stick.

I an I alone
a trod through creation,
Babylon on me right, Babylon on me lef,
Babylon in front of I an Babylon behind I,
an I an I alone inna de middle
like a Goliath wid a sling-shot.

'Picni-dem a bawl,
rent to pay,
wife to obey,
but only Jesus know de way!
De meek shall inherit de earth
an de fulness thereof!'

But look what she inherit?
Six months pregnant, five mout fi feed,
an her man deh a jail, no bail.

'Cho, Roy, man! Let me go, no, man?
Me no want no man inna '81!'
'So wha happen? It was only '80
yuh did a teck man? Cho, Doris, man,
consider dis late application.'

Dem waan meck love pon hungry belly
jus fi figet dis moment of poverty
but she mus get breed
an dem haffi go face dem calamity.

'Joshua did seh oonoo fi draw oonoo belt tight.'
'Which belt, when me tripe a come through me mout?'
'What happen, sah, yuh get deliver? Yuh naw answer?'
'Hi, lady, yuh believe in Socialism?'
'No, sah, me believe in social livin.'

'Calaloo! Shoppin bag! Thyme!'
'Dinner mints! Cigarettes an Wrigley's!'
'Hi, Albert, which part Tiny?'
'Hi, sah, beg yuh a ten cent, no?'
'Meck yuh no leave de man alone?'
'Hi, sexy! Honey-bunch! Sugar-plum!'
'Dog-shit! Cow-shit!'

I an I alone
a trod through creation,
Babylon on I right, Babylon on I lef,
Babylon behind I an Babylon in front of I,
an I an I alone inna de middle
like a Goliath wid a sling-shot.

Lawd, a find a ten cent.
Lawd, we naw go get no sentance.

Give Me Little Dub Music

Give me little dub music
right ya so
tonight

Give me little dub music
right ya so
tonight

A have dis haunted feelin
so meck we bat een
an ketch a reasonin

No bodder talk bout anyting too tough
Skip de usual stuff
dat yuh out a luck
a look fi wuk
an meck we seat up

We no mourners
We naw go watch weself
go down de road
like witherin flowers

An jus
give me little dub music
right ya so
tonight

Give me little dub music
right ya so
tonight

For we search we head an we heart
down to we very soul
an we still waan someting else fi hold
We naw go stop
an come off a Brutas Pass
We waan someting
dat will last

An de more dis-ya system-ya squeeze we
fire boun fi gush outa we

So jus excuse me
an give me pass
an meck a chat to yuh boss
for im a rock out me
for im a rock out me
me rass

fi jus
give me little dub music
right ya so
tonight

Give me little dub music
right ya so
tonight

dat anytime we have a power cut
a no lies an deceit an hypocrisy
full up I-man gut

So jus
give me little dub music
right ya so
tonight

Give me little dub music
right ya so
tonight

Say, Natty-Natty

Say,
Natty-Natty,
no bodder
dash weh
yuh culture!

Say, Natty-Natty,
no bodder
dash weh
yuh culture!

For de teacher man know it
but im naw tell de sheep
dat ratta ratta
no bring back new teet
when yuh dash weh de spliff
an yuh teck up de sniff.

Remember yard is yuh mumma,
pon groun yuh sleep,
a seh she teck yuh picni
when yuh tired fi breed,
an if yuh no sleep
yuh mumma no sleep
an if yuh a go die
she a beg Gawd
meck she die too.

So say,
Natty-Natty
no bodder
dash weh
yuh culture!

Say,
Natty-Natty,
no bodder
dash weh
yuh culture!

Yuh no country-come-to-town,
yuh born a Jam-down,
so no figet yuh gal a yard
an teck one from abroad
an lick out pon de beach
an ejaculate
between a *Time* magazine.
Dem will spread it
pon a Boo York scene
seh yuh's a dollar-a-day dread.
A better yuh bald yuh head!

So say, Natty-Natty,
no bodder
dash weh
yuh culture!

So say, Natty-Natty,
no bodder
dash weh
yuh culture!

A know yuh disillusion
when yuh see de politician
im teck out yuh daughter
an im buy her supper
an im get her fat
an im call it culture.

But say, Natty-Natty,
be aware of de cultural smuggler!
Say, Natty-Natty,
be aware of de cultural smuggler!

No bodder teck we revolution, man,
so tun touris attraction!

GRACE NICHOLS

Grace Nichols was born in 1950 in Guyana, where she grew up and worked, among other things, as a journalist. She came to Britain in 1977, and has since published three books of poems. Her first, *I is a long memoried woman* (Karnac House, London, 1983), won the 1983 Commonwealth Poetry Prize. *The Fat Black Woman's Poems* (1984) and *Lazy Thoughts of a Lazy Woman* (1989) are published by Virago, who also brought out her first adult novel, *Whole of a Morning Sky* (1986), which is set in Guyana.

Her books for children include: two collections of short stories published by Hodder, *Trust You Wriggly* (1980) and *Leslyn in London* (1984); a book of poems, *Come On In To My Tropical Garden* (A & C Black, 1988); and an anthology, *Black Poetry* (Blackie, 1988; reissued as *Poetry Jump Up* by Penguin, 1989). She was awarded an Arts Council bursary in 1988 to work on a new cycle of poems.

Home Truths

by GRACE NICHOLS

If I have to describe myself as coming from a particular part of
the world I like to think of myself as a Caribbean person; because
the Caribbean embraces so much it's like saying you're a poet of
the world. For psychically, you're at once connected to Africa
(which I see as a kind of spiritual homeland), Europe, Asia, and
the Americas.

My early childhood was spent in a small country village along
the Guyana coast and my most treasured memory is of myself,
around the age of six, standing calf-deep in rippling goldish brown
water, watching the moving shapes of fish just below the sunlit
surface. This picture stands out like an oasis in my memory and
whenever I return to it, it's still one of infinite beauty, magic and
grace.

When I was eight years old I moved to the city, Georgetown,
with my five sisters, brother, mother and father. My mother was
a warm, intelligent, loving woman who was full of stories, anec-
dotes and songs from her own childhood. People loved being
around her and I can't remember a single day when our home
wasn't visited by some friend, neighbour or relative who had drop-
ped in 'just fuh a minute' but ended up staying hours (much to
our delight) and sharing in whatever was being cooked. I'm sure
my father, who was more private and reticent, didn't welcome as
many people present in our house all the time. But we relished
it. There were no distractions like television and I for one was
always in the midst of friends and relatives listening to their every
word, all the jokes, stories, some a bit on the bawdy side. My
mother's half-hearted attempts to drive me from the room on
these occasions nearly always failed.

As a child, at home, with a lot of books, I was a regular book
hound. My father who was a headmaster managed to get boxes
of old books from the Public Free Library from time to time for
his school and would keep some of these for his own and our
reading.

My early exposure to poetry was very much in the English
tradition, which would have been the norm in any British colony.
Through our school text books, West Indian and Royal Readers,
I was thrown into contact with 'The boy stood on the burning deck

whence all but he had fled.' But curled safely between the pages
of discarded library books I also discovered the soulful weariness
of the home-ward-plodding ploughman whose heartful sadness I
identified with completely; the magic and mystery of Christina
Rossetti's *Goblin Market*; and a little later, Shakespeare's beaut-
iful sonnets. These to my young ears were the music of poetry.

I left high school when I was sixteen without taking my A Levels,
as I was eager to start earning my own money, so I escaped having
to dissect poems and am only vaguely conscious of words like
scansion. I guess my poetry comes out of my own perception of
what is poetry — a heightened imagistic use of language that does
things to the heart and head.

After high school I worked among other things, as a primary
school teacher, a clerk at a telephone company, a reporter and
freelance journalist. I had also done a Diploma in Communica-
tions at the University of Guyana. I was lucky that part of the
course work meant spending some time in the hinterland of our
vast and ruggedly beautiful country. No one who experiences the
Guyana hinterland remains unchanged — the magnitude and
density of the forests, the sudden sheer drop, when flying by
helicopter, over a mountain's stark face, the dark mysterious
rivers and waterfalls, all leave their primeval imprint on the
psyche forever.

It wasn't surprising that the very first adult short story I ever
wrote was set in this region. I also began research into collecting
Guyanese folktales and Amerindian myths, some of which appear
in a small self-published collection for children, *Baby Fish and
other stories*. It was only after coming to England in 1977 that
poetry began to play a bigger and bigger part in my life. I started
to read more of the work of other Caribbean and Black American
poets. Having been surrounded by a lot of English poetry as a
child I found that Caribbean poetry helped to put me in touch
with the different rhythms, orality and atmosphere of our own
culture. I myself like working in both standard English and
Creole, and tend to want to fuse the two tongues because I come
from a background where the two were constantly interacting.

Though I still enjoy the work of some English poets, there comes
a time when I feel like something that sounds different to the ear.
Something that looks different to the eye on the page. Something
with a different rhythm. But in writing a poem I don't consciously
set out to write it in Creole or standard English. The language,
like the form and rhythm, dictates itself.

In both my fiction and poetry, women characters figure strongly, for I am conscious that Caribbean female characters have largely been portrayed by men. But while exploring my female heritage does excite my imagination at a conscious level, writing is also very much an unconscious process.

I is a long memoried woman in fact owes its inspiration to a dream I had one night of a young African girl swimming from Africa to the Caribbean with a garland of flowers around her. When I woke up I interpreted the dream to mean that she was trying to cleanse the ocean of the pain and suffering that her ancestors had gone through in that crossing from Africa to the New World. So the book sprang from that dream which is echoed in one of the poems:

> even in dreams I will submerge myself
> swimming like one possessed
> back and forth across that course
> strewing it with sweet smelling
> flowers
> one for everyone who made the journey

As the cycle of poems began to develop I was aware that I was dealing with my whole female history but I don't see my work as limited to women. In my novel for instance, the main character is Archie Worrell, inspired by my father. And when I give poetry readings both men and women respond to the Fat Black Woman with her quirky tongue-in-cheek look at the slimming and fashion industries. Poetry thankfully is a radical synthesising force. The erotic isn't separated from the political or spiritual.

[1989]

Those Women

Cut and contriving women
hauling fresh shrimps
up in their seines

standing waist deep
in the brown voluptuous
water of their own element

how I remember those women
sweeping in the childish rivers
of my eyes

and the fish slipping
like eels
through their laughing thighs

Extract from *I is a long memoried woman*

1
From dih pout
of mih mouth
from dih
treacherous
calm of mih smile
you can tell

I is a long memoried woman

2
We the women who toil
unadorn
heads tie with cheap
cotton

We the women who cut
clear fetch dig sing

We the women making
something from this
ache-and-pain-a-me
back-O-hardness

Yet we the women
whose praises go unsung
whose voices go unheard
whose deaths they sweep
aside
as easy as dead leaves

Night is her Robe

Night is her robe
Moon is her element

Quivering and alert
she's stepping out behind
the fields of sugarcane

She's stepping out softly
She's stepping out carefully
She's bending she's stalking
She's flitting she's crawling

Quivering and alert
she's coming to the edge
of her island forest

Now, with all the care
of a herbalist
she's gathering strange weeds
wild root
leaves with the properties
both to harm and to heal

Quivering and alert
Quivering and alert
she's leaving the edge
of her island forest

Sugar Cane

1

There is something
about sugarcane

He isn't what
he seem −

indifferent hard
and sheathed in blades

his waving arms
is a sign for help

his skin thick
only to protect
the juice inside
himself

2

His colour
is the aura
of jaundice
when he ripe

he shiver
like ague
when it rain

he suffer
from bellywork
burning fever
and delirium

just before
the hurricane
strike
smashing him to piece.

3

Growing up
is an art

he don't have
any control of

it is us
who groom and
weed him

who stick him
in the earth
in the first place

and when he
growing tall

with the help
of the sun
and rain

we feel the
need to strangle
the life

out of him

But either way he can't survive

5

He cast his shadow
to the earth

the wind is
his only mistress

I hear them
moving
in rustling tones

she shakes
his hard reserve

smoothing
stroking
caressing
all his length
shamelessly

I crouch
below them
quietly.

Epilogue

I have crossed an ocean
I have lost my tongue
from the root of the old one
a new one has sprung

*   *   *

From **The Fat Black Woman's Poems**

The Fat Black Woman's Motto on Her Bedroom Door

IT'S BETTER TO DIE IN THE FLESH OF HOPE
THAN TO LIVE IN THE SLIMNESS OF DESPAIR

Tropical Death

The fat black woman want
a brilliant tropical death
not a cold sojourn
in some North Europe far/forlorn

The fat black woman want
some heat/hibiscus at her feet
blue sea dress
to wrap her neat

The fat black woman want
some bawl
no quiet jerk tear wiping
a polite hearse withdrawal

The fat black woman want
all her dead rights
first night
third night
nine night
all the sleepless droning
red-eyed wake nights

In the heart
of her mother's sweetbreast
In the shade
of the sun leaf's cool bless
In the bloom
of her people's bloodrest

the fat black woman want
a brilliant tropical death yes

The Fat Black Woman's Instructions to a Suitor

Do the boogie-woogie
Do the hop
Do the Charlestown
Do the rock
Do the chicken funky
Do the foxtrot

Do the tango
Drop yourself like a mango
Do the minuet
Spin me a good ole pirouette
Do the highland fling
Get down baby
Do that limbo thing

After doing all that, and maybe mo
hope you have a little energy left
to carry me across the threshold

Small Questions Asked by the Fat Black Woman

Will the rains
cleanse the earth of shrapnel
and wasted shells

will the seas
toss up bright fish
in wave on wave of toxic shoal

will the waters
seep the shore

feeding slowly the greying
angry roots

will trees bear fruit

will I like Eve
be tempted once again
if I survive

Island Man

*(for a Caribbean island man in London
who still wakes up to the sound of the sea)*

Morning
and island man wakes up
to the sound of blue surf
in his head
the steady breaking and wombing

wild seabirds
and fishermen pushing out to sea
the sun surfacing defiantly

from the east
of his small emerald island
he always comes back   groggily groggily

Comes back to sands
of a grey metallic soar
                              to surge of wheels
in dull North Circular roar

muffling muffling
his crumpled pillow waves
island man heaves himself

Another London day

Shopping

I'm guilty of buying too little food

1 carton milk
1 carton juice
1 half chicken
a little veg and fruit

Why can't you buy
for more than one day
at a time
my old man whines

Still blank as a zombie
I wander supermarket aisles

The chunky red odours
behind the cellophane
cannot revive
the spritely apples
the lady reluctantly urging samples

Between the bulge of the shelf
and the cast of my eye
between the nerve of my trolley
and the will of my mind
I'm always paralysed

Winter Thoughts

I've reduced the sun
to the neat oblong of fire
in my living room

I've reduced the little
fleshy tongues of the vagina
to the pimpled grate
and the reddening licking
flames

I've reduced the sea
to the throbbing fruit
in me

And outside
the old rose tree
is once again winterdying

While I lay here sprawled
thinking
how sex and death
are always at the heart
of living

Two Old Black Men on a Leicester Square Park Bench

What do you dream of you
old black men sitting
on park benches staunchly
wrapped up in scarves
and coats of silence
eyes far away from the cold
grey and strutting
pigeon
ashy fingers trembling
(though it's said that the old
hardly ever feel the cold)

do you dream revolutions
you could have forged
or mourn
some sunfull woman you
might have known a
hibiscus flower
ghost memories of desire

O it's easy
to rainbow the past
after all the letters from
home spoke of hardships

and the sun was traded long ago

Be a Butterfly

Don't be a kyatta-pilla
Be a butterfly
old preacher screamed
to illustrate his sermon
of Jesus and the higher life

rivulets of well-earned
sweat sliding down
his muscly mahogany face
in the half-empty school church
we sat shaking with muffling
laughter
watching our mother trying to save
herself from joining the wave

only our father remaining poker face
and afterwards we always went home to
split peas Sunday soup
with dumplings, fufu and pigtail

Don't be a kyatta-pilla
Be a butterfly
Be a butterfly

That was de life preacher
and you was right

Never Enough

But where are my days
of leaning through window
parting the cool trades

Breezing out with Bo
In the shade of the back steps
Dress lapped between legs
Like a river. Loud ice in lemonade.
Bird-picked mangoes hiding in foliage.
Fowls grazing the back yard
Clean-neck, feather-neck,
Each solitary, eyes pulled down,
From the glare of the sun.
And Hibiscus, queen of all the flowers,
Cupped red and rude against the paling.
Still glistening with little mercuries
From the earlier shower
Of earth-smelling rain
But never enough to keep us rooted.

Possession

Europe has become part of my possession
but how to come to terms with the architecture

The walls too sealed and solid
the closed door against the cold

The ivy of my voice
can no longer climb towards the ceiling

To overhang
            green and listening.

Because She Has Come

Because she has come
with geometrical designs
upon her breasts

Because she has borne five children
and her belly criss-crossed
with little tongues of fire

Because she has braided her hair
in the cornrow, twisting it upwards
to show her high inner status

Because she has tucked
a bright wrap
about her Nubian brownness

Because she has stained her toes
with the juice of the henna
to attract any number of arrant males

Because she has the good sense
to wear a scarab
to protect her heart

Because she has a pearl
in the middle
of her lower delta

Give her honour
Give her honour, you fools,
Give her honour.

FRED D'AGUIAR

Fred D'Aguiar was born in 1960 in London of Guyanese parents, and grew up in Guyana. He returned to London in 1972, and later trained and worked as a psychiatric nurse before reading English with African and Caribbean Studies at the University of Kent. He was writer-in-residence for the London Borough of Lewisham in 1986-87, and at Birmingham Polytechnic in 1988-89, and is the Judith E. Wilson fellow at the University of Cambridge for 1989-90. He received a Guyana Prize for Poetry in 1988.

He has published three collections of poems: *Mama Dot* (1985) and *Airy Hall* (1989) from Chatto, and *British Subjects* (1993) from Bloodaxe. His play *High Life* was produced at the Albany Theatre in 1987, and *A Jamaican Airman Foresees His Death* was commissioned by the Royal Court Theatre in 1989. He has recently held a number of writer's residencies in the USA.

Zigzag Paths

by FRED D'AGUIAR

As children we used to try and catch fireflies by locking onto their zigzag, lights-on, lights-off flight in the dark, the same zigzag uncles told us to run in if chased by an alligator. When the lights of a firefly came on we dashed to it, in the brief dark that followed we slowed then stoodstill, momentarily lost in directionless night, left only with an afterglow. Then it would spark again forming an imaginary necklace of light that faded on itself.

Some of these poems arrived singly, in odd lines that resonated for me because tied to a childhood memory, lines with built-in images which burnt with a beacon's clarity in my mind's eye... in my eye and in my heart. I mean the lines *felt* as much as *meant* something; meaning and feeling occupied the same space.

Somehow these images have intensified with time, rather than blurred as might be expected. The concentrated light in the mind that allows some images and feelings to keep as-new, defying matter and time is owed in part to an early activity which demanded a similar effort of will and concentration. Fishing with makeshift rods, twine and tin hooks with anything for bait held the gaze for whole afternoons. You'd see first how once the string hit the water a wet creeps up it to the rod, seeing too the expanding rings of water made by the tin hook piercing the water's face, how the rings bounced off the pond's edge to return on themselves, and finally when a fish took the bait how a whirlpool seemed to begin at the centre of all that calm where the cork had bobbed daintily over the pleats ruffled up by any breeze.

Some of this charge is owed, too, to my efforts to catch the tsetse fly – an almost impossible task given that none of us knew where the tsetse slept, if it ever slept. Already convinced that our grandmother never closed her eyes except to blink (we'd tried staying awake more than once for as long as we could but she just kept on pottering around until the sound of her long dress on the floorboards and her weight creaking some of them sent us to sleep; or else rising so early we heard what we took to be the whistling of the only bird in the world, then realising, since it came from the kitchen and it was the sound of every bird that ever was, all rolled into one, it could only be her), we knew that the tsetse had the additional advantage of a compound eye, able to see behind as well as above its head, 360° vision, but not quite. Talk had it that a blind spot or more accurately a line continued along the tail of the tsetse. We therefore imagined a tightrope drawn from the tail to us as our walkway to it, an approach made sideways on and dead slow. This would take as long as it took to catch a wise old fish with our telltale rods. With patience and luck it was possible to get close to a tsetse, so close in fact you'd make out clearly the rigging of veins in its see-through wings and count the splinters on the paling fence the tsetse loved to use for its food-vigil. The last inches between us and the tsetse did not involve movement in the usual sense of the word, so much as a delicate adjustment of muscles in the toes clutching the grass as the weight shifted from the heel of the trailing leg to the ball of the foot that was forward, lengthening the arm and fingers for imminent capture. To lose the tsetse then, in that awkward pose, in the middle of nowhere, with it gone from the tip of the paling fence was compar-able only to having to bring in off the line the women's period-stained clothes, made into strips from old sheets, at a time of month when the moon was just past full and all the women in the house seemed to bleed at once.

On those full mooned nights it was possible to walk outdoors and believe we were walking on the clear bed of the shell pond. The body cut through light. Thought itself was somehow exter-nalised; we could see each other's thoughts in the slivers of moon emanating from each of us. Consequently we moved in unison and communicated without uttering a sound, each intuiting what the other would do next as the light formed one unbroken shaft after another from one mind across the solid night air to the next.

In the day the spell broke, though sun and moon frequently sat in the same sky. It was the sun which opened again the distances closed at night. This depth made by sunlight did not compromise clarity and definition in any way. If anything we were able to distinguish the faded colours in a dress or terylene shirt hundreds of yards away because the sun put back the colour repeated wash-ing had extracted. This trick of the light meant the horizon was not a zinc haze but a mosaic. A coin was visible from far by the glint it threw off acting as a daylight moon. A blade of grass set itself out from the rest of the field like a solitary whisker on an otherwise clean-shaven face. Don't ask me how. That was how the facts presented themselves to me then: an uncle stepping across a trench on a log that moved sprouting four legs a long tail and jaws that separated opening a poles'-gap. What I will always see is him springing into the air and seeming to run in air for the nearest tree in that famous zigzag.

[1989]

From Mama Dot

Born on a sunday
in the kingdom of Ashante

Sold on monday
into slavery

Ran away on tuesday
cause she born free

Lost a foot on wednesday
when they catch she

Worked all thursday
till her head grey

Dropped on friday
where they burned she

Freed on saturday
in a new century

Oracle Mama Dot

I am seated at her bare feet.
The rocking chair on floorboards
Of the verandah is the repeated break
Of bracken underfoot. *Where are we heading?*

Who dare speak in these moments before dark?
The firefly threads its infinite morse;
Crapauds and crickets are a mounting cacophony;
The laughter of daredevil bats.

Dusk thickens into night.
She has rocked and rocked herself to sleep.
She may hold silence for another millennium.
I see the first stars among cloud.

Angry Mama Dot

I

She gesticulates and it's sheet lightning on our world.
Our ears cannot be stopped against her raised voice.
All the crying we ever did is a roof, soaked through.
With no gaps for thought, we save the night trembling
A string of prayers in gibberish for her rage to quell.

II

The powdery collisions of moths round a lamp.
Us, out first thing, upturned face and palm.
So her peace comes. We stick close, watching.
Busy and humming with it, she throws us clean.
I am years later fighting to break my fall.

Obeah Mama Dot
(her remedies)

I

I am knotted in pain.
She measures string
From navel to each nipple.

She kneads into my belly
Driving the devil
Out of my enforced fast.

II

For the fevers to subside,
I must drink the bush
Boiled to a green alluvium,

In one headback slake;
And return to bouncing around,
Side-stepping bushes for days.

III

A head-knock mushrooms
Into a bold, bald,
Softened bulb.

Her poultice filled
At the end of a rainbow –
The sun above Kilimanjaro;

The murderous vial drawn,
Till the watery mound
Is a crater in burnt ground.

IV

Our rocking-chair counsellor:
Her words untangling us
from bramble and plimpler notions

Into this sudden miles-clearing.

Mama Dot's Treatise

Mosquitoes
Are the fattest
Inhabitants
Of this republic.

They suck our blood
From the cradle
And flaunt it
Like a fat wallet.

They form dark
Haloes; we spend
Our outdoors
Dodging sainthood.

They force us
Into an all-night
Purdah of nets
Against them.

O to stop them
Milking us
Till we are bait
For worms;

Worms that don't
Know which way
To turn and will
Inherit the earth.

Mama Dot Warns Against an Easter Rising

Doan raise no kite is good friday
but is out he went out an fly it
us thinkin maybe dere wont be a breeze
strong enouf an widout any a we to hole it
fo him he'd neva manage to get it high-up
to de tree top ware de wind kissin
de ripess sweetess fruit we cawn reach
but he let out some string bit by bit
tuggin de face into de breeze
coaxin it up all de time takin a few steps back
an it did rise up bit by bit till de lang tail
din't touch de groun an we grip de palin
we head squeeze between to watch him
an trace its rise rise rise up up up in de sky
we all want to fly in like bird but can only kite
fly an he step back juss as we beginnin
to smile fo him envy him his easter risin
when bap he let out a scream leggo string
an de kite drop outta de sky like a bird
a sail down to de nex field an we runnin to him

fogetting de kite we uncle dem mek days ago
fram wood shave light as bird bone
paper tin like fedder an de tongue o kite
fo singin in de sky like a bird an de tail
fo balance string in de mout like it pullin
de longess worm an he a hole him foot
and a bawl we could see seven inch a greenhart
gone in at de heel runnin up him leg
like a vein he groanin all de way to de haspital
on de cross-bar a bike ridden by a uncle
she not sayin a word but we hearin her
fo de ress a dat day an evry year since
doan raise no kite is good friday
an de sky was a birdless kiteless wait fo her word

Mama Dot Learns to Fly

Mama Dot watched reels of film
Of inventor after inventor trying to fly.
She's so old, she's a spectator in some.

Seeing them leap off bridges straight
Into rivers, or burn
Strapped to backfiring rockets,

Or flap about with huge wings
Only to raise a whole heap of dust,
Makes her cringe: what conviction!

How misguided. Right then, she wants
To see an ancestor, in Africa; half-way
Round the world and back through time.

Her equipment's straightforward,
Thought-up to bring the lot
To her: *Come, leh we gaff girl.*

From Farewell Mama Dot

Her rocker halted,
Is earth's spin lost.

Her stripped bed,
Our world became savannah.

Her coffin dances down
Six feet to a wailing chorus.

Her shovelling over
Scores on greenhart, amplified;

Her ground rising-up oh Jah,
From sweet diminuendo to bass.

Her rounding off by delicate pats
With the backs of shovels.

Her new-made bed of flowers.
That second shadow *is she.*

Papa-T
(for Reginald Messiah)

When Grandad recited the Tennyson learned at sea,
I saw companies of redcoats tin-soldiering it
Through rugged country, picked off one by one
By poison-tipped blow-darts or arrows from nowhere:
Their drums' panicky rattle, their bugler's yelp,
Musket-clap and popping cannons, smoke everywhere.

He'd cut short to shout, *If yu all don't pay me mind,*
I goin ge yu a good lickin an sen yu to bed, resuming
As he breathed in, his consonants stretched past recall,
Into a whales' crying place, beginning polyp kingdoms,
Shipwrecked into Amerindian care for months. We'd sit tight,
All eyes on our sweet seasalter, for that last-line-sound,

Someone mistimed once, making him start again.
These days the perfect-lined face of a blank page,
Startles at first, like Papa-T's no-nonsense recitals;
It has me itching to bring him reeling-off in that tongue –
Honour the charge they made! Honour the Light Brigade,
Noble six hundred: to hear, to disobey.

Masquerade

His passage of time is a series of dustclouds.
Streets widen at the end of town
Into sheer savannah, rolled bundles of bracken.

He watches a crow dip its beak and imagines
A living quill as its head throws back to swallow.

His cadillac is a well-kept secret
Plunged thirty feet to the bottom of this ravine.
The steering-wheel has him jacked to plush upholstery.

It's a B-road past disused miles of track
Running deep into exhausted mines.

As a child he skipped those sleepers
Or lay in wait for Black Boy, the daily steam-express
To flatten a six-inch nail into a knife.

It left a thick smoke trail that swept
Rice-paper-thin over ripening paddy.

It whistled at the crossroads where a woman
And child in a cart were carried
A quarter of a mile up the track.

He fished his brother out of a gully, found the mule
Grazing; his mother, no memory would want to account for.

Before a fit the skinned spider-monkeys
Failed to cure, he smells cut-grass and sees purple,
And a train, approaching his ear on the line.

Airy Hall

The red sand road, houses well back,
Trees there to collect dust
Whipped by traffic and flung at them,
The log bridge I am forever crossing
For a sound logs make as they shuffle
Underfoot, the lop-sided main gate
That has to be lifted into place,
Palings you can swing-up and duck
Sideways through if loose and if known,
Tsetse flies stickled on their spikes
We take all afternoon approaching
Just to pincer the papery tails
Between the thumb and index fingers:
How many pushed off those tips
Leaving us all open and mannered,
As I am left now, now and always.

Airy Hall Barrier

Many deny what we see
Has anything to do with anything:
The imperialist who will not let us forget;
The runner crossing the city ahead of taxis;
Fireflies whose phosphorus belongs everywhere.

I follow the sound to a door,
One that opens on approach
To my room in water,
Pooled and swirling as if plunged
From a falls: Kaiteur.

Water sounding again,
This time a cliff-face,
Scaffold and men blasting rock

To the year of nought;
Somehow the sonic genius of a bat,

To stay latched to that sound
And find the true falls.

Airy Hall Iconography

The Tamarind hangs its head,
stings the eyes with its breath.

The Mango traps the sun by degrees,
transforms its rays into ambrosia.

The Coconut's perfect seal lets in rain,
bends with solid milk and honey.

The Guava is its own harvest,
each seed bound in fleshy juice.

The Guinep's translucence is all yours
if you skin its lips, chew its seed for the raw.

The Stinking-toe might be lopped off a stale foot,
on the tongue it does an about-turn: myrrh.

The Paw-paw runs a feather along your nose,
you want it to stop, you want more.

The Sour-sop's veneer is the wasp
treading air at the vaulted honeycomb.

The Sapadilla ducks you twice in frankincense,
you are fished out fighting to go down a third time.

Airy Hall's Dynasty

The house added to wing by wing
Has lost its symmetry. Marriages
Under the one roof are an upward
Curve. Children count from great
Grandchildren in dozens, half-dozens,
Not twos or threes. Paint on wood
Go back to another age, one
Sewn up inside the pitch a gas-lamp,
Signing arms and voices map.

> Boundaries you had to respect,
> Fictions you now inspect.

So many layers has the wood spongy,
A feel you double-take everytime.
To restore banisters and stairs,
You move through captured rainbows
Picking up sheer grain at last.
Brace yourself for the names;
Eraser, not restorer; rubbing out
Your own thumbprint and the dead's,
Defenceless save your belief in ghosts.

> Boundaries you had to respect,
> Fictions you now inspect.

Later, you examine your thumbs,
Naked, you'd clothe them in those
Several layers against the years:
A first brushstroke steered by
Your guide's steady pressure,
Your hand in his, fleshy and warm.
A direction you learn then resist,
Resisting until it lets you go,
To find a groove all yours.

> Boundaries you had to respect,
> Fictions you now inspect.

Airy Hall Ward

There will be days when you or I are bedridden,
Unable to stomach direct light or a voice.
Who fly-posts town?
Word spreads faster than the virus
Rusting the joints; weeks' worth of picked fruit
Turns the whole place into an orchard.

It's enough to make anyone get up.
All this loving and understanding
That's just there for when
You're in a bad way
And all the time I'm thinking
They must have the wrong house altogether:

The door-knocker that had to be silenced
With a bandage, the children shooed
From the sick part of the house –
Partitioned, horticulturally sound,
And a solid stillness
You had to whisper in and labour through.

The Cow Perseverance

I

Here I am writing to you on old newspaper against a tide of print,
In the regular spaces between lines (there are no more trees).
I've turned it upside-down to widen the gap bordering sense and
    nonsense,
For what I must say might very well sound as if it were topsy turvy.
I put myself in your shoes (unable to recall when I last set eyes on a pair);
You read everything twice, then to be doubly sure, aloud,
Testing their soundness: *we wash cow's dung for its grain*,
And I feel your stomach turn; it's not much unlike collecting it for fuel,
Or mixed with clay to daub cracks in our shelters and renew door-
    mounds

That free us of rain, insects and spirits. They no longer drop the milk
We let them live for; their nights spent indoors for safe keep,
Their days tethered to a nearby post. People eye them so, they are fast
Becoming our cross; you'd think they'd fallen out of the sky.

II

Hunger has filled them with what I can only call compassion.
Such bulbous, watery eyes blame us for the lack of grass and worse
Expect us to do something; tails that held the edge of windscreen
     wipers
In better days, swishing the merest irritant, a feather's even,
Let flies congregate until the stretched, pock-marked hide is them.
That's why when you asked how things were I didn't have to look far,
I thought, *Let the cow explain, its leathery tongue has run this geography*
Many times over; how milk turns, unseen, all at once, so lush pastures
Threw-up savannahs. The storms are pure dust or deep inside the
     rowdiest
Among us, virtually dead and rowdy because they know it, they're
     not sure
What else to do. You fathom why, when a cow croons we offer it
What we can't as a bribe for it to stop; *silence is perseverance.*

III

We watch its wait on meagre haunches, ruminating on what must be
Imperishable leather, some secret mantra, our dear buddha, for the
     miracle
We need; and us with nowhere to turn find we believe. God knows
It's a case of choosing which pot-hole in the road to ride; knowing
We export the asphalt that could fill them; knowing too the one thing
We make these days that is expressly ours is whipped in malarial
     water
And forced down our throats for daring to open our mouths.
Give us the cow's complicity anyday: its perfect art of being left
In peace; its till-now effortless conversion of chewy grass to milk;
And its daft hoof-print, ignored for so long though clearly
     trespassing.
Then and then alone, we too can jump over the moon, without
     bloodshed.
Its raised-head and craned-neck attempt to furnish an exact account
Is a tale you and I are bound to finish, in flesh or spirit.

Acknowledgements

Thanks are due to the copyright holders of the following poems, essays and interviews for permission to publish them in this anthology:

Louise Bennett: Poems from *Selected Poems* (Sangster's, Kingston, 1982), reprinted by permission of the author and publisher: copyright © Louise Bennett 1966, 1982. Interview with Dennis Scott reprinted from *Caribbean Quarterly*, 14 nos.1-2 (1968).

Martin Carter: Poems from *Poems of Succession* (New Beacon Books, London, 1977), reprinted by permission of the author and publisher: copyright © Martin Carter 1954, 1982. 'Conversations' reprinted from *Kyk-over-al*, no.28 (December 1961). Extract from an interview with Peter Trevis from the Caribbean Focus writers conference recorded by ILEA (Unit 6) at the Commonwealth Institute, London, on 23-25 October 1986: copyright © ILEA 1986.

Derek Walcott: Poems from *Sea Grapes* (Cape, 1976), reprinted by permission of the author and publisher; from *In a Green Night* (1962) and *Another Life* (1973), reprinted by permission of the author and Faber & Faber Ltd: copyright © Derek Walcott 1962, 1972, 1973, 1976, 1986. 'Self Portrait' reprinted from *Caribbean Quarterly*, 26 nos.1-2 (1980). Extract from 'Leaving School' (VIII) reprinted from *London Magazine* (September 1965).

Edward Kamau Brathwaite: Poems from *Rights of Passage* (1967), *Islands* (1969), *Mother Poem* (1977) and *X/Self* (1987), reprinted by permission of the author and Oxford University Press; from *Third World Poems* (Longman Drumbeat, 1983): copyright © Edward Kamau Brathwaite 1967, 1969, 1977, 1983, 1986, 1987. 'Stone' reprinted from *Artrage*, 12 (1986). 'Rohlehr on Brathwaite' reprinted from an interview with E.A. Markham in *Artrage*, 18 (1987). Extract from 'Timehri' reprinted from *Savacou*, 2 (September 1970).

Dennis Scott: Poems from *Uncle Time* (University of Pittsburgh Press, 1973) and *Dreadwalk* (New Beacon Books, London, 1982) reprinted by permission of the author and publishers: copyright © Dennis Scott 1973, 1982. Interview with Mervyn Morris reprinted from *Caribbean Quarterly*, 30 no.1 (March 1984).

Mervyn Morris: Poems from *The Pond* (New Beacon Books, London, 1973), *On Holy Week* (Kingston, Jamaica, 1976) and *Shadowboxing* (New Beacon Books, 1979) reprinted by permission of the author and publishers: copyright © Mervyn Morris 1973, 1976, 1979. 'Riding Pillion with the Poet' was commissioned for *Hinterland* and first published here: copyright © Mervyn Morris 1989.

James Berry: Poems from *Fractured Circles* (New Beacon Books, London, 1979), *Lucy's Letter and Loving* (New Beacon Books, 1982) and *Chain of Days* (Oxford University Press, 1985) reprinted by permission of the author and publishers: copyright © James Berry 1975, 1979, 1982, 1985. 'Defendant in a Jamaican Court', 'Words of a Jamaican Laas Them' and 'Faces Around My Father' are reprinted from *Poetry Review*, 'What Is No Good' from *Poetry* (Chicago), and 'Ol Style Freedom' from the *Poetry Book Society Anthology 1988-89* (PBS/ Hutchinson, 1988); 'Signpost of the Bluefoot Man' was commissioned for *Hinterland* and first published here: copyright © James Berry 1989.

E.A. Markham: Poems from *Human Rites* (1984), *Living in Disguise* (1986) and *Towards the End of a Century* (1989), all published by Anvil Press, reprinted by permission of the author and publisher: copyright © E.A. Markham 1984, 1986, 1989. 'A Date on the Calendar', 'Letter to Kate' and 'Hinterland' are from a forthcoming collection, *Letter from Ulster*. 'Random Thoughts' and 'Many Voices, Many Lives' were commissioned for *Hinterland* and first published here: copyright © E.A. Markham 1989.

Olive Senior: Poems from *Talking of Trees* (Calabash, Kingston, 1985) reprinted by permission of the author and publisher: copyright © Olive Senior 1985. Extract from an interview with Anna Rutherford reprinted from *Kunapipi*, 8 no.2 (1986).

Lorna Goodison: Poems from *I Am Becoming My Mother* (1986) and *Heartease* (1989), both published by New Beacon Books, London, reprinted by permission of the author and publisher: copyright © Lorna Goodison 1986, 1989. 'A Far-Reaching Voice' by Anne Walmsley reprinted from *South's Book People*.

Linton Kwesi Johnson: Poems from *Voices of the Living and the Dead* (Race Today, 1974), *Dread Beat An' Blood* (Bogle-L'Ouverture, London, 1975) and *Inglan is a Bitch* (Race Today, 1980) reprinted by permission of the author and publishers: copyright © Linton Kwesi Johnson 1974, 1975, 1980. 'Di Great Insohreckshan' reprinted from *Race Today*. Interview with Mervyn Morris reprinted from *Jamaica Journal* (1988).

Michael Smith: Poems from *It A Come* (Race Today, 1986) reprinted by permission of Nerissa Smith and the publisher: copyright © Nerissa Smith 1986. Interview with Mervyn Morris reprinted from *Jamaica Journal* (1982).

Grace Nichols: Poems from *I is a long memoried woman* (Karnac House, London, 1983) and *The Fat Black Woman's Poems* (Virago, 1984) reprinted by permission of the author and publishers: copyright © Grace Nichols 1983, 1984. Three other poems are published by permission of the author. 'Home Truths' was commissioned for *Hinterland* and first published here: copyright © Grace Nichols 1989.

Fred D'Aguiar: Poems from *Mama Dot* (Chatto, 1985) reprinted by permission of the author and publisher: copyright © Fred D'Aguiar 1985. Six other poems are published by permission of the author. 'Zigzag Paths' was commissioned for *Hinterland* and first published here: copyright © Fred D'Aguiar 1989.

Thanks are also due to the following for photographs of the poets: Louise Bennett, page 43 (Louise Bennett) and 44 (Sangster's); Martin Carter, pages 64 and 65 (ILEA); Derek Walcott, page 87 (University of Kent) and 88 (Jonathan Cape); Edward Kamau Brathwaite, page 107 (Julian Stapleton) and 108 (Oxford University Press); Dennis Scott, page 136 (Networking Public Relations) and 137 (New Beacon Books); Mervyn Morris, pages 155 and 156 (Julian Stapleton); James Berry, page 173 (James Berry) and 174 (Julian Stapleton); E.A. Markham, page 191 (Lori Sauer/Anvil Press) and 192 (David Hunter); Olive Senior, page 210 (Longman Group) and 211 (ILEA); Lorna Goodison, pages 229 and 230 (Julian Stapleton); Linton Kwesi Johnson, pages 260 and 261 (Julian Stapleton); Michael Smith, page 273 (Race Today) and 274 (Julian Stapleton); Grace Nichols, page 294 (Fanny Dubes) and 295 (Julian Stapleton); Fred D'Aguiar, page 312 (London Pictures Service) and 313 (Chatto & Windus).

Of the many people and organisations who have assisted me in compiling this book, I wish to thank specifically Dr Edres Bird at the University Centre, Antigua; the Staff at the University Centre, Montserrat; Chris Keane and others at the Commonwealth Institute, London; Louis James, Errol Lloyd and Eve Williams for help with locating materials; Race Today Collective, Walter Rodney Bookshop and New Beacon Books for assistance, and MAAS and the University of Ulster for the use of resources.

I wish to thank, also, Peter Fraser and Mimi Khalvati for having read the introduction and (MK) bits of the text and making valuable suggestions.   EAM

Index of Titles and First Lines

(Titles are italics. The numbers refer to pages.)

ERRATA

Page 40, note 13: for 'Claud' read 'Claude'; for 'Austen' read 'Austin'.

Page 91, line 35: for 'booket' read 'booklet'.

Page 95, epigraph, line 1: for 'though' read 'since'.

Page 97, 'A Letter from Brooklyn', line 2: for 'trembing' read 'trembling'.

Page 99, title should read '*Extract from Sainte Lucie:* For the altar-piece of the Roseau Valley Church, St Lucia'.

Page 110, line 25: for '*Masks*' read 'masks'; line 32, for 'allusive' read 'elusive'; line 37, for 'moles' read 'modes'.

Page 157, line 2: insert 'high-rise' before 'window-cleaner'.

Page 171, 'I Am the Man', line 7: for 'choice' read 'voice'.

Page 252, line 20: for 'Science' read 'Silence'.

Page 263: insert 'from' before title: this is an extract from 'Bass Culture'.

Page 271, penultimate line: insert 'di' before 'smashin'.

Page 285, line 25: insert 'a' before 'modder'.

Page 287, line 5: for 'the middle' read 'de middle'; line 14, for 'can' read 'cyann'.

Page 301: insert 'from' before title: section 4 is omitted from this extract.